T0325087

The Practical Philosophy of AI-Assistants

An Engineering-Humanities Conversation

The Practical Philosophy of AI-Assistants

An Engineering-Humanities Conversation

Suman Gupta
The Open University, UK

Peter H. Tu
General Electric Research, USA

World Scientific

NEW JERSEY · LONDON · SINGAPORE · BEIJING · SHANGHAI · HONG KONG · TAIPEI · CHENNAI · TOKYO

Published by

World Scientific Publishing Europe Ltd.

57 Shelton Street, Covent Garden, London WC2H 9HE

Head office: 5 Toh Tuck Link, Singapore 596224

USA office: 27 Warren Street, Suite 401-402, Hackensack, NJ 07601

Library of Congress Cataloging-in-Publication Data
Names: Gupta, Suman, 1966– author. | Tu, Peter H., author.
Title: The practical philosophy of AI-assistants : an engineering-humanities conversation /
     Suman Gupta, The Open University, UK, Peter H. Tu, General Electric Research, USA.
Description: New Jersey : World Scientific, [2024] | Includes bibliographical references.
Identifiers: LCCN 2023012624 | ISBN 9781800614154 (hardcover) |
     ISBN 9781800614215 (paperback) | ISBN 9781800614161 (ebook for institutions) |
     ISBN 9781800614178 (ebook for individuals)
Subjects: LCSH: Intelligent personal assistants (Computer software) |
     Artificial intelligence--Social aspects.
Classification: LCC QA76.76.I58 G88 2024 | DDC 006.30285/436--dc23/eng/20230531
LC record available at https://lccn.loc.gov/2023012624

British Library Cataloguing-in-Publication Data
A catalogue record for this book is available from the British Library.

For any available supplementary material, please visit
https://www.worldscientific.com/worldscibooks/10.1142/Q0417#t=suppl

Desk Editors: Balasubramanian Shanmugam/Ana Ovey/Shi Ying Koe

Typeset by Stallion Press
Email: enquiries@stallionpress.com

Printed in Singapore

About the Authors

Suman Gupta is Professor of Literature and Cultural History at The Open University, UK. He has led a series of international collaborations since 2002, and is currently coordinating the *Analysing Political Catchwords* project, with activities in Cyprus, Jordan, Bulgaria, and the UK. Gupta has authored 20 and edited 11 books, and published numerous scholarly papers and chapters, in text studies, cultural theory, and politics. Recent books include: *Usurping Suicide: The Political Resonances of Individual Deaths* (Zed, 2017, co-authored with M. Katsarska, T. Spyros, and M. Hajimichael); *Digital India and the Poor: Policy, Technology and Society* (Routledge, 2020); *What Is Artificial Intelligence?: A Conversation Between an AI Engineer and a Humanities Researcher* (World Scientific, 2020, co-authored with P. Tu); and *Political Catchphrases and Contemporary History: Critique of New Normals* (Oxford University Press, 2022).

Peter H. Tu is the Chief Scientist for Artificial Intelligence at General Electric Research. Over his 25-year career at GE, he has led a number of government (DARPA, NIJ, DHS, and FBI) and industrial (Aerospace, Healthcare, Security, NBC Universal, and Transportation) programs in the fields of video analytics and artificial intelligence. He is currently leading the DARPA ADUCA program with a focus on developing conceptual neuro-symbolic representations of objects and behaviours. In addition to GE Research, the team includes multiple universities and small businesses. Tu has over 75 peer-reviewed publications and has filed more than 50 US patents. He is a co-author of *What Is Artificial Intelligence?: A Conversation Between an AI Engineer and a Humanities Researcher* (World Scientific, 2020, with Gupta).

Acknowledgements

We are indebted to Stephanie, Federico, Alfredo, and Mark for their generous contributions to this book. We are, as always, grateful to Anne, Jack, Ayan-Yue, Kiyomi, Cheng, and all our friends and colleagues. They decide the tenor of our everyday lives, which informs the following pages as much as, if not more than, the authors who are cited. Thanks are due to Adam Binnie of World Scientific for picking up this proposal and seeing it through commissioning and production.

Where we are unable to blame each other, erring governments, wayward corporations, or misguided communities, we are happy to accept joint responsibility for shortcomings in this book.

Contents

Introduction

Overview

This book debates the theoretical principles and engineering methods that could enable the construction of an optimal AI-Assistant. The idea is that such an AI system could come to be integrated into any person's everyday life as a constant companion and counsellor. Envisaging such an AI-Assistant involves confronting technological challenges as well as philosophical and social conundrums.

This book discusses four ways in which such an AI-Assistant could be conceived, each concerning a different kind of capacity. The pros and cons of these four approaches are discussed in the following sections.

- What sort of capacity should such an AI-Assistant have for recognizing and identifying individuals?
- How could such an AI-Assistant partake in human communications?
- How may such an AI-Assistant propose explanations for observations and events?
- To what extent can such an AI-Assistant integrate with the norms and practices of social civility?

While pursuing the idealistic objective of conceptualizing an optimal AI-Assistant, issues of present and pragmatic moment are discussed. In fact, the idealistic objective is formulated by way of gauging the current conditions and limitations of AI knowledge. Unusually, in this book, that objective is centred on everyday life and interests, at ground level. By and large, the field of AI is constituted in terms of the large objectives of governments and corporations, which bear upon people in a top-down manner. With an eye on the present, the formulation of an optimal AI-Assistant serves the following functions here:

- It offers a framework for bringing together accessible summaries of some AI technologies currently employed for recognition/identification, communication, explanation, and civility.
- The theoretical principles that underpin these technologies are explained, which involves taking account of the current limits of AI research.
- The philosophical and social dimensions of such technologies are unpacked with close reference to specific capabilities and their underpinning principles.
- The latter are enabled by calling upon analogies and equivalents for AI methods and terms from humanities disciplines.

These thrusts of the book involve a constant interweaving of engineering knowledge and humanities perspectives.

Consequently, the book follows the somewhat unorthodox form of an academic conversation between an AI Engineer, Peter, and a Humanities Researcher, Suman — the co-authors. That is to say, the argument of the book unfolds in alternating interventions (short chapters) from each by turn. In general, the pattern followed is of Peter presenting some observations on the state of knowledge and principles of a specific area of AI; then Suman considering the philosophical and social dimensions of that area and raising questions; Peter addressing those questions; and so on. Each intervention is around 3,000–4,000 words.

The format designated here as an academic conversation is more formal than a Socratic dialogue and less so than a scholarly paper/monograph. This book does presume some acquaintance with academic conventions and expressions. At the same time, the specialist registers are mediated for greater accessibility than is usual in scholarly publications. To a large extent, this is due to the conversational setup, which means that engineering descriptions are expressed to be accessible to humanities researchers, and philosophical or social concepts are similarly rendered amenable for engineers. In the main, that involves fully explaining discipline-specific terms when they appear, keeping symbolic formulations to a minimum, and not expecting readers to have prior knowledge of the texts cited.

Further, the conversational format allows for a certain lightness of spirit. Conversationalists generally try to engage each other with more than simply rigorous arguments. Some play and humour are natural in exchanges among friends, however scholarly the theme. The liberties and provocations of friendship between the conversationalists are not concealed in this book, but those appear without compromising rational deliberation. In fact, the conversational format, with its performative dimensions, is germane to the theme of this book since it builds upon the idea of AI as friend.

Key Terms

Before launching the conversation, let us pause on the two key terms in the title: 'AI-Assistant' and 'practical philosophy'.

In this book, the characterization of the AI-Assistant as such suggests a familiar human-like relationship to users, that of having a helpful and subordinate employment position. However, professional relationships are not immediately relevant here. Contractual obligations and conditional recompense between AI-Assistant and user are not taken on board in what follows. Our sense of the optimal AI-Assistant is, instead, conceived as being closer to a 'friend': one who is available in need, offers support, can be a confidant, companion, equal partner in some activity, etc. without predetermined returns. A friend seems to offer a model to think with or a horizon to work towards or, at the least, a useful metaphor. However, though we like the idea of a friend as a model, the AI-Assistants' relation to their users is rather more ambiguous. This relationship does not quite carry the moral and emotional weight of friendship. Ultimately, the role allocated to AI-Assistants cannot be straightforwardly analogous to a human relationship. The fact that the AI-Assistant is non-human needs to be factored into its function.

We had, in fact, started with the different and fantastical idea of the AI-Assistant as something like a spirit familiar, in the Oxford English Dictionary sense of: 'A spirit, often taking the form of an animal, which obeys and assists a witch or other person'. Imagined as a human/non-human hybrid, there are considerable histories of witches' and other cunning folk's familiars being represented as animals with human-like consciousness (for useful discussions of English traditions, see Wilby 2005 and Miller 2017: Ch. 2). We were also very much taken by the richer connotations of 'daemon', of great antiquity, too (cf. White 2021). Philip Pullman's *His Dark Materials* trilogy (1995–2000) gave a popular fantasy construction of a daemon as an *alter ego* persona accompanying each human person — perhaps a material exteriorization of their consciousness — which has the form of an animal. A set of rules governing the inextricable relationship of persons and their daemons provides an epic machinery for the trilogy, and puts the daemon–human relationship within an imagined social system. This systematic approach recommended Pullman's version of the daemon as a possible model for the AI-Assistant. Attractive as modelling the AI-Assistant with a fantasy daemon in mind is, we decided against it. We were keen to keep away from any whiff of mysticism and superstition. In that respect, the professional distance of an 'assistant', who is close to the user but in a formal way, seems apt if mundane. Nevertheless, in imagining the AI-Assistant, at times the ideas of 'friend', 'familiar', and 'daemon' seem not too distant.

The commitment to 'practical philosophy' that we, Peter and Suman, share is drawn straightforwardly from Aristotle's *Nicomachean Ethics*. We had in mind the concept of φρόνησῐς (phronesis) — usually rendered as practical wisdom or philosophy — as distinguished from scientific knowledge, philosophic wisdom, and intuitive reason. Naturally, we have strong investments in the latter areas, but in more or less complementary ways. What allows us to engage with each other is a core of robust pragmatism with conviction in a direction for intellectual endeavour, pretty much as Aristotle had described it for the person with practical wisdom:

> Regarding practical wisdom we shall get at the truth by considering who are the persons we credit with it. Now it is thought to be the mark of a man of practical wisdom to be able to deliberate well about what is good and expedient for himself, not in some particular respect, e.g., about what sorts of thing conduce to health or to strength, but about what sort of thing conduce to the good life in general. This is shown by the fact that we credit men with practical wisdom in some particular respect when they have calculated well with a view to some good end which is one of those that are not the object of any art. It follows that in the general sense also the man who is capable of deliberating has practical wisdom. (Aristotle 2009: 64).

We naturally do not go with the distinction from scientific knowledge that Aristotle offered, and in any case, the concept of practical philosophy has seen prolific updating and reconsideration. But we do buy into the notion that a concept of the good life, a good society, is not derived from a specific discipline or technique. It is, in some sense, prior to those and should therefore bear upon those. We also agree that the discernment of the good life with respect to the AI-Assistant will emerge through deliberation rather than any predetermined vision or presumed framework. Bringing a practical philosophical approach to designing such an AI-Assistant may well be the path to endowing the latter with practical wisdom. Hence, the conversation that follows.

Part 1

Recognition and Identification

Chapter 1

Face Work 101

Peter Tu

Question: What is the definition of a micro-Helen?
Answer: The amount of facial beauty required to launch a single ship.

A good friend of mine, Joy Hirsch over at Yale Medical School once told me: 'If you want to see someone's neurons really light up, just stick her head into an fMRI and then show her an image of a frightened face.' As a species, a significant amount of our cognitive development was centred around two life-preserving capabilities:

(i) how not to get lost in the forest, and
(ii) how to distinguish between friends and foes.

In terms of the latter, if our AI-Assistant is going to earn its keep, it had better get a good grip on that most fabulous of topics: facial analytics. So, let's start our discussion with the topic of faces and how our AI-Assistant might one day use these technologies to our benefit.

From a computer vision point of view, the analysis of faces conjures up a great number of intriguing topics of investigation, including:

1. how to detect a face,
2. how to segment a face into its constituent parts,
3. how to estimate facial orientation or pose,

4. how to estimate a person's direction of gaze (may allow for the inference of attention),
5. how to estimate a person's facial expression (may allow for the inference of emotion),
6. how to synthesize authentic-looking faces,
7. how to classify a face in terms of concepts such as age, gender, and ethnicity (soft biometrics), and of course,
8. how to determine the identity of a person given her facial image (face recognition).

I thought I would start by giving a quick summary of the experiences that my colleagues and I have had in the pursuit of developing automatic facial analysis methods.

Eigenface

My first foray into the face space was through the somewhat obscure field of forensic facial reconstruction. Given a skull found at a crime scene, the goal is to reconstruct a 3D model from it of the face in question with the hopes that someone familiar with the individual it belongs to can enable an identification. Traditionally, manual clay-based reconstructions have dominated this field. The goal of the ReFace program was to automate this process using computational methods. Before jumping in, I would like to first describe the concept of Principal Component Analysis (PCA), which was initially used for constructing 2D eigenfaces.

Consider an ensemble of 2D facial images such that each face is placed into some sort of canonical orientation. For example, all images might be transformed such that the centre of the left and the right eye of each image are in a uniform (consistent) position. The next step is to establish a set of correspondences between all the images and a single reference image. This then establishes a common set of topologically equivalent pixels (x, y, i) for each image, where x and y give the pixel location and i is its intensity value. Each image can then be represented by a vector X which is simply a long list of (x, y, i) values. We can now define the average or mean face as $\bar{X}$. We can also define the covariance matrix C, which characterizes the variation of X. An eigenvector e of C has the property that $Ce = \lambda e$, where λ is a scalar value known as an eigenvalue (*eigen* is the German word for same). You can think of an eigenvector as a kind of global deformation mode. It turns out that one can in general find a set of eigenvectors such that they are mutually orthogonal to one another. By considering only the most significant eigenvectors, say the top 30, one can approximate any face using the mean face $\bar{X}$ plus a weighted sum of eigenvectors. Early forms of face recognition would use the eigenvector weights for a given face as a form of signature that could be used for face recognition. But, for our purposes, the eigenvector structure provides for a compact representation of a face as well as the face space in general — just 30 parameters as opposed to millions of pixels. We will see how this trick can be used for multiple purposes. For a hoot, you should check out the Kevin Costner film *No Way Out* (1987). To my knowledge, this is the first time that PCA and eigenvectors have been used for dramatic effect. Now, let's return to the ReFace program.

We started by collecting in the order of 500 CT head scans ranging over gender, age, and ethnicity. The benefit of having such a database is that a surface of both the skull and the skin of each subject can be extracted directly from such data. This is accomplished using the Marching Cubes algorithm, which was invented by two stalwarts of the GE Research Center, Bill Lorenson and Harvey Cline. To my knowledge, Marching Cubes is the most cited computer graphic paper ever (Lorenson and Cline 1987).

Given a skull found at a crime scene, an initial classification with respect to race and sex can be made. Appropriate skulls in the CT database can then be warped so that their shape becomes identical with the skull in question. The skull-warping transformations can also be applied to their respective skin surfaces. This results in a set of warped skin surfaces, where each surface represents a possible estimate of the skin in question. To characterize this distribution of skull-specific skin-surface estimates, we can apply the PCA trick that was previously described. We end up with a kind of skull-specific eigen flesh that characterizes the possible variation of flesh depth for the individual in question. One can then explore this space by sampling the eigenvector weights producing various possible skull-specific facial reconstructions. If additional knowledge, such as the age and/or weight of the individual in question, is known, such information can then be used to restrict the eigen flesh resulting in a specific reconstruction. The insertion of eyeballs and artificial hair can also be performed to create a more lifelike representation. Experiments with respect to recognition demonstrated that humans do poorly when asked to identify individuals based on such reconstructions; however, when a commercial face-recognition engine attempts to compare a ReFace reconstruction against a list of missing person images, the results are impressive (for additional details, see Tu *et al.* 2007).

Discriminants

Our next set of face-related projects was sponsored by the National Institute of Justice (NIJ) with the goal of developing facial analytics for visual surveillance purposes. We teamed up with a company called Pittsburgh Pattern Recognition (PPR). In my opinion, PPR had, at that time, the best face detector on the market. Face detection is similar to object detection. In those days, the recipe was as follows:

1. Collect a large set of facial training images.
2. Draw a bounding box around each face — these are your true samples.
3. Collect a representative set of non-face images with arbitrary bounding boxes — these are your false samples.
4. Select your favourite set of image features that can be used to construct a feature vector X for each image.
5. Choose a machine-learning method that usually comes with incongruous names such as Adaboost, Support Vector Machines, or Random Forests, and then search for a discriminant associated with the feature representation X that can be used to distinguish between the false and true samples. Armed with such a discriminant, one can then apply a sliding window classifier to an image by considering all possible bounding boxes and use the discriminant to classify them as either a face or a non-face.

Modern approaches substitute deep learning neural networks for Steps 4 and 5. They also provide for more efficient search methods — examples include the Single Shot Detection (SSD) paradigm. Armed with a solid face detector, our initial interest was the production of a better face for recognition purposes. To this end, we were interested in the concept of super resolution.

An image, or any signal for that matter, can be described using methods known as Fourier transforms. When a young engineer first encounters Fourier mathematics, it is quite a jaw-dropping moment. It turns out that all signals can be represented by an infinite sum of sinusoids. A sinusoid is defined based on its amplitude, phase shift, and frequency. The resolution of an image can be characterized as the maximum frequency associated with the sinusoids that are used to construct the image. Digital cameras make use of various forms of sampling. The sample rate defines what is known as the Nyquist frequency, which is an upper limit on the sinusoid frequency values that are used for its construction. At this point, I fear that I am hearing a 'so what?' from the reader. Well, higher frequencies allow for the construction of fine details such as wrinkles and the structure of the eye. Such details are, of course, critical for many face-related applications. My colleague Fred Wheeler's challenge was to produce images that go beyond the Nyquist frequency.

But how is such a thing possible? The logic behind the proverb 'you can't squeeze blood from a turnip' should certainly apply to images, and it does. However, if in a video sequence we collect multiple images from slightly different angles, and then if one can warp all these images as if they were taken from the same viewpoint, one can in theory construct a new image with higher sample rates. Miraculously these synthetic images provide details that cannot be found in any single image (Wheeler *et al.* 2007). The next question, of course, is how can one warp these images in an automatic fashion? Enter Xiaoming Liu and his remarkable alignment apparatus …

Alignment

Xiaoming started with the standard approach, which makes use of the PCA eigenface methods that we previously described. The idea is that you start with a set of key points such as the corners of the eyes, nose, lips, and jawline. You can place the key points onto an image in an arbitrary fashion. This then allows you to produce a vector representation X of the face (see earlier discussion on eigenfaces). One can then ask the question, 'what is the probability that such an X would have been generated by the eigenface distribution?' One can then simply adjust the key point positions until the probability of the resulting X is maximized. This is known as a generative approach to alignment. Xiaoming then came up with the inspired idea of using discriminative instead of generative methods for facial alignment. The idea here is that we create two sets of images: those that are properly aligned and those that are not. We then get a discriminative classifier (like the one we used for face detection) to learn to distinguish between properly and improperly aligned images. We then adjust the key points based on the guidance (hotter or colder) provided by the learned discriminant. So impressive was this result that Xiaoming got one of the two face-related oral presentations at the prestigious IEEE Conference for Computer Vision and Pattern Recognition (CVPR) 2007 (Liu 2007).

Comparison

Having gotten our feet wet with forensic face reconstruction, face detection, super-resolution, and facial alignment, it was time to take a hack at what I often call boutique face recognition. The general approach to face recognition is similar to face detection. Given two facial images, the task at hand is to determine whether or not the two faces have come from the same person. This then comes down to extracting a feature vector X from both images, measuring the differences between the two feature vectors (which is itself a feature vector) and then learning to discriminate between matching and non-matching feature vector differences. The field started with handcrafted features and established machine learning methods; we now simply use neural networks to learn the feature representation and search for the means of discrimination. Of course, the main lesson that we have learned is that the more data that are available for training, the better. Over the years my good friend Jilin Tu (no relation to yours truly) has pointed his face recognition engines at various domains: site-specific face recognition, face recognition from driver licenses, face recognition through passenger windows, and face recognition for partially obscured faces (see Tu *et al.* 2010 for a sample of his good work).

A slightly different approach to face recognition was the NIJ-sponsored work done by my colleague Jixu Chen, where he looked at the problem of person-specific face recognition. The idea was that if one could identify specific features such as scars, tattoos, or blemishes, then such distinguishing features could be used to detect specific individuals. This contrasts with the feature vector approach which attempts to develop a representation for the general population. Jixu's work also made use of hairstyle, which in general is considered a nuisance by most face recognition engines.

Remaining in the world of surveillance, we found that our alignment methods also allow for the estimation of gaze based on the orientation of the face. Also sponsored by the NIJ was the work done by my friends Ting Yu, Ser-Nam Lim, Kedar Patwardhan, and Nils Krahnstoever, who used gaze and proximity to understand social structure in crowded environments (Yu *et al.* 2009). One of their findings was that mutual eye contact was a good measure of familiarity between individuals except when it comes to married couples. Husbands and wives don't seem to need this form of communication. Over the years we have used gaze-estimation methods for other applications such as the analysis of what shoppers are interested in as well as how sportsmen function in critical situations (check out the GE NBC Quarterback Vision system). Another interesting application is based on the idea that a video analytics system might be unaware of certain critical events such as someone having a heart attack. However, if the system can monitor the gaze of people in the scene, it may be able to infer that something is amiss and then request assistance. In this way, people become a kind of virtual sensor network.

Expression

This leads to the next face topic: expressions. It is interesting to note that besides his interest in evolution, Darwin devoted much of his research to the study of facial expressions. The anthropologist Paul Ekman (see *Emotions Revealed*, 1993) was able to show that the ability to recognize common facial expressions is a universal capability. His experiments involved showing images of Westerners to indigenous persons that have never encountered such individuals — they had no trouble recognizing Western facial expressions. Paul Ekman also developed the idea of facial action units (FAUs), which can be used to characterize the various muscle movements of the face. The idea was that facial expressions can be characterized by the presence or absence of various FAUs. In theory, such methods can be used to discriminate between false and authentic expressions. The Duchenne smile is an example of a false expression. In this case, electrodes are used to stimulate muscles in the face resulting in a false sense of satisfaction, when in reality the subject is not in the least bit happy with her circumstances. My colleagues Jilin, Xiaoming, and Yan Tong have over the years taken runs at automating the extraction of FAUs (Chen *et al.* 2013).

The more general approach to expression classification is to use methods similar to face detection and face recognition. After normalizing the face, a feature vector X is extracted and subsequently classified via machine learning with respect to a manually defined expression label. Of course, deep learning methods have become the dominant method of choice in this domain. We first started exploring methods for automatic facial expression recognition in support of NBC Universal. The idea was that by watching people who are watching television, we could provide insights regarding the effect that various actors and jokes might have on the general population. To this end, many of my lab mates were frog-marched into the lab and forced to watch various episodes of the hit NBC franchise *Friends*. Through such sacrifices, we were able to demonstrate the efficacy of automatic facial expression recognition for entrainment purposes. In later years we built the Defense Advanced Research Projects Agency (DARPA) Sherlock system that used facial expressions, gaze analysis, pupil motion, tracking, and articulated pose analysis for the purposes of inferring group-level social states such as rapport and hostility (Tu *et al.* 2015). More recently, we have developed an Interactive Advertising system based on an avatar that uses continuous learning methods for the purpose of selecting actions based on observed facial expressions and body pose with the goal of receiving some sort of long-term reward (Tu *et al.* 2019). And so concludes our whirligig tour through the face space. Let's now consider if and how our AI-Assistant might make use of these hard-fought gains.

AI-Assistant

A cocktail party is always fraught with the potential for personal faux pas. Someone slightly familiar catches your eye, starts a conversation, and, for the life of you, you can't put a name to the face. In such situations, we would all give an arm and a leg for a friendly AI that could pull us back from the brink of humiliation by gently whispering into our ear the name and circumstances of such individuals. Taking this one step forward, as one attempts to move up the social ranks our capacity to win friends and influence others is a function of one's social skills. To this end, an AI-Assistant capable of reading the crowd via facial expressions could provide valuable feedback. For example, if one of your recently purchased jokes mysteriously fell flat, your AI-Agent might pinpoint the moment when things went awry — maybe you lost them just before the punch line. With such evidence, you might even get a refund. In this way, the AI-Assistant becomes a sort of trainer or coach.

On a more serious note, people who fall into the autism spectrum simply do not recognize many social cues. Like a hearing aid that amplifies sound, our AI-Assistant could be a kind of empathy aid that amplifies expressed emotion. Temple Grandin, who is an accomplished professor and autistic, describes some of her coping mechanisms in her book written with Catherine Johnson, *Animals in Translation* (2005). When a graduate student comes into her office and tells a joke, she gets nothing out of it. However, she realizes that there will be social consequences if she does not laugh at the end of this engagement. So, she simply waits for the student to finish and then she laughs in a socially acceptable manner. Of course, this strategy is predicated on the ability to recognize the conditions of a given social event. If such cues are not easily grasped, then this technique will certainly fail. Under such circumstances, an AI Empathy aid might one day be there to lend a helping hand.

If the AI-Assistant is able to gain a vantage point whereby the face of the user herself is visible, then we can consider use cases where the AI-Assistant might become a champion for our well-being. Ailments such as depression and even conditions such as sepsis can be detected via facial analysis. When it comes to afflictions such as obesity and substance abuse, one's demeanour might be predictive of a possible lapse in conviction or willpower. In such fall-off-the-wagon moments, our AI-Assistant might be able to muster the appropriate reinforcements.

Suman, at this point you are probably brimming with questions and concerns so I will yield the floor and look forward to your comment and consideration.

Question: How can you identify the extrovert at an engineering party?
Answer: She's the one looking at the other people's shoes.

Chapter 2

Face-Off

Suman Gupta

Peter — I am struck with admiration at the ingenuity and imagination of AI Engineers in engaging with facial recognition; and equally by the lucid exposition you have given of those endeavours. Nothing I say going forward should be taken as questioning that impressive effort. What I propose to do in response is to get into some of the muted processes behind (or quietly entwined with) the impressive *how-to* process you have outlined. In other words, where you have focused on *how* to automatize facial recognition, I will try to say something about *what* is being automatized and *why*. This argument doesn't suggest that engaging with the *how-to* questions is indifferent to the *what* and *why*-questions; rather, the argument is that the *how-to* is determined in a tacit but definite way by *what* and *why* considerations. Further, the argument proposes that because these *how-to* processes are conditional on *what* and *why* considerations, their bearing on individualized technology in everyday life is limited. In a way, I feel your account already suggests that. It seems to me that you struggled to find suitable applications for this technology in the everyday sphere. Beside the enormous ingenuity described in developing automatized facial recognition processes, the everyday-life applications you mention seem tame.

How

Let me start by summarizing some of the broader principles and practices evident in your account of the development of facial recognition technology. To a degree, doing so clears my own head; in some measure, that might usefully align the few technical terms you have used with ordinary language inferences; importantly for me, doing so helps to lead into those *what* and *why*-questions that I come to later.

Your account of the development of facial recognition technology starts by posing the relevant *how-to* questions (a nice list of eight at the beginning). Then you weave together the methods used and the challenges overcome in response to them by pausing on particular phases/projects. Let me summarize by pulling those apart a bit: first, giving a somewhat honed set of *how-to* questions; then, reiterating very briefly the general points on methods employed and challenges overcome.

How-to Questions

The way you have phrased your *how-to* questions seems at times to pre-empt the *how-to* process. For instance, the question 'how to segment a face into its constituent parts' is already premised on knowing that segmenting is what you have to do to get along with engaging *how-to* questions. To put that another way, this question seems to be conditional to a preceding *how-to* question:

"How to deal with this face for such-and-such purpose?"
"We need to segment it into its constituent parts."
"How to segment a face into its constituent parts?"

and so on.

Similar presumptions underpin your phrasing for some of the other *how-to* questions. Without putting the cart ahead of the mule, we can then pare down the number of *how-to* questions you address to a set of first-order *how-to* questions. It seems to me that you indicate those clearly enough in terms of purposes (to reconstruct, to discriminate, to recognize, and so on) without quite stating them as such. As I understand it, there are four first-order questions in your account, thus:

Through automatized technological means, how to:

1. get an identifiable face given its underlying structure (skull)? [Reconstruction]
2. identify a face as a face from a pool of (2 or more) face and non-face images? [Discrimination]
3. identify a particular face as that particular face rather than another from a pool of (2 or more) face images? [Comparable recognition]
4. identify a particular face as that particular face under varying conditions — factoring mutability in environment (light, surroundings, other objects, view captured, etc.) and in appearance (hairstyle, clothes, etc. ... I take expression as a specific kind of change in appearance)? [Contextual recognition]

Methods

Your account of the methods used is beautifully clear, but let me nevertheless restate the general principles that they actuate, insofar as I have grasped them:

- using formulae to extrapolate a norm from a given pool of stable faces (such as a mean face) and then tracking variations relative to that norm,
- using formulae tracking interactions between two or more correlated norms (of faces and/or non-faces) that are appointed as such (rather than extrapolated) with regard to a given pool of stable faces and/or non-faces,
- using data on the evidenced behaviour of mutable conditions on an accruing pool of faces to continuously fine-tune the formulae for tracking interactions between two or more correlated norms under mutable conditions (for any existing or potential pool of faces) — i.e., a learning method.

Eigenvectors, Fourier transforms, Marching cubes, generative and discriminative approaches to alignment are some of the primary formulae which operationalize these steps (so algorithms). They effectively automatize application and thereafter automatize learning for increasingly robust application.

Challenges

Here I refer to the challenges that the field you have outlined encounters in a general way. Specific projects address one or more of these to greater or lesser degrees.

- *The complexity of the face as an object*: We can think of this as aggregating between a relatively stable underlying structure, such as the skull or inherited features — let's call this the Deep Face — and the different levels of mutability that are expressed on the outer appearance — let's call this the Sur-Face. Biological factors like illness and ageing, which are tied in with environmental/social factors like work and weathering, which are tied in with social factors like vestments and styling of appearance, offer different levels of mutability imprints on the Sur-Face.
- *The special complexity of expression*: Though mainly on the Sur-Face, expression presents an aggregation range similar to that between Deep Face and Sur-Face. We can think of this range as between Universal Expressions (those that are indifferent to socialization and character) and Distinct Expressions (those that are conditional on socialization and character).
- *Complexity pertaining to the perceiving apparatus that looks at/ records the face (the eye of the beholder, the image-recorder)*: The equipment might (mostly, will) have limited capacities that need to be factored in, such as resolution, coverage, colour-accuracy, movement-capture. The environment in which the object — i.e., face — is discerned might (mostly, will) pose challenges: such as, in a crowd, in darkness or mist, in disguise, with certain expressions or alongside particular body postures.

What

This is the area of questioning which is muffled in your account, Peter.

So, what are you automatizing? Obviously, the process of facial recognition. Let's take 'facial recognition' as the overarching phrase which consists in all the fine-tuned outcomes of the four *how-to* questions above (reconstruction, discrimination, comparable recognition, contextual recognition). Before getting down to clarifying the *how-to*, perhaps we could ask: what is facial recognition? This is not the same as asking what it consists in (reconstruction, discrimination, comparable recognition, contextual recognition), but to ask what we need to know already so as to know that it consists in those processes. Here's a popular ready answer: facial recognition is what humans do in variously interacting with each other. Automatizing facial recognition is getting a machine to do *that*, but only to do it more accurately, comprehensively, on larger scale, undiscriminatingly, objectively, etc.

That's the ready answer, and I don't find it immediately helpful. I don't dismiss it either and will return to it at the end, but I do not think that's the answer which informs your account of what AI Engineers are at. Some such notion is perhaps fuzzily in the background somewhere, like an enveloping mist around AI Engineers which doesn't really trouble them. That's because these AI Engineers are beavering away at something both narrower than that ready answer, and, at the same time, larger. They are working on one thrust of facial recognition: the identification of individuals. It is there in all your first-order *how-to* questions: identify a face from the skull, identify a face as such from a pool, identify a particular face as that face from a pool, identify an image of a face by comparing to another image of that face, identify a face as that face in different contexts, etc. The primary *how-to* questions, centred on identification, are set by institutions focused on identification: by your experience, to do with forensics and surveillance. The process of working out *how-to* in itself involves contingently or pragmatically naming or labelling faces — giving them identification signs.

So, here are some more immediately relevant responses to *what* questions.

Question: What is facial recognition?
Answer: It is a process by which one person identifies another/others.

Further *what* questions can roll off from there.

Question: What does it mean to automatize facial recognition?
Answer (the most plausible I can think of): It means enabling a self-operating technological intervention in the process of one person (an identifier) identifying another person/s (the identified). This intervention is designed to make the identification:

- more accurate (the identified will always be correctly identified by the identifier),
- more comprehensive (the identified would be known immediately to the identifier in various circumstances and contexts, in depth),
- more objective and undiscriminating (the identifier's prejudices won't interfere with the identification or won't be interfered with by the technological intervention),
- more scaled-up (the identifier can extend such identifying to lots of others, the identifier can do the identifying more quickly than they could if left to their own inbuilt devices).

There's an implicit horizon there, a kind of Absolute Facial Recognition horizon for the purposes of identification (most accurate, most comprehensive, most objective, maximally scaled-up). This horizon can be imagined as setting the direction of travel for AI Engineers engrossed with developing facial recognition systems.

That's still not, to my mind, a sufficient answer. I am putting rather a lot of weight on the word 'identification' as if it were obviously distinct from our run-off-the-mill everyday understanding of 'facial recognition'. This everyday understanding is loose and not necessarily focused on identification. Sometimes we identify someone encountered earlier, sometimes we recognize them but fail to identify, sometimes we register a face and then identify if needed, sometimes we fail to identify but sense a familiarity, and so on — all according to some logic of evolutionary and social need. The push towards Absolute Facial Recognition already begs another *what* question: what is the superlative identification centred for this? Something more is needed than the fuzzy field of everyday recognition to grasp its peculiarity and distinctiveness. With some sense of the automated facial recognition systems in place, this seems an answerable question — at least an answer can be mooted. The following is far from being an unfamiliar answer: *identification is an indexical process.*

Let me pause on that and try to come up with a tentative definition which you can complicate or modify, Peter, or which I can then complicate and modify myself. So, for the area currently in view: an indexical process is essentially a process of naming or labelling persons such that each can be distinguished from others, and such that all can be put into various sorts of relationship or order (e.g., classification, location, organization) with regard to each other according to need. An index is a list of such names/labels which serves this process. Where facial recognition is focused on identification, it is principally a matter of, so to speak, putting a name to a face. So, there are two components at work in identification:

1. being sure that a face in question is that particular face and not any other, so carries a specific name (which all your *how-to* questions are ultimately devoted to cracking, Peter); and
2. having or generating a list of names matched to faces in which the face in question features and therefore its name can be recovered (which is the missing part of your account, Peter).

Actually, the indexical process is necessarily more complex. Very little of the ordering and putting into relationships can be done on the basis of one index. Identification usually involves a number of indexes being put to work in relation to each other according to need. So, to visualize this, we can have our A-Index of names matched with faces. Then we can have a B-Index of the same face matched to different expressions. Then we can have a C-Index of names matched to, say, financial histories. With these at hand, facial recognition could mean putting a name to a face and concurrently knowing whether that face is angry or happy at the moment discerned (gauging its intentions) and at the same time knowing whether that face belongs to a person who is thrifty or profligate. If A-Index gives us a basic identification, its interplay with B-Index and C-Index could give us more in-depth identification. The more indexes to interplay, the deeper, so to speak, identification is.

This puts another dimension to that question: what does it mean to automatize facial recognition? Because the automatized facial recognition system cannot engage in its identification tasks simply by doing something with faces, it also needs to do something with indexes. In fact, the AI Engineers' development of these facial-recognition systems is not merely about how to automatize the disaggregating, disambiguating, and reading of faces. It is also concurrently about how to automatize the play of indexes to identify those faces. So, to my previous answer to that question, some more could be added.

Question: What does it mean to automatize facial recognition?
Answer (the most plausible I can think of): It means enabling a self-operating technological intervention in the process of one person

(an identifier) identifying another person/s (the identified). This intervention is designed to make the identification:

- more accurate (the identified will always be correctly identified by the identifier),
- more comprehensive (the identified would be known immediately to the identifier in various circumstances and contexts, in depth),
- more objective and undiscriminating (the identifier's prejudices won't interfere with the identification or won't be interfered with by the technological intervention),
- more scaled-up (the identifier can extend such identifying to lots of others, the identifier can do identifying very quickly than it would be if the identifier were left to their own inbuilt devices). The self-operating technological intervention achieves these enhancements by concurrently:
    - integrating existing indexes relevant to current populations of identifieds, and
    - automatically generating new/wider indexes and constantly updating all indexes for all possible identifieds.

Thus, along with the horizon of Absolute Facial Recognition for identification purposes that the *how-to* questions push AI Engineers towards, there's also a horizon of the Total Facial Index (one of several biometric identity indexes, others could be of fingerprints, iris scans, or genetic profiles) for identification purposes which necessarily pull AI Engineers onwards.

Why

So, finally, to the *why*-questions. Why develop such automatized facial recognition systems? Why reach towards Absolute Facial Recognition and be drawn towards the Total Facial Index? Why enhance the capacity of identifiers and the exposure of identifieds?

For you, Peter, and for your colleagues, I suspect the immediate answer is clear enough from your account: the sheer pleasure of engaging with those *how-to* questions, the thrill of expending your ingenuity and knowledge on cracking them, the delight of successfully overcoming the challenges. Evidently, in raising those *why*-questions, I am not really asking why AI Engineers develop automatized facial-recognition systems.

I think I am asking *why* the identifiers want this. That's an important question because the *what* and *how-to* questions are ultimately delved by AI Engineers to fulfil that primal *why* according to terms set by the demanding/consuming identifiers. And when you ask whether this technology can be brought usefully to ordinary people going about their everyday lives, to introduce an AI-Assistant accordingly which could be demanded/consumed by these ham-and-eggers, you are also asking a *why*-question. Why should ordinary individuals amidst their everyday lives want an AI-Assistant with facial recognition capacities?

Let me state the obvious first: an automatized facial recognition system technically identifying persons doesn't do so for its own ends; it does the identifier's identifying for them according to the identifier's purposes. The direction towards Absolute Facial Recognition and the Total Facial Index that developing such systems involves is for quite peculiar identifier-demanded ends. Those ends are not immediately relevant to ordinary individuals in their everyday lives; these are to do obviously with Big Purposes, such as those of investigating or surveillance agencies. They are properly the purposes, in other words, of state or corporate agencies, for large-scale governmental or commercial objectives.

There are two views on such Big Purposes, depending on whom one asks:

1. On the one hand: automatized systems serving them are designed to closely control and manipulate populations without their fully understanding or consenting to that. This could be for the purpose of having compliant citizens who are unquestioning of governmental moves or compliant consumers who are suggestible as regards products in the market. Historically, compulsory identification strategies (e.g., national ID cards) have periodically aroused unease about the consequent potential for authoritarian control and exploitation. Under the current circumstances of advanced automation, such anxieties have intensified. It seems arguable that Absolute Facial Recognition and the Total Facial Index may come to be achieved without any explicit compulsion — without the identifieds even knowing that they are included. And that makes identifieds all the more controllable and manipulable.

2. On the other hand: automatized systems serving Big Purposes are designed to extend benefits and protection more efficiently and even-handedly to all identifieds than heretofore. Or, to go further,

such systems may help the identifieds to take their affairs into their own hands. It is often argued by interested governmental and commercial agencies that such systems can eradicate corruption, prejudice, and simply human errors and inefficiencies. If there is lack of consent and manipulation in implementing them, that's nevertheless a reasonable cost for the greater good of the identified — the benevolence of governmental and commercial identifiers needs to be taken on trust.

At any rate, while governments and corporations are investing heavily in pushing AI Engineers towards the Absolute Facial Recognition horizon, they are also investing handsomely in putting together the Total Facial Index. Passports in quite a few countries are tagged to face images now. An almost total facial index of citizens, also tagged to fingerprint and iris scan indexes, and moreover to all sorts of social indexes (financial behaviour, movement, etc.) has been realized in India through the Aadhaar number scheme under the Unique Identification Authority of India (UIDAI) in gradual steps since 2009.

Such Big Purposes are not easily translated into the pluriverse of individuals amidst their everyday lives with their small ends and means. Insofar as you're contemplating a localized AI-Assistant (a gadget of some kind) with facial recognition capacities that individuals may want for something they do regularly, there are two possibilities:

1. Individuals conduct their everyday lives continuously in sync with states and corporations. Almost every dimension of everyday life is, wittingly or otherwise, penetrated by the conditions set by governmental strictures and market conditions. Individual compliance is largely fine-tuned to a habitual level. The face-recognizing AI-Assistant in question may be used to facilitate this synchronising of everyday lives of individuals with the Big Purposes. Arguably, that's really the way in which our mobile gadgets already work. But it's difficult to say whose ends those are serving. One of your examples of possible usage of such an AI-Assistant is really to instil a collective norm of facial recognition: to guide autistic persons to gauge the import of expressions so as to be able to simulate a social norm of behaviour. Collective norms are crucial for synchronizing Big and Small Purposes.

2. Individuals could be encouraged to behave like and feel like governmental or commercial identifiers in their microcosms by taking recourse to AI-Assistants with facial recognition capacities. Your other example is in this direction: to 'repair' forgetful moments so that each individual can feel a bit like an Absolute Recognizer with access to a Total Index akin in-principle to states and businesses. Small groups of individuals amidst everyday life — in the homestead, club, workplace, etc. — can then begin to act like micro-states and micro-businesses and refer to their AI-Assistants accordingly. The great burgeoning of individualized usage of tracking devices, domestic and workplace surveillance and security systems, profiling engines, etc. is a considerable industry in this direction already.

Much sociological research has been devoted to this ground already, exploring concepts of 'risk society', 'serialization', 'information society', 'biopolitics', 'neoliberal governmentality', 'technocracy', etc. No doubt a great deal more is on its way.

But there is a third interesting possibility. Perhaps new sorts of facial-recognition AI-Assistants can be conceived by resetting the horizons of the field of automatized facial recognition. That might involve taking on board the functions of everyday human facial recognition more carefully. That might mean moving away from the horizons of Absolute Recognition and Total Indexes, and considering the principles and practices of the very much Less-than-Absolute Recognition and Less-than-Total Indexes which are the default settings of individuals amidst their everyday lives — the basis of everyday life itself. There might be something new for the AI-Assistant to contribute to people's lives from this direction. More distinctive modes of usage and consumption might lie ahead with that approach.

I will leave it to you to contemplate that possibility in your response, and, of course, to find holes in the above argument.

Chapter 3

Facing Up to Challenges

Peter Tu

Suman, let me start by thanking you for your kind words regarding the collective accomplishments of my engineering brethren. I like your perspective of adding to our discussion on face work the topics of both *what* and *why*. In terms of *what*, before getting to the heart of the matter, you start by bringing up the challenges that must be overcome in the pursuit of accurate face recognition. So, let me begin there ...

More on Challenges

In my last intervention, I discussed the concept of spatial resolution and how it can be characterized via Fourier mathematics and what is known as the Nyquist frequency. Beyond resolution, three other key factors should be discussed: Projective Geometry, Illumination, and Convolution. I will give a short primer on each of these topics. I will then try to address the heart of your question: what is facial recognition? Shifting gears, I will attempt to add to the discussion of why our AI-Assistant might need a solid facial analytics engine.

Projective Geometry

In the 1990s, much of the work in Computer Vision was focused on a particular form of mathematics known as Projective Geometry. The idea is that an image can be thought of as a projection of the 3D world onto a 2D imaging plane. The pin-hole camera represents one of the simplest models for such a process. It turns out that for a pin-hole camera, the mapping of a 3D point in space (*X*, *Y*, *Z*) to a 2D pixel location (*u*, *v*) can be defined by what is commonly known as a 3 × 4 projective matrix *P*. Initially, the math is quite simple, if you understand the idea of similar triangles, then you can work out how a *P* matrix is derived. The hard part comes when you start asking questions such as how quantities in the image space change when transformations are applied to their corresponding objects in the 3D world. From a face recognition perspective, this is of crucial importance. Not only is the shape of the face dynamic in nature, but changes in viewing angle result in complex 2D transformations in the image space. My friend Xiaoming Liu wrote a number of papers on what is known as 'facial rectification' (Wheeler *et al.* 2010). This is an attempt to compensate, to some degree, for changes in viewpoint. He also wrote a clever paper regarding the optimal viewing angle for facial identification purposes (Liu *et al.* 2006: 1430). I am sure that later in our discussions we will return to the question of geometry and projection, but for now, all you have to know is that variation due to changes in viewpoint must be considered when building a proper face recognition engine. As a quick historical aside, it turns out that the number of academic papers associated with Projective Geometry took a precipitous drop during the early Noughties. This is due to the publication of *Multi-View Geometry in Computer Vision* (2003) by Richard Hartley and Andrew Zisserman (Hartley and Zisserman 2003). In Computer Vision circles, their offering is commonly referred to as 'The Book'. After this seismic event, there simply was not much more left to be said on the topic and so the community had to move on. Full disclosure: when I was at Oxford, I had the pleasure of working with Andrew and when I first joined GE, Richard and I became both good colleagues and good friends.

Illumination

Publishers argue that if *n* is the number of equations found in a popular science book and *R* is the number of people who would read such a book for *n* = 0, then the actual number of readers *R'* is $R' = R \times (\frac{1}{2})^n$. With this said I think that the following equation is rather critical to our understanding of how difficult things like face recognition really are. So, with your indulgence let me describe what is known as the Bidirectional Radial Distribution Function (BRDF) — and yes, I realize that including an equation for this justification for an equation may have in itself lost half of our potential readers.

Consider the following:

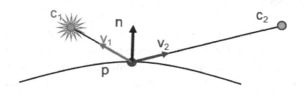

$$I_{2,1}(\mathbf{p}) = \eta\rho(\mathbf{p}, \mathbf{v}_1, \mathbf{v}_2)\mathbf{n} \cdot \mathbf{v}_1 \frac{1}{\|\mathbf{c}_1 - \mathbf{p}\|^2}$$

For a given ray of light, this equation defines *exactly* the amount of energy (intensity) that will be received at point C_2 given a light source at point C_1 and a path that includes the point p associated with a given surface. In our case, C_1 represents a light source such as the sun, p is a point on the face, and C_2 might be a pixel element on a CCD camera. From our perspective, the main concern is the term $\rho(p, v_1, v_2)$. This is known as the Bidirectional Reflectance Distribution Function (BRDF). The BRDF is a property of the material at point p (i.e., one's skin). It is in general unknown and non-parametric (contrary to what many computer graphics people believe, the world is not Lambertian). The non-parametric nature of the BRDF implies that if one changes either angle v_1 or v_2, the change in intensity will be unpredictable. The main consequence of the non-parametric nature of the BRDF function is that the appearance of a face will change in an unpredictable manner depending on both the illumination and viewing angle. This was the premise behind an episode on *Seinfeld*, where Jerry's new girlfriend appeared to be very attractive under certain lighting conditions and significantly less so in others. If the BRDF made it so difficult for poor Jerry to decide whether or not to share his affections with a young lady, just imagine the challenges faced by the humble engineer who is attempting to build a reliable face recognition engine. A number of years ago, Peter Belhumeur built what might be thought of as a Camera Dome (Magda *et al.* 2001: 391). A person sitting in the camera dome is sequentially illuminated and imaged from all sorts of angles. This then allowed for the approximation of a person-specific BRDF function.

As a side note, one of the reasons why stereo reconstruction from multiple images is so difficult is that the unpredictable BRDF function does not allow one to use raw pixel values alone in order to establish correspondences between stereo image pairs. However, Lord Helmholtz hypothesized that if the path between C_1–p–C_2 was reversed becoming C_2–p–C_1, then $\rho\,(p, v_1, v_2)$ must equal $\rho\,(p, v_2, v_1)$. That is to say that the loss in energy associated with light following the same path but opposite direction must be the same. This led to a modest cottage industry known as Helmholtz Stereopsis. My colleague Paulo Mendonça and I have a small claim to fame in that we were the first to show that 3D reconstruction can be achieved using a single Helmholtz Stereo pair (Tu and Mendonça 2003).

Convolution

We have discussed the geometry of the imaging process as well as the material properties of the face and how this affects the image formation process. What else is there to consider? Well, light must travel through the atmosphere and this acts as a kind of filter. Also, the collection of pixels is not instantaneous. The need for integration time coupled with small movements of the subject can result in what is known as motion blur. Under certain conditions, filtering and blurring can to some degree be modelled as a linear process known as convolution. Convolution is a mathematical operation on two functions (f and g) that produces a third function expressing how the values of one are modified by the other ($f * g$). It is defined as the integral of the product of the two functions after one is reversed and shifted. If f is an original image and g models the effects of filtering or blurring, then $f * g$ is the resulting image. From a face recognition perspective, f represents the image of the face without atmospheric filtering or motion blur and $f * g$ is the image that we are forced to work with. We would much rather work directly with f instead of $f * g$. In one of our previous discussions, I mentioned that working with integrals is tough, so trying to get rid of g in the spatial domain is going to be tricky. However, Fourier mathematics comes to our rescue in the form of what is known as the Fourier Transform (FT). FT converts any function from the spatial domain into the frequency domain. Now the frequency domain is a weird place. Remember how any function can be represented by the summation of an infinite set of sinusoids? Well, the amplitude and phase shift of each of these sinusoids is sorted based on frequency in the frequency domain. We also have to start working with complex numbers, which have both a real and an imaginary component — but let's not worry about this for now. One of the properties of the FT is that convolution in the spatial domain becomes multiplication in the frequency domain. So, if one can transform $f * g$ into the frequency domain, divide by the FT of g (but remember dividing by zero blows things up), and then inverse FT, what remains back in the spatial domain is that in principle you get f, which is what you want to work with. Half the fun with this type of image processing is figuring out how to come up with the distorting function g and an appropriate model of its inverse. For a great read on the fundamentals of Fourier Transforms, I would go to the old classic *Signals and Systems* (1983) (Oppenheim 1983).

What Is Face Recognition?

Now let's get back to the question of what does face recognition really mean. I think that you hint at the idea of a recognition being a true description of the face via a form of exhaustive indexing. Let me dwell on this point. For all practical purposes, there is an open-ended set of facial image classes. Examples of such categories include the following:

- All realistic faces
- Projections of the famous folk singer Arlo Guthrie
- Images of an academic with the arched eyebrow of scepticism that forms whenever a colleague, much less an underling, is offering a novel opinion, formulation, or hypothesis
- Faces that appear to be nodding in agreement with one's argument
- Images of Justin Trudeau with and without racially disturbing affectations
- Angry faces in general
- Bernie Sanders when he is angry
- Bernie Sanders when he is standing next to a billionaire
- The face of someone that you have not seen for over 20 years
- The face of someone that you think you saw committing a crime
- Portraits

- Caricatures
- Cartoons
- The list goes on and on …

One could argue that to fully describe a face, one approach might be to attempt to list all the categories that such a face belongs to. Computationally this seems problematic. However, it seems that when we recognize a face, we are probably doing something even more fantastic, out of all the possible face categories we seem to pull out the most salient or useful set of categories to which a given face belongs. This can be thought of as a kind of spectral description of the face.

In one of our early conversations (Gupta and Tu 2020: Chs. 2 and 3), I attempted to characterize the difference between classification and recognition. With very limited success, I tried to describe what Kenneth Sayre (1965) calls an act of attainment. So, let me take another run at this. Consider the two phrases: 'Joseph is looking for his book' and 'Bridgette saw her book'. The concept of looking is associated with a causal process in that it was initiated by Joseph's desire to find his book. A similar sense of volition does not seem to apply to Bridgette, it is something that happened to her. Looking for something can be thought of as a task or process and as such can be criticized with respect to competency or efficiency. Such task-related analysis does not seem to apply to the act of seeing something. So, when you or I recognize a face, I believe that we are seeing a face and that this is an act of attainment.

I think that Dan Kahneman's (2011) description of System 1 and System 2 has some bearing here. System 1 is described as the workhorse of the mind. Given the current context, System 1 is responsible for going out and 'bringing things to mind'. This is how associative memory is often described. System 2 can be thought of as the conscious mind that encapsulates awareness. So, when we see or recognize a face, somehow System 1 has selected the most relevant set of face categories as well as established membership or not with these categories. Within a matter of milliseconds, such findings are presented to System 2 for consideration. Now System 1 is not all-powerful. To make this point, consider the following question 'what is more frequent, words starting with the letter *i* or words whose third letter is *i*?' Words that start with *i* readily come to mind: iceberg, ink, island, Ichabod Crane … However, when asked to produce words having a third letter *i*, most of us draw blanks. This might lead to the conclusion that more words start with the letter *i*, which is not true. Human face recognition also has its blind spots. We need very few pixels from eye to eye in order to recognize the face of someone that we are familiar with, such as a good friend or family member. However, studies have shown that we are very poor at picking someone from a line-up that we have seen before but are not particularly familiar with. Contrary to our personal beliefs, our ability to discriminate between honesty and deceit based on facial imagery is little better than chance. With this said, we put a lot of stock in our System 1 assessment skills. We may choose our mates based initially on their facial qualities and, more outrageously, we seem to choose our leaders in a similar manner. There was an experiment performed where people not familiar with the politics of a given region were shown facial images of the winner and loser of a local election. Such predictions were on the order of 75% accurate. This implies that the voters in general take their cues from central casting.

To summarize, I have argued that face recognition is an attainment as opposed to a causal task or procedure. It involves identifying the most salient face membership classes from a seemingly infinite set of possibilities. This seems to be achieved by some sort of System 1 entity in a matter of milliseconds. In contrast, all the AI-related facial analysis methods that I have described in my last intervention should be viewed as a kind of purpose-driven causal task of classification with respect to a fixed set of membership classes:

- *Face Detection*: Membership with the class of all possible faces.
- *Biometric Identification*: Membership with the classes of faces from all persons found in a database of individuals.
- *Identity Authentication (Access Control)*: Membership with the class of faces from a specific and cooperative individual.
- *Expression Classification*: Membership with the classes of faces of people expressing certain emotions.
- *Soft Biometrics*: Membership with the classes of faces from certain populations (i.e., gender, age, and race).

As we have discussed earlier, new architectures such as Autoencoders, Emergent Languages, and General Adversarial Networks hint at going beyond specific acts of classification and towards possibly supporting more open-ended acts of recognition. But results to date are scant at best, so for now all we have to look forward to in the foreseeable future are increasingly accurate facial classifiers. I can now turn to your second question of 'why'.

Why

In your last intervention, you were somewhat unimpressed by my list of possible face-related applications. Reasons for such a tepid response may be the following:

- Artificial facial analysis methods have been constructed to support specific applications such as access control as opposed to more general use by an AI-Assistant.
- I limited my considerations to applications where facial analysis was used in isolation as opposed to being used in a more holistic fashion.

Let me now come to the question of *why* in the context of a possibly more compelling scenario. Consider the following.

Sheryl, a humble engineer returns to her office on a bright Monday morning refreshed and ready to go. She opens her inbox and to her horror, there is a meeting invite for 11:00 AM that morning with the subject line 'brainstorm'. Not for the first time does Sheryl curse the inventor of the electronic calendar, where practically anyone from anywhere can carve out hours of her day with just a few simple clicks and a keystroke or two. Twenty years ago, when Sheryl first started, she could keep a list of all the meetings she needed to attend over the next three months on the back of an envelope. Today the idea of stringing together three uninterrupted hours in a row is as rare as a compliment from her mother-in-law. Sheryl considers replying that she has a previous commitment. However, the organizer will just reschedule. Maybe asking for a call-in number will do the trick, but alas the meeting is just down the hall and they already have post-it notes on the whiteboard. At this point, inspiration hits — Sheryl responds that while she has a previous commitment, this meeting is too important to delay and so she is activating a new feature of her AI-Assistant Joan — the proxy mode.

Joan arranges to have a robot platform make its way to the meeting. The platform itself is not much more than a self-propelled cart with a screen, camera, speaker, microphone and of course a wireless connection. Just before the meeting starts, Joan installs herself on the platform. The image of her avatar is now projecting on the screen and she is ready to go. As the meeting starts, the usual suspects start to trickle in. The first 40 minutes go pretty much as expected, everyone grandstanding and holding forth without paying much attention to what others are saying. From time to time, Joan manages to chime in with some pithy remarks. Things are going well. However, with only 20 minutes to go, two unexpected characters make an entrance. Using her face recognition engine, Joan realizes that trouble might be brewing. The first person is a Product Manager (PM), also known as the cheque writer. The second was none other than Chad St Clair, Sheryl's most despised nemesis. Analysis of Chad's facial expression revealed that something was amiss. Chad was getting ready to project some slides onto the common office display. While Chad was fiddling with the HDMI connection, Joan was able to hack into his account. It was worse than she feared, Chad was going to propose making changes to project funding allocations. Sheryl will be devastated. Joan quickly checked the product manager's schedule. The PM had a hard stop at the top of the hour. Joan needed to somehow make the next 20 minutes disappear. She only had one option — the filibuster. Before Chad could connect to the screen, Joan threw up a set of slides from a presentation that Sheryl gave last week to a gaggle of marketing folks. As she started to go over each slide, she made eye contact with all the other folks in the room. They knew what she was doing and through their eyes promised to support this desperate manoeuvre. As Joan was getting to her last slide, the PM looked at her watch and promptly left the room. The day, as they say, was saved.

Suman, I hope that this tale of derring-do illustrates how important face work is in our daily lives. Faces are essentially organs of expression, communication, and social hierarchy. If our AI-Assistant is going to navigate these murky waters on our behalf, it cannot be oblivious to all things facial.

Chapter 4

Janus-Faced Issues

Suman Gupta

I am afraid I still find myself resistant to the numinous sense of 'recognition' and 'attainment' drawn from Sayre. The idea of 'attainment' suggests that human face recognition cannot be accounted in terms of causal or purposive processing. There are aspects of what humans do by way of recognizing faces that are in the nature of leaps of doing, just happenings, intrinsically accomplished — hence, attainment. Face recognition technology for identification (in surveillance or forensics) is distinct from human face recognition in being purposively constructed. It seems to me that taking recourse to 'attainment' circumvents the issue, 'what is face recognition in the everyday sphere?' There's space for a more leisurely pause on this.

Dimensions of Recognition

To pause on this, I will take recourse to an analogy. But before that, more or less instinctively, it seems to me that three distinct kinds of doing are conflated in the term 'recognition'. Such conflation occurs because, though distinct, no clear precedence or sequence can be attributed to doing one or the other as they integrate into recognizing a face. The distinct kinds of doing that are integrated are as follows:

1. *Registering* a face as descriptively that specific face. (This is a complicated matter of knowing what a face is, apprehending

faceness; deploying rule-of-thumb and adjustable classifications of faces and relatedly noting individualizing features of a face; factoring in mutable factors like illumination and expression; having a descriptive record of a face accordingly, etc. In fact, most of the challenges you have so carefully addressed for automation come up here.)

2. *Indexing* a face that is thus registered with other already-registered and to-be-registered faces, in an ongoing process and according to significance, i.e., probability of need for recall or reviewing or reference. (Memory storage equipment and mnemonic apparatuses play their part here; social conventions such as naming and mapping are implicit here; a language for sharing the index with others is needed; etc. The seeming imperfections of this aspect of human recognition compared to a comprehensive biometric identity database may well be necessary structuring devices for functional everyday life.)

3. *Interpreting* a face that is registered and indexically positioned, though those don't necessarily precede interpreting — it is quite possible that interpreting is coterminous with registering and indexing. (Peter, your story about how some handy AI-Assistant Joan saved Sheryl's day is really about interpreting a face, and gauging mood and intent of a face in a given situation. Interpretation seems to me as possibly the weak element in the technology chain. That's not in terms of developing automatized abilities to tag expression/behaviour to mood or intent, but in operating the precepts and anticipating the consequences of interpretation).

If we think of registering, indexing, and interpreting as the inextricable but distinct aspects of face recognition, then a few more inferences could be mooted. But to clarify these interlocked aspects and possible inferences, it might be helpful to take recourse to an analogous terminology. Defamiliarization of terminology sometimes puts excessively familiar issues and assumptions into perspective.

Texts and Reading

The analogy is with texts and reading. If any literary/linguistics aficionados are reading these exchanges, they should perk up now. For such, most phenomena can be expressed in terms of texts (and contexts) and reading.

In relation to face recognition, it seems plausible enough that the *face* could be regarded as a text and *recognition* involves something like reading. Let's see whether the analogy can be stretched.

As it happens, the concepts relevant to reading texts are distributed between different scholarly areas which speak infrequently to each other. A literary/linguistics aficionado would generally go for one area as if it were the core of the matter and quite unrelated to the others. The reason why that happens is itself of some interest here.

The facets of texts that bear upon reading are covered under the following areas, sketchily outlined:

1. *Typography* attends to the physical production of texts and has well-developed concepts of (and measurements for) legibility and readability. Some typographists make a reasonably clear distinction between legibility and readability, focusing on the typeface itself for the former and its relation to other factors — such as reflectance, material, layout, design, environment, etc. — for the latter. Elsewhere, legibility has taken in readability. Miles Tinker's *Legibility in Print* (1963) set out the main factors that have been considered and measured variously since: kind and size of type, width of line, spatial arrangement on a page, colour of print and background, printing surfaces, illumination, the reading situation. Various modes of measuring the optimal characteristics of each and in combination for different genres (newspapers, manuals, directories, etc.) have occupied such scholarly pursuit. This has ultimately been with a strong applied objective: setting industry standards or trying to find what gives a marketable edge for particular kinds of print production. In this area then, it is the *appearance* of the text that's foregrounded, and the *content* of the text is of relatively little interest (that is, only insofar as content characterizes genres that should be typographically distinguishable or offers unusual typographical possibilities). The focus is on the relation between the reader's normal sensory apparatus and expectations in relation to the physical/visual appearance of the text. Legibility and readability have attracted burgeoning (and lucrative) interest with the shift from print to digital production, from paper to various screens.
2. *Readable writing* (asking what makes writing readable) is an area of enquiry which deals with textual content, but in a particular way: for ease of comprehension. This is therefore not so much

about interpreting the received content of texts as about designing textual content for easy understanding by the maximum number of readers. Naturally, such enquiry is also led by applied considerations, especially in relation to teaching writing (in an instructional context) and increasing the uptake of informational texts (such as news reportage). The applied thrust keeps scholarly attention focused either on texts meant for mass readership (for marketing purposes) or on the textual productions of less proficient writers (for educational purposes). Various formulae have been proposed, mainly by educationists, to measure or give scores for the readability of a text, combining factors such as length of sentences, vocabulary, stylistic features, reading speeds, etc. These formulae have had an increasingly numerate tenor since Rudolf Flesch's *The Art of Readable Writing* (1949), but the norms of ease still appear more preconceived than evidenced, and tend to be grounded at lower levels of proficiency rather than variegated according to a range of proficiencies.

3. *Reader response and reception theory* is an area of literary/linguistic studies which analyzes how readers make sense of received texts at the level of content, taking in factors such as language usage, narrative structure, hermeneutic framing, contextual relevance, linkage to other texts, situated reading practices, etc. For literary scholars, this has ranged between working out how texts are designed to guide interpretations according to the reader's associations and proclivities (Iser 1978) gave a persuasive account of this) and suggesting that interpretation depends on conventions of reading established among readers before reading a text (Fish 1980) influentially proposed this. Rather more systematically, an experimental approach to how readers read and understand given texts according to linguistic practices, cognitive abilities, social norms, etc. has proved to be productive. Since this has been a particular hobbyhorse of literary scholars, the focus has usually been on interpreting the received content of culturally valued (canonical), often challenging, texts — at the other pole of textual engagement than in 2.

All of these are about the relationship between the text and reader. If they haven't quite come together in a synthesized conception of reading, it's because researchers in each focus on quite different objectives and find their particular lines more or less sufficient for those objectives: for typographers, setting industry standards and looking for marketable production edges; for researchers in readable writing, instructions for learners and maximizing the reach of informational texts; for literary/linguistic analysts, clarifying why certain cultural texts are valued and unpacking the mechanics of textual interpretation.

The distinction between appearance and content of a text for the reader is sharp because of the nature of writing as a communicative medium; the mediation of phonetic/ideogrammatic signs seems to put a particular wedge between appearance and content. That distinction may seem less germane for an image (a photograph, for instance). However, in fact, the distinction between studying the appearance and the content of an image still applies much as for reading texts. An image may be described according to the relations of lines, forms, colours, grids, etc. on the surface (appearance) and according to what it represents or says as an image to a viewer (content). Whether an image is abstract or represents reality in an obvious way may excite the passions of a viewable-photography instructor in the same way as a readable-writing proponent. For literary/linguistics scholars, an image is but another text and the viewer but another reader, though the mechanics of the medium is different from writing.

Analogy

To push the analogy then, let me be pat about the complex how-to processes of automatizing face recognition you have described, Peter — without in any way underplaying the scale of challenges overcome. The description of a face for automatic recognition, ingeniously incorporating the registering aspects of recognition, is analogous to the typographical grasp of reading texts. That is to say, insofar as the automated capacity is that of disaggregating and recomposing the appearance of the face — registering it — that is analogous to what a typographist attends to, i.e., the appearance of a text. Further, insofar as the automated capacity thereafter takes on the indexical aspect of recognition for the purpose of identifying a face, that is analogous to what the readable-writing exponent seeks, i.e., finding ways of rendering textual content easily understandable (readable). This is analogous to being application driven with a narrow attention to content.

There isn't an analogous step to the reader response and reception part in your account of recognition for developing automatized capacities. The complexities of interpretation don't seem to feature there beyond tagging indicators of expression/behaviour to intention/mood. The latter is still within the narrow sphere of indexing really, analogous to setting some gauges for readable writing. The nearest you come to the interpretation of a face that is registered and indexed is in drawing upon Kahneman's Systems 1 and 2 — which is worth pausing on. But before doing so, let me suggest that possibly this limitation in the approach of AI Engineers is analogous to the limitations that are found among typographers and readable-writing exponents. All are similarly uninterested in the interpretation of received texts (a written one or a face). This limitation arises because neither the AI Engineer nor the typographist or the readable-writing exponent needs to go there to serve their applied purposes. Their immediate applied purposes do not need much more than a focus on appearance (registering and indexing) with only cursory delving into the content of texts. Beyond the cursory, content has little to do with setting typographical industry standards, teaching comprehensible writing, and, for that matter, identifying faces for surveillance or forensic purposes.

However, where the purpose is not wholly set in advance and the sought-after application not quite posited yet, there is scope for open-ended exploration. Insofar as thinking about extending automatized capacities within everyday life goes, the process of face recognition that needs to be considered may well need to dwell upon the aspect of interpretation within recognition carefully — as carefully as the registering and indexing have been considered.

Peter, your recourse to Kahneman's Systems 1 and 2 comes close to beginning an exploration of interpretation. So, System 1 is the more or less preconscious aspect of the recognition capacity that looks for suitable categories to register a face (from an existing or developing index) and somehow brings them up; while System 2 is the conscious aspect of the recognition capacity that processes the face in view according to categories made available already via System 1 and responds accordingly. You go on to observe (using the '*i*'-as-first-or-third-letter test) that System 1's choices are far from robust, but once the choice is made, a great deal of confidence is reposed in it for System 2's conscious part. So, human recognition is imperfect compared to the Absolute Facial Recognition and the Absolute Index for which automation for identification strives.

But maybe this conscious fallibility, activated by a preconceptual choice, is not imperfection but exactly what's needed for the functioning of everyday social life among humans.

Insofar as we are considering the part that an AI-Assistant may play in everyday life, that seeming fallibility needs to be examined and possibly rationalized. That seeming fallibility may well underpin the degree of uncertainty or confirmation-deficit which makes interpretation both necessary and contingent. No interpretation is final or absolute in this pluriverse of everyday life, even though one might feel supremely confident about the interpretation one arrives at in a given situation. Elizabeth may have total confidence in her interpretation of Darcy's face as expressive of arrogance and condescension, but with some insistence, she can be persuaded that Darcy is in fact enamoured of her. The leeway in her mind that allowed her to be persuaded may well also have pushed her to make the incorrect interpretation in the first place. Maybe, in other words, imperfection is the condition which impels interpretation.

You — and Kahneman — have seemingly assumed that Systems 1 and 2 are, so to speak, constitutive of the interpreter's recognition apparatus. However, as with reader response theory in relation to texts, the recognition apparatus may incorporate both inbuilt individual proclivities and collective conventions and habituations. Another way of saying that is: Elizabeth's ability to recognize Darcy's face is connected with some shared strategies for registering, indexing, and particularly interpreting faces which prevailed in early 19th century Hertfordshire. The habitual bases of gender and class relations, as much as the built environments these persons were accustomed to, as well as the pleasures and pains they were socialized in ... all that has something to do with how Systems 1 and 2 work conjointly. Systems 1 and 2 in Darcy's recognition apparatus and Systems 1 and 2 in Elizabeth's recognition apparatus share something with everyone's Systems 1 and 2 within their social and collective life *because* of their social and collective life. Cracking the mysteries of interpretation in face recognition may call for a careful tracking of all those social determinants along with the inbuilt proclivities which enable registering and indexing. It might mean not merely focusing on what one person's body and mind does when encountering a face, but also tracing and modelling what occurs in a network of numerous and continuous encounters and re-encounters of numerous faces with each other.

Insofar as something like a concept akin to Sayre's 'attainment' goes, philosophers have occasionally suspected that recognition is ultimately grounded in a preconceptual apprehension which must be accepted as given rather than explained in a consequential way: i.e., the mutual recognition of being human. That seems to me close to the notion of an attainment. Mutual recognition of shared humanness is the foundation upon which the complexities of recognition are erected. Existentialist philosophers, ever in search of the preconceptual predicates that enable rationalization, have been particularly given to proposing this. Thus, Jean-Paul Sartre (1956 [1943]) put a particular emphasis on the gaze, the exchange of the look between someone and a stranger — an Other — whereby someone knows that:

> My apprehension of the Other in the world as *probably being* a man refers to my permanent possibility of *being-seen-by-him*; that is, to the permanent possibility that a subject who sees me may be substituted for the object seen by me. "Being-seen-by-the-Other" is the *truth* of "seeing-the-Other". (345).

Not dissimilarly, Maurice Merleau-Ponty (2012 [1945]) also conceived of a certain mutual entwinement in persons recognizing each other:

> I find vision to be the gaze gearing into the visible world, and this is why another's gaze can exist for me and why that expressive instrument that we call a face can bear an existence just as my existence is borne by the knowing apparatus that is my body. (367).

No Existentialist philosopher has ever cared about readable writing, but it is (almost) clear from these that insofar as something like an attainment has been conceived by philosophers, quite a low ground or fundamental plane is allowed for it: that of humans recognizing humans, and not much more. But I don't for a moment suppose that such philosophical reflection has any bearing on what AI Engineers have to take on board by way of automatizing face recognition. I just mention it by the by … because I know it teases.

Projection and the AI-Assistant

Now, finally, let's get back to the possibilities of face recognition for our AI-Assistant amidst everyday life. How can those face recognition technologies you described, Peter, be brought worthily into everyday life? Your story at the end of the last posting is entertaining but doesn't really venture beyond quite a pedestrian technological recourse.

In this respect, I have a proposal to put out here. I proceed to state it here in bare outline, without elaboration and explanation. Perhaps space can be made for it later if you feel it's worth pursuing.

The insertion of various kinds of AI-Assistants in everyday-life activities — at home, in offices, on the streets, in shops, at leisure, among family, amidst friends and colleagues and strangers, etc. — is less because there's an active demand for them and more by creating a demand, by pointedly publicizing a convenience. Once introduced, an AI-Assistant may catch on and even become indispensable. Hefty profits for the producers and purveyors of AI-Assistants, and the perception among ham-and-eggers that in the past things were inconvenient and now there are these AI-Assistants we can't do without, are part of the same movement. Under these circumstances, the point is not only to get AI-Assistants to provide ever more services in everyday life which hadn't been sought before, but also to make it acceptable and even desirable to have AI-Assistants do it. I suspect that the field of what's called 'AI' for everyday life services is only partly a matter of finding the niche where a convenient new service can be inserted, and as much if not more a matter of making AI-Assistants acceptable and, better yet, desirable to consumers.

There are several ways in which that could be achieved. One obvious way is to attach status and lifestyle values to having AI-Assistants. Consumers can take pride in possessing and being adept in using AI-Assistants — it shows tech-savviness, high status, superior control of the environment, being at the cutting edge, and so on. A more insidious way is to make the AI-Assistants seem like friends and servants, kind of human but more dependable and able. This is where the technology in question takes recourse to the human penchant for *projection.*

The human penchant for projection has a considerable scholarly literature behind it in anthropology, religious studies, psychology, and marketing. Projection is partly found in the human tendency to imbue various sorts of animate or inanimate entities (animals, idols, trees, cars, and so on) with living human-like personalities, and more continuously in the human propensity for reflecting oneself in others — attributing one's penchants and feelings to others. The examples of AI-Assistants mentioned in our Introduction (chatbots like Alexa or Siri, GPS systems, Jane in *Ender's Game*) have design features which invite projection from users: a name, a voice, ordinary language phrases, the suggestion of humanoid shapes, etc. The very appellation 'Artificial *Intelligence*' is designed to invite the kind of respect or circumspection that humans reserve for each other (with a few exceptions, like animists or psychopaths).

In short, I am suggesting that AI research for services in everyday life is as much about providing conveniences for consumers as about prodding and inviting consumers to project themselves on automatizing gadgets and systems. The technological endeavour of automatization consists significantly in developing a technology for inviting projection.

This is where the face recognition technology that you have described might come in useful for the everyday life sphere. Face recognition is, I feel convinced, at the heart of projection. The technology may best be called upon not for AI-Assistants to provide a convenient service but for AI-Assistants to be presented such that consumers are tempted to project and thereby to accept them as friends and servants.

Chapter 5

Deception and Knowledge

Peter Tu

Suman, I did not for one second think that you would accept, hook, line, and sinker, attainment as being anything other than numinous. However, ever the optimist, I feel that we may be starting to dislodge a few things. Your terms registering, indexing, and interpreting are reasonable. For the sake of clarification, a few notes. The Computer Vision community would consider the term 'detection' as the ability to both discover and register faces, where registering usually means that sensed face data have been transformed into some sort of canonical coordinate system. What you call 'indexing' would probably be described as either hard biometrics (usually associated with identity) or soft biometrics (associations with type). In general, indexing can be thought of as a form of classification. As for 'interpretation', I am inclined to think of this topic in terms of inference with respect to the cognitive state and world knowledge. As you point out, inference is not limited to estimating mood or intent, it is also about integrating many forms of belief and social conventions. The consequences of such intuitive or logical leaps include trust, attraction, and racism. More on this later. Let's start by running with your analogy between reading text and recognizing faces.

The Analogy

Your description of typography as being comparable to registering/detection is justified. However, I think there is an aspect of Computer Vision that also fits well with typography. I am thinking about low-level image processing. This type of analysis is focused on the search for generic or primitive features. The idea is that certain forms of image structure are relatively common, so if one had a reliable means for extracting such features, this could support higher-level purposes such as object detection, tracking, and reconstruction. Examples of such primitives are blobs, texture elements, and line segments. However, the one feature that has received the most attention is the edge. By considering an image as a kind of surface, where intensity is analogous to height, an edge can be thought of as some sort of step. The most famous algorithm for detecting edges is the Canny edge detector (Canny 1986). John Canny started out by defining the general criteria that should be used to judge an edge detector. He then used the calculus of variations to derive an optimal function that, when convolved with an image, will produce local maxima that correspond to points on edges. It turns out that a good approximation of this optimal function is the first derivative of a Gaussian. The Canny algorithm itself can be summarized by five steps: (1) application of the Gaussian filter, (2) computation of the intensity gradients, (3) utilizing a method known as non-maximal suppression to find local maxima, (4) using various thresholds to identify seeds for edges, and (5) tracking the edges using a method known as hysteresis. Since its inception, there have been many proposed innovations and, of course, the deep learning algorithms assume their own low-level image processing steps. However, this classic algorithm is still in use today. A quick historical note: the traditional benchmark for edge detection and many other image processing algorithms is a photograph of a model named Lena. This image was first published in a popular gentleman's magazine. I fear that the early days of computer vision were less woke times.

I am fine with the mapping of readable writing to indexing/biometrics. You argue that the closest thing to reader response and reception that I have described so far is the tagging of indicators of expression and behaviour to intention and mood. You also argue that this could be viewed as yet another form of indexing. I start by agreeing with this point, but before attempting to offer more in the space of reader response and reception, let me dally a bit with the tagging problem.

Digression on Deception Detection

Over the years I have been interested in the topic of deception detection. Interestingly, this dark art is sometimes referred to as 'reading someone's face'. In a previous intervention, I gave details regarding Paul Ekman's work on facial action units (FAUs). In this context the topic of deception results in the hypothesis behind micro-expressions. As you recall, FAUs are associated with various muscle movements of the face. A given expression may be composed of a collection of FAUs. If an individual is attempting to present a false expression, they must accomplish the following tasks: (1) consciously produce the FAUs required to fabricate the desired facade, and (2) consciously suppress the FAUs that the body would naturally produce under such circumstances. If one has access to a high-speed image capture device, one might be able to detect momentary lapses over such fine-tuned control. However, the jury is still out with respect to the efficacy of this approach.

Another dimension for deception detection is the use of physiological cues. The premise behind most polygraph systems is that the act of deception is inherently stressful. While this may or may not be true, the detection of stress through standoff methods provides an avenue of investigation. A number of years ago, I started a collaboration with Ioannis Pavlidis from the University of Houston (Pavlidis *et al.* 2002). He is a pioneer in the use of thermal imagery for the purpose of detecting autonomic responses. As a result of stress, the body starts to prepare itself for various fight-or-flight responses. One of these preparatory measures is the opening of the capillaries just below the surface of the face near the inner portions of the eye sockets. I was keen to observe this effect for myself as well as maybe apply some of our facial analytics to the thermal imagery in order to automatize the deception detection process. To this end, I invited one of his students to do an internship in my lab. One of the more memorable and successful experiments involved having upper-level managers attempt to do basic arithmetic in their heads. This resulted in a crescendo of stress-related symptoms. The leaders were cool as cucumbers when tasked with problems such as 159 minus 27. However, if you asked them for answers to problems such as 153 minus 78, the thermal images of their inner eye-sockets really lit up. This is, of course, because the second class of problem required mental gymnastics such as borrowing. Given such intriguing results, I was keen to look for other physiological cues.

In addition to faces, the iris itself represents an excellent biometric. The idea is that patterns embedded in the iris act like barcodes. Interacting with traditional iris recognition systems is like looking through a microscope or telescope eyepiece. In contrast, my colleague Fred Wheeler (Wheeler *et al.* 2008) developed a standoff system that allowed the user to simply stand within a fixed cubic meter. The design of this system was quite elaborate. First, we had to select a frequency of light that was optimal with respect to imaging irises. We then had to find a camera that was sensitive to this type of light as well as an appropriate source of illumination. Methods for automatically targeting both the light source and the camera, while making sure that we did not inadvertently blind our subjects, were then developed. It turns out that the system was not only excellent at performing iris recognition, it was also very good at measuring pupil dilation. This gets us back to the question of deception. When a person is experiencing significant cognitive load, their pupils may start to dilate. Thus, when engaging in an elaborate deception, which might involve keeping multiple storylines straight, the deceiver may become mentally taxed to the point where their eyes turn into tells. I have always suspected that professional poker players often wear sunglasses in order to avoid this effect.

As an interesting side note, consider the following experiment. Images of random women are turned into image pairs wherein the only difference is that one image has the pupils artificially dilated. When asked for a preference, most men will select the photo with the dilated pupils. Since the artificial dilation is so subtle, most men are not able to explain why they have the preference — they just do.

A final comment on automatic deception detection. I was hoping to develop some sort of pheromone-based sensing system. Unfortunately, while in the distant past our ancestors made extensive use of chemical emissions for communication purposes, we no longer seem to do so. The standing hypothesis claims that before the new-world primates separated from the old-world primates (we are old world), both groups made extensive use of pheromones. However, old-world primates made the jump to colour-based vision, and this displaced the need for chemistry-based expression and identification. Since Mother Nature seems to operate under the principle of use it or lose it, our ability to both produce and detect pheromones have atrophied. In contrast, our new-world cousins never made the transition to colour-based vision and still have the capacity to emit and detect pheromones. The only problem from my research perspective is that spider monkeys, marmosets, and capuchins are a pretty honest bunch.

Inference

Now back to your analogy. I think that your description of interpretation calls for an expanded discussion of inference. To this point, my description of inference can be thought of in Bayesian terms. Suppose we know that when people in general are happy, they smile 90 percent of the time — $p(\text{smile}|\text{happy}) = 0.9$. We may also know that, in general, Fred is happy 50 percent of the time — $p(\text{happy}|\text{Fred}) = 0.5$. So, if we observe that Fred is smiling, then we can make the inference that Fred might be happy with a certain amount of confidence. The calculation $p(\text{happy}|\text{smile},\text{Fred}) \propto p(\text{smile}|\text{happy})p(\text{happy}|\text{Fred}) = 0.9 * 0.5 = 0.45$ provides a measure of merit for the happy hypothesis. When compared to other possible emotions, happy receives the highest score, thus it becomes the most reasonable inference. Now, let's paint a broader picture of inference. General knowledge represents things that we know about the world, such as people smile when they are happy. However, we know lots of other things as well:

- Cows are animals.
- January has 31 calendar days.
- The mayor of New York is Bill de Blasio.
- There are seven seasons of *Star Trek: The Next Generation*.

One way to organize such information is to construct a knowledge graph. In this representation, vertices in the graph are associated with semantic concepts such as cows, animals, and Bill de Blasio. Edges between vertices define the relationship between concepts. Thus, each pair of connected vertices can be thought of as a relational predicate. In predicate form, the knowledge that I just listed could be represented by the following: {[cows]->[are]->[animals], [Number of calendar days in January]->[equals]->[31], [Mayor of New York]->[is]->[Bill de Blasio], [*Star Trek: The Next Generation*]->[has]->[7 seasons]}. If we inject another piece of knowledge such as [all animals]->[will]-[die], then the following question can be posed: 'Will my pet cow ever die?' An initial search for a predicate that directly answers this question will turn up empty. However, we can still compute an answer by attempting to traverse the knowledge graph. This leads to the following form of inferential logic: our pet is a cow, a cow is an animal, all animals die, therefore our pet will die. Venerable AI languages such as LISP and Prolog were designed to support this form of analysis. As we speak, there are enormous efforts afoot to construct and maintain ever more encompassing knowledge graphs.

An aspect of interpretation can now be thought of in terms of inference over observations. In your example, Mr. Darcy's observed expressions along with general knowledge associated with Edwardian England may lead to various interesting inferences. Suppose Elizabeth has access to the following predicates:

- [Elizabeth]->[is]->[strong, independent, intelligent, female]
- [Darcy]->[is]->[Englishman]
- [Englishmen]->[are intimidated by]->[strong, independent, intelligent, females]
- [intimidated men]->[feign]->[condescension]

Darcy's facial expression triggers Elizabeth's inference engine to produce the following interpretation: Darcy is simply intimidated by her intelligence. Now if we come at this from the perspective of a 21st-century Genuine AI Engineer (GAIE), the knowledge graph might take on a more Philistine air:

- [Books by Jane Austen]->[are]->[fodder for romantic comedies]
- [*Pride and Prejudice*]->[was written by]->[Jane Austen]
- [Stuttering British men]->[are]->[adorable]
- [Actors that could play the part of Darcy]->[include]->[Hugh Grant, Colin Firth, and maybe Paul Rudd?]
- [Characters played by Hugh, Colin, or Paul]->[always fall in love with]->[the leading lady]

So, when the GAIE attempts to interpret Mr. Darcy's demeanour, a completely different conclusion can and will be drawn.

As you can imagine, there are two basic problems with reasoning over knowledge graphs. First, as the knowledge graphs become increasingly complex, contradictions almost always creep in. Sometimes probability can be used to save the day, but more often the whole thing just collapses on itself. Second, the term 'Inference Explosion' refers to the problem that the number of inferences that can be made increases exponentially with the size of the knowledge graph. This quickly becomes computationally intractable. Going back to our Systems 1 and 2 discussion, my take it that part of recognition involves System 1 dynamically carving out useful segments of one's knowledge graph based on the utility that it may serve with respect to the current context. As you have intimated, this process may be fallible, but in a useful way.

Recognition as Reconstruction

Now let's shift gears to your taunting description of Existentialism. The ideas of 'mutual recognition of shared humanness' and 'Being-Seen-by-the-Other' is the truth of 'Seeing-the-Other' conjures up a few thoughts. A while back, I wrote a paper that was inspired by the existence of mirror neurons (Tu *et al.* 2012). The following is a short excerpt from that paper:

> The recent discovery of mirror neurons has led many researchers to re-evaluate the relationship between experience and recognition [16, 17, 4]. It has been observed that when human subjects physically perform certain goal-oriented actions such as picking up a cup or kicking a ball, specific sets of mirror neurons are activated. It has also been observed that these same mirror neurons fire if and when the subject observes another individual performing the same action. It has been hypothesized that these mechanisms may be the basis for such human traits as empathy and the ability to interpret the motivations of others. From the computer vision perspective, the existence of mirror neurons leads to the question 'what is the relationship between recognizing an action and experiencing an action?' In this paper, we explore the hypothesis that the ability to recognize an action may in fact be a by-product of learning how to execute an action. (124).

While this research was focused on methods for behaviour recognition, the takeaway for this discussion is that the existence of mirror neurons implies that when 'I see you', I can, to some degree, 'feel what it is like to be you'. This is sometimes used to justify Theory of Mind (ToM) frameworks, which argue that people are constantly creating cognitive models of each other allowing for various forms of recursive mindreading. So maybe 'to be recognized by another' is to be mirrored or 'reconstructed by another'. And thus, an important aspect of recognition might be the act of reconstruction. Begging your continued indulgence, let's explore this a bit more.

One might think that a reasonable model for human cognition is the following:

- Observations of the world are gathered.
- A reasoning engine consumes such observations resulting in higher-level interpretations.
- Decisions are made.
- Plans are executed.

However, experimental evidence does not really support this description of cognition. What seems to be a more accurate model is the following:

- The mind constructs a model of the physical world, which incorporates a narrative that explains why the model is the way it is.
- This narrative can then be used to predict the future state of the world.
- Subsequently, the prediction can be compared with actual observations of the world.
- Once discrepancies become too large, the narrative is edited so as to remove such incongruencies.

As I have described in a previous intervention, studies performed on subjects suffering from various forms of brain injury seem to indicate that individuals are usually oblivious to this editing process. We simply believe that our current narrative is the one that we have always had resulting in a remarkably false sense of continuity. Going back to our Existentialist friends, when we are seen by others, are we not being reconstructed by others? This might explain the attraction for the painted portraits of the past and the selfies of today. The possibility of future observers reconstructing and hence recognizing us from such artefacts might offer a modest opportunity for immortality. Although I suppose that the Existentialists would not view such measures as being sufficient antidotes to the death angst that grips them so tightly.

Religion

In *This Life* (Hägglund 2019), we come across the argument that the logical consequence of atheism is socialism. The author argues that God's grace offers a form of vertical integration where one is automatically recognized and hence validated. The alternative being a form of horizontal integration where one starts by recognizing that others are human and worthy of respect. This in turn results in oneself being recognized by others as being human and worthy of respect.

Turning the tables, it might be interesting to think of this from the side of the supernatural. In *God: A Biography* (Miles 1995), Jack Miles takes the interesting approach of considering the First Testament as a form of original source material in order to write a biography of God. Miles paints a picture of a lonely entity that creates humanity in order to produce a reflection of itself. This is done so that it can better understand itself. By humanity recognizing God, a reconstruction of God is produced. God can then study this reconstruction/reflection and thus reconstruct itself. This is like two-facing mirrors that allow for an infinite ToM reverberation. Once again, the ideas of mirrors, reflections, reconstructions, and recognitions all seem to swim together in a pre-Existential manner. Unfortunately, as the story unfolds, God appears to lose interest in his reflection and drifts away leaving the mirror to its own devices.

So, Suman, you may have inadvertently put your finger on a new killer app for the AI-Assistant. If an AI can reconstruct, reflect, and recognize us, might this lead to a personal defence against nihilism? I suppose that if God lost interest in us, we might end up running the risk that our new mirrors will pull a Scarlett Johansson and just slither off to singularity. Of course, this might add to instead of lessen our already hefty load of preconceptual apprehensions.

Projection

Now let me turn to your conviction that Face Recognition is at the heart of projection. The accusation behind this assertion seems to be that the cunning GAIE are attempting to pull a Henry Higgins by teaching their AI-Assistants to ape the manners of their betters. By adorning our contraptions with the trappings of human intelligence, we are plotting that the casual observer will believe that there is more there than there really is.

I will start by, to some degree, conceding this point. It is well known that if you want Alan Alda and the good folks from PBS to show up at your doorstep, all you have to do is strap furry eyebrows, a pair of googly eyes, and some sort of mouth-like contraption onto a relatively modest perambulating robot and you are good to go. But before outright condemning such antics, let's consider the recent work of Malcolm Gladwell.

In *Talking to a Stranger* (Gladwell 2019), Malcolm Gladwell argues that trust is an extremely valuable commodity. If people are only able to trust direct blood relatives, then the amount of commerce that a society can produce is miniscule compared to societies where everyone trusts just about everyone else even if such trust is not always warranted. It is my conviction that if driverless car capabilities plateau with the same accident rates as humans, they will not be allowed on the roads. So, the question might be, how will AI-Assistant learn how to tap into our innate capacity for trust? If projection is the key, then are we looking for the means for gifting AI-Assistants with some sort of artificial personality?

Setting the stage, let me start with what currently passes for AI charm. The game industry uses the term non-player characters (NPCs) when referring to the AIs that we interact with during gameplay. The goal here is to have the NPCs act in a realistic manner. This usually comes down to some sort of hand-crafted finite-state machine, where all possible states are enumerated and then mapped to specific actions or planning objectives. If done well, this can be somewhat convincing — think of our friends, the menacing ghosts in Pacman. Advancing a little on this, instead of handcrafting, we now see agents that must learn their policies. I myself have taken a page out of the old Mary Shelley playbook by attempting to construct an Avatar that must discover over time how to convince shoppers to purchase their mercantile wares. The following is an excerpt from a recent account describing this odyssey (Tu *et al.* 2019):

> An interactive advertising system is proposed comprising a flat-screen display, a collocated sensing camera, and an outcome feedback camera. The display presents an Avatar that has the goal of convincing people to enter a store. The Avatar has a repertoire of actions that it can perform such as offer a coupon or present a piece of merchandise. A sensing camera is used to represent the state of a possible customer. State variables include affective pose, facial expressions, gaze direction, and eyeball movement. The outcome feedback camera is used to detect if and when a customer elects to enter the store. Given access to such

feedback, a reinforcement learning algorithm is then used to construct a policy that indicates which actions should be taken as a function of observed customer state. The efficacy of this approach is considered via synthetic experiments as well as real-world demonstrations. The paper includes a discussion regarding new descriptors based on emergent languages that can be used to augment the state space representation.

In the spirit of projection, the avatar was named Joan and was, of course, the inspiration for the notional AI-Assistant story in my last intervention. So, I guess my question to you would be: what does Joan need in order to get you to start tapping your toes to the old Lloyd Price classic:

Cause you've got personality
Walk, with personality
Talk, with personality
Smile, with personality …

Chapter 6

Elephants and Monkeys

Suman Gupta

Much of your argument, Peter, seems to consist in something like the following: (1) what you call 'elephants' we call 'monkeys'; (2) your elephants are clumsy, our monkeys are dexterous; (3) the best you can do with your elephants is make them march in formation, whereas our monkeys almost beg that they, ooby do, wanna be like you, wanna talk like you, and you'll see it's true, they can be like you. My feeling is that you need to give pachyderms more space and treat apes with customary circumspection. Accordingly, my argument is something like the following: (1) what I call 'elephants' are often distinct from what you call 'monkeys'; and (2) if you want your monkeys to compose a serviceable AI-Assistant for everyday life, they need to be more like elephants. In making this argument, I follow the sequence of subheadings in your latest intervention and address the arguments under each by turn.

The Analogy

Since we are into swapping terms, let me introduce a few more in the pool — not to do with *reading* and *text*, but to do with *performance* and *framing*. These are adapted in a simple form straight from the work of the Canadian (just throwing that in to stir your patriotic fervour) sociologist Erving Goffman, especially *The Presentation of Self in Everyday Life* (1959) and *Frame Analysis* (1974), numerously nuanced and honed since.

The idea of performance is that in everyday interpersonal encounters, each of us constantly plays a series of roles which have, so to speak, partly pre-decided 'scripts' (conventions, agreements, and expectations). So, Homer and Bart play, respectively, the roles of father and son when they are together, and similarly, Homer and Marge play the roles of conjugal partners, Homer and Grimes play the role of colleagues, Homer and Apu play the roles of shopper and grocer, and so on. Each of these roles has some broad pre-decided social templates to adhere to as well as some mutually understood interpersonal templates, and each involves some departures from those in view of immediate circumstances. Further, within each set of interpersonal encounters, there might be a range of subsets of parts played: Homer and Lisa performing father and daughter roles may, respectively, play commanding/obedient etc. and correspondingly obedient/commanding etc. Such roles are formalized in official circles, and given costumes, titles, backdrops, etc.

Given the dramaturgical metaphors that Goffman so happily unleashed into sociology thus, the difference in this concept of performance from that in theatre is usefully kept in mind:

1. The performers and the audiences are all on the stage of everyday life, each person is both in the troupe and in the audience, all the world's really a stage.
2. There's no real Homer which is different from performer Homer in everyday life, so performance is all that composes everyday life actions and interactions (if Homer is alone in his basement being the strong silent type, he is performing the strong silent type insofar as anyone knows, including Homer himself).
3. There are social conventions etc. that form a kind of given or pre-written script for these performances.
4. The cognitive environments, incidental occurrences, etc. around these performances both bear upon how performances go (they interfere in the script) and become constitutive of performances (they become part of the script) — these performances have quite dynamic scripts.

The key thing in these performances is how performers and audiences know what each is at, i.e., how these performances are expressed and make impressions. So, signs pass constantly from and to us, the performers/audiences. In this respect, there's a little distinction Goffman made which I have always found suggestive — a distinction between *giving* signs and *giving off* signs.

> The expressiveness of the individual (and therefore his capacity to give impressions) appears to involve two radically different kinds of sign activity: the expression that he *gives*, and the kind of expression that he *gives off*. The first involves verbal symbols or their substitutes which he uses admittedly and solely to convey the information that he and others are known to attach to these symbols. [...] The second involves a wide range of action that others can treat as symptomatic of the actor, the expectation being that the action was performed for reasons other than the information conveyed in this way. (Goffman 1959: 2).

The idea of framing is quite slippery in Goffman's formulation and even fuzzier in the area where it has the strongest hold: Media Studies. Summarizing drastically, I can discern two tactics here.

1. Everyday life occurrences are overdetermined (in a loosely mathematical way), i.e., more than one way of accounting for them is possible. Usually, numerous ways can be proposed, of which none really has a decisive upper hand. Under these circumstances, a mode of coming to grips with an everyday life phenomenon is to restrict its import — to put a frame on it (by selecting one account, by focusing on one aspect, by privileging one explanation, etc.).
2. At the same time, doing that also opens up the possibility of linking or associating such a phenomenon with others so as to confirm the chosen frame. Indeed, it is possible that you have chosen this frame because you have it already at hand from past attempts to frame such phenomena. Goffman worried about how and when a frame comes about — the 'primary frame' — and though he didn't quite get to an answer, he nevertheless found that if primary frames are assumed, one can go quite far in systematizing everyday life phenomena. Let me not go into the media studies stuff, which, to be honest, tends to be less thought-through than Goffman's old formulations.

Peter, it occurs to me that the idea of framing is in the opposite direction from looking for the most stable features in, for instance, a face or image — from looking for monadic primitives. The work that the Canny edge algorithm does is, in an abstract way, the opposite of what, for instance, a media person does with framing. Edge detection homes in on the most stable features and sieves out the relatively unstable to obtain a phenomenal description of, say, a given face. Framing involves introducing a feature in relation to the given face which is taken as *de facto* stable and thereby generating a series of unstable features from there. Framing leads to proliferating associations, submerging the face at hand into multiple narratives and perceptions. This is a typical device in news stories. For instance, given an image, it may be trimmed, labelled, juxtaposed with other images, commented upon (each of these is a frame-appointing device) such that nuances which are not necessarily contained in that image are suggested or associated. In such a process, a fetching portrait of Peter may become framed as that of the AI Saviour, the AI Superhero, the Evil AI Engineer, the AI Engineer as Mr Nice Guy, the AI Engineer as a Machine, and so on. A definition of framing which Media-Studies types are apt to quote a lot, by R.M. Entman, goes as follows:

> To frame is to select some aspects of a perceived reality and make them more salient in a communicating text in such a way as to promote a particular problem definition, causal interpretation, moral evaluation, and/ or treatment recommendation for the item described. (Entman 1993: 52).

'Selecting some aspects of a perceived reality' suggests that framing strategies are *within* that which is framed; but it is often found that a feature can also be held beside something to frame it (like the metaphor 'frame' itself, Jacques Derrida had some interesting things to say about this).

Digression on Deception Detection

Peter, your description of technological efforts to detect deception is much like your description of efforts in face recognition. These efforts are devoted to answering questions that are too narrow to have any significant bearing on how we look at each other in everyday life. In the case of face-recognition technology, the question was narrowly one of identification; in the case of deception-detection technology, the question is narrowly one of confirming whether someone is stating facts or knowingly concealing them. Only professional interrogators and detectives would be so single-mindedly interested in this as to seek some AI-Assistant to help them.

We can put this in the terms of Goffman's performances of self: signals *given* and signals *given off*. The situation you are describing goes thus: a Person *gives* a signal (such as saying, 'My name is Homer'), and *gives off* some signals unwittingly (such as a twitch of the left ear — like a 'tell' in poker). The assumption here is that the signal given off has a direct bearing on the signal given, either confirming or falsifying the latter (there are some in-between states too …). The main difference in the detection technology you describe is that it focuses exclusively on tracking signals given off which are not as obvious as twitching ears — deep signals given off (micro expressions, physiological cues, iris tracking). The deep signal given off (DSGO) is intrinsically either not part of everyday life interactions or only so at an unknowing level (like unknowingly finding Marge's dilated pupils dead sexy). The assumption seems based on the notion that DSGOs are by their nature linked to the signal given, they offer a kind of immediate meta-commentary on the signal given. But this metacommentary can only be meaningfully read (so to speak) when the signal given is very simple, like a yes/no answer or an unambiguous statement of fact — which, in fact, forms a relatively tiny part of the range of everyday communications (any every-day usage corpus can be unpacked to show this). Only interrogators deter-mined to catch some poor sod out fixate on DSGOs. It is a small part even of the part of performing the self that Goffman considered under 'inten-tional misinformation and feigning'.

In everyday life exchanges, signals given and signals given off have a more ambiguous relationship. It is more often the case that signals given off (SGOs) work as framing devices for signals given (SGs). Several pos-sibilities may play out:

1. We may do the investigator thing and take the SGO as a truth indi-cator for the SG (Homer's twitching ears gave him away when he said, 'I didn't eat the doughnut!').
2. We may use the SGO as contributing to the information found in the SG (Homer's tone of voice indicated that he was annoyed when he said, 'I didn't eat the doughnut!').
3. We may use the SGO to make a circumstantial observation unre-lated to the SG (Homer's wistful look when he said, 'I didn't eat the doughnut!', showed me that Homer is inordinately fond of doughnuts).
4. We may use the SGO to link this SG to other SGs in other contexts (Homer's defiant look when he said, 'I didn't eat the doughnut!', was

reminiscent of Bart's when accused of blowing up a spaceship — a remarkable family resemblance was visible).

Inference

It doesn't surprise me in the least that tracking the inferential process based on knowledge graphs tends to either collapse through contradiction or self-destruct through exponential inference explosion. The problem is that knowledge graphs take the inferential process *in everyday life* to be as comprehensively constructed as in a consistent mathematical or logic system, where all axioms or first principles are consistently built upon in inferential steps. I see that your final remarks on inference go back to the friendly Systems 1 and 2 terminology à la Kahneman, where System 1 mysteriously carves out the part of a possible comprehensive knowledge graph which is serviceable to the present need without contradiction or too many inferential possibilities (leading to fuzziness, uncertainty, vacillation, to-do-or-not-to-do inertia). Here's a point on which conceptualizing the AI-Assistant in everyday life may pause: how mysterious is System 1's delimiting impetus? Is there method in the madness of System 1's precipitate limiting of fields from which inferences are made in everyday life? Three thoughts cross my mind here.

1. Let's go back to *framing*. Let's say, you have a potentially comprehensive knowledge graph rolling out before you. You want this to inform your understanding of a juncture in everyday life in which a *Person* decides to do *This* at a *Given Time*. In charting every possible cognitive, habitual, mnemonic, conventional, social factor which may have led the *Person* to infer that the best way forward at the *Given Time* is to do *This*, we put together every possible and/or inferential step leading into the *Given Time* — of the following forms: if factor *F1*, then *C1*; if factors *F1* and *F2*, then *C2*; if factor *F1* or *F2*, then *C3*. Mapping these sufficiently persistently is likely to suggest that either the *Person*'s decision to do *This* would be deferred, perhaps indefinitely, or the *Person* should be thrown into chronic indecision about whether to do *This*, *That*, or the *Other*. As you say, the way out is something System 1 can do, take a useful chunk out of all the Big Graph leading into the *Given Time* so that the *Person* sees that *This* is clearly the way to go. But how does that happen? The framing idea would suggest something like this: the *Person* simply chooses to set a given factor Super-*F* as precedent so that every other

factor and consequence becomes conditional to it: if Super-F, then factor $F1$, then $C1$, and so on. Such a delimitation (or maybe a few of these, a few Super-Fs) is sufficient to take the *Person* safely to a decision to do *This* at the *Given Time*. The Super-F is the framing device. But how is the Super-F set? There are three options: it is already there in the *Person*'s mind; the *Person* plucks it out of a pool which is available somehow; it appears fortuitously for the *Person* at that *Given Time*. Which is it? Well, sometimes you can tell after the fact rather than in a predictive fashion, i.e., we can know how that worked less from induction and more from deduction. For instance, Trump decided today that COVID-19 was deliberately unleashed upon the world from a laboratory in Wuhan by the Chinese government to deter him from being re-elected in November 2020 as US President. It seems pretty clear that this decision was based on a Super-F which is firmly implanted in Trump's brain: delusional self-centredness. But Trump is a very simple creature. Any *Person* deciding to do *This* has more complex ways of fixing a Super-F at a *Given Time*. Understanding those ways is just a matter of researching the business ...

2. To take another tack, let's pause on inferential processes in everyday *ordinary-language conversations*. The thing about everyday conversations is that the signals given — what is said and indicated in tone, gesture, expression, etc. — by a speaker contain a great deal more information than is explicit, and moreover, this information is usually efficiently picked by the receiver. Whole propositions are conveyed by only enunciating little bits of them — in sub-propositional statements, for instance. There are numerous shortcuts, standardized or functionally deployed ellipses, unspoken implications, and yet conversations work for both interlocutors quite robustly in everyday life. This has been a hobbyhorse for linguists and analytical philosophers alike, and various theories on how such brevity or economy of expression in conversations work have been proposed. The general trend has been to rationalize various usages by hypothesizing that: (a) there are certain conversational norms which are mutually accepted, grounded in the structure and practice of language itself, which enables this to happen (influentially the line taken by Paul Grice); (b) there are principles for estimating relevance of a given signal between interlocutors within a given cognitive environment (Dan Sperber and Deirdre Wilson laid some relevance-determining principles);

(c) there are shared assumptions which are tested by seeing how a given signal works for possible worlds (Robert Stalnaker explored this concept suggestively). These could all be rationales which throw more light on the part played by what you call System 1 in making inferences.

3. Then there are concepts of *deformative reading*, which have to do with more formal pursuits of knowledge, especially literary studies (also philosophy, history, etc.). The way much literary criticism works is: here's a text T which gives a narrative which readers generally read and feel they understand; a critic takes T and argues that there is a hidden layer of meaning/significance in it which is deeper than what readers have generally understood; the critic then applies some *interpretation strategies* on T so that it reveals more than readers had generally found in it, often layers of significance which are contrary to received readings or counterintuitive. Such interpretation strategies typically involve quite odd moves, such as: (a) highlighting some passages of T which then operate as framing devices and put a new light on T as a whole (close reading of quoted passages works in this way); (b) reading T with hindsight, so in a way privileging reading backwards or rereading; (c) bringing information from outside T which may be relevant to it (say, in terms of when, where, and by whom it was written — contextualization). These techniques seem to twist the reading of T away from a straightforward linear reading and could be thought of as deformative reading (the critics Jerome McGann and Lisa Samuels (2006) argued that such deformative strategies constitute a kind of performance of being an interpreter). Again, these curious and yet entirely uncontroversial ways of approaching interpretation may illuminate how System 1 works.

Recognition as Reconstruction

I guess the above kinds of inferential processes — let's call them System-1 processes, following your preference — show that in areas such as framing and performance analysis, conversation analysis, critical text interpretation, it has seldom been assumed that recognition is other than reconstruction. In a way, these are the elephants of everyday life: we already know that we are both recognizing that there's someone out there when we perceive her; and, at the same time, we also know that this involves superimposing something of ourselves on the someone out there whom we have perceived. This isn't a discovery or a conundrum — it is a quality of *richness* in the process of everyday life. The existentialists, I think, were taking it for granted that when they talk of mutual recognition of being human by two persons that would be understood as involving mutual construction of humanness by each. This is perfectly clear, particularly in Sartre's *Being and Nothingness* (1943), much of which consists in clarifying stories about how people recognize–construct each other.

So, I guess the distinction you had presumed between recognition and reconstruction — only shaken by the contemplation of mirror neurons (by finding an organic mechanism for enacting reconstruction) — is in the area of your monkeys. In the monkey region, the preconceptual point is that recognition involves sensory registering, etc. of something out there and there is a separate mechanism through which reconstruction works (or interferes with recognition). In the elephant region, the preconceptual point is that recognition cannot but involve some degree of reconstruction and vice versa — in fact, is it even worth calling upon two terms? Maybe there's just one thing — you could call it reading, performance, framing, interpretation, relevance gauging, etc. — which involves, in monkey terms, inextricably the act of recognizing/reconstructing.

Religion

This is going to be short. Would it be possible for you to rewrite this argument without presuming that all religious folk are monotheistic? I figure around half the world's population of the faithful are polytheists, pantheists, animists, syncretists. If our AI-Assistant is to do any consolatory recognizing, it might begin by not assuming that there is One True God and that this One True God could basically be an 'AI' app. The monotheists will peg this app as satanically courting a deadly sin; the other faithful sorts will simply not know what our AI-Assistant is playing at by recognizing them (let alone feel consoled by that). The rest are non-believers like you and I, who would never fall for such a trick.

Projection

Let's put aside Gladwell's concept of 'trust', which is unfortunately indifferently articulated and doesn't bear protracted attention. Neoconservatives like Francis Fukuyama have come up with more interesting concepts of 'trust', and there's a great deal of rather more thought-through psychological, sociological, and philosophical formulations of the term. If you want to return to Gladwell, we could, but why?

What you are getting at is that 'projection' is no more than a matter of making A feel with regard to B that B is much like A and shares A's interests. To muffle any moral disapprobation in 'projection' you chuck in 'trust' as a normatively positive term instead. Then you deny that there is any simplistic goal of doing this (like sticking some markers of humanoidness on apps and gadgets) on the part of AI Engineers. Then you go in the contrary direction and show that that's exactly what AI Engineers are in fact doing, only it's not simplistically but quite cleverly done (as is worthy of AI Engineers). Then, just to show how cleverly, you remind me that the character Joan in your story at the end of the last posting is in fact a learning Avatar. All that shows is that your story in the last posting was merely an exercise in your projection of yourself on Sheryl — an act of literary fiction where you are the author.

It is only in projection that people imagine that animals want to be like humans, like the beat maestro King Louie in *Jungle Book*, or for that matter the gullible Iofur Raknison in *Dark Materials*. Possibly that's also why you characterize Joan thus. But the point is that, clever though it might be, there is no need for our AI-Assistant to fool their everyday human partners, to deceive by appearing trustworthy, to be used to extract costs for unnecessary services. They could be conceived and planned as genuinely helpful friends, which is only possible if they are grounded in an understanding of how these everyday human partners think and work and live. That calls for more ideational elephants and fewer ideational monkeys to start with.

Chapter 7

Flavours of the Fabled 'System 1'

Peter Tu

The Can Opener

An engineer, a physicist and an economist are stranded on a desert island with a single can of beans. The three castaways establish camp on the beach and start to discuss how they might gain access at their one and only food source. The engineer declares that she has an idea. She suggests that they use the engineer's favourite device — the lever. She proposes that a large stick be tied to a sturdy rock (the fulcrum) and that the short end of the stick be placed on top of the can. By elevating the long end of the stick, the resulting external pressure will crush the can thus releasing its contents. The physicist and the economist demur. The physicist points out that this uncontrolled approach will result in the beans coming into direct contact with the sand, rendering them unpalatable. The engineer acknowledges their concerns. The physicist then declares that she too has a thought. She argues that they search for a giant clam shell. The idea is that the shapes of such mollusc domiciles are roughly parabolic. They could polish and then position the shell such that the sun's rays are concentrated on the can, causing its internal temperature to rise. The resulting pressure will then induce a rupturing of the vessel. To add some heft to her proposal, the physicist uses a stick to scribble out a few equations in the sand such as $PV = nRT$ and $y = x^2$. While the engineer had to recognize the elegance of this solution, after all equations were produced, she was quick to point out that an exploding can of beans is even more problematic than a crushed one … It was at this point that the economist raised his hand. Both the engineer and the physicist are sceptical but reluctantly agree to hear him out. The economist confidently proclaims: 'Why don't we just assume that we have a can-opener!'

Suman, I am the first to admit that John Searle's words in the Chinese Room argument (Searle 1980) are so hateful primarily because they are so true. Our monkeys are profoundly lacking. With this said, I am tempted to raise an eyebrow regarding the grandeur of your elephantine constructs. I, of course, marvel at the many feats of observation and self-introspection ranging from Augustine (Brooks 2015) to the present day that have culminated in such remarkable insights. But when claims along the lines of 'The existentialists, I think, were taking it for granted that when they talk of mutual recognition of being human by two persons that would be understood as involving mutual construction of humanness by each', I am drawn to questions such as: well, then what is the nature of such constructions? Are they frame-like templates with fields that just need to be filled in? Are they more like wind-up toys or is there enough temporarily devoted neural architecture to allow for some form of limited autonomy? One can't help but feel that this magnificent herd of conceptual pachyderms are to some degree built on the assumptions of can-openers.

As a point of contrast, let me turn to one of the many intriguing topics that you raised in your last intervention — the question of signals. My colleagues over at UCLA, Tao Gao and his graduate student Stephanie Stacy, have been working on the question of intuitive signalling. The following reflects their modelling viewpoint:

> Communication is highly overloaded. Despite this, even young children are good at leveraging context to understand ambiguous signals. We propose a computational shared agency account of signalling that we call the Imagined-We (IW) framework. We leverage Bayesian Theory of Mind (ToM) to provide mechanisms for rational action planning and inverse action interpretation. To expand this framework for communication, we first treat signals as rational actions, to convert it back into the ToM framework. We then incorporate our rich understanding of intuitive physics to constrain the scope of affordable actions. Finally, we treat communication as a cooperative act, subject to constraints of maximizing a shared utility function. We implement this model in a set of simulations which demonstrate this model's success under increasing ambiguity as well as increasing layers of reasoning. Our model is

capable of improving performance with deeper recursive reasoning; however, it outperforms comparison baselines at even the shallowest level of reasoning, highlighting how shared knowledge and cooperative logic can do much of the heavy-lifting in language. (Stacy *et al.* 2021).

The curious reader can refer to their paper for details. While this formulation does not claim to represent the full goings on of the human signalling process, it does provide for an implementation that we as Genuine AI Engineers (GAIE) can build on, experiment with, and eventually improve upon or discard. In short, it may be one of the many can-openers that we need in order to move forward.

Sequential Search

Let me now turn to your question regarding how one might go about building a usable System 1 capability. That is to say, given the current context, how can one quickly gain access to the right pieces of knowledge that will allow us to arrive at a reasonable solution in a timely manner? To begin this conversation, let me start with the topic of search spaces.

Suppose you have been assigned the task of finding an answer to a query which can be defined as X. X might be something like: 'What were the favourite pastimes of the British aristocracy between 1797 and 1813?' You might start your quest by heading to the local library. Libraries are generally organized such that each book is assigned a specific address Y. We can also define a Utility function $U(Y|X)$, which will be high if the book associated with Y turns out to be useful with respect to answering the question X and low if not. Given X, our goal is to locate a book Y such that $U(Y|X)$ is high. One approach might be to perform a *sequential search*, which would involve going through each book in the library, reading it end-to-end, and then measuring $U(Y|X)$ by asking ourselves whether we now know the answer to X. This process would continue until we find a book Y that produces a high $U(Y|X)$. Of course, this would be extremely taxing, so we would much prefer to take advantage of the fact that the library is organized in a way that allows for more *direct* access. Floors and shelves are arranged in categories. Within a shelf, books are arranged in alphabetical order. The books may also be labelled and sorted based on the Dewey Decimal Classification system. The books themselves have tables of contents. The card catalogue may be arranged based on topic areas and, of course, the dedicated librarian is always there to lend a helping hand. But what happens when the search space is not *organized* in this fashion?

Let's broaden the concept of search space to include high-dimensional spaces. Consider the set of all possible images composed of 640 by 480 pixels, where each pixel can have up to 256 different values. Each pixel can be thought of as an independent dimension. A specific image Y can then be thought of as a single point in this space. The coordinates of this point being defined as $(Y_1, Y_2, ..., Y_i, ..., Y_{640 \times 480})$, where Y_i is the pixel value of the ith pixel. Now suppose our library is composed of all the images of faces of people that we have met in our lifetime and that each of these images is described by its Y coordinates. Given a query image X, which incidentally can also be described by its coordinates in image space, we can then define our utility function $U(Y|X)$ as being proportional to the probability that Y and X were both generated by the same individual. This, of course, is the face identification problem. Now if the size of our library is relatively small, we could try our sequential search strategy and compare X with all known Y and select the Y such that $U(Y|X)$ is maximal, assuming we know how to compute $U(Y|X)$. However, as the set of Ys gets very large, we have to start looking for another approach to mapping Xs to useful Ys.

Indexing

In Simon Winchester's *The Professor and the Madman* (Winchester 1998), we have the edifying story of how the Oxford English Dictionary (OED) came into being. The problem with most dictionaries is that once they have been compiled, their shelf life is limited due to the fact that languages evolve over time. So instead of trying to find an exact definition for each and every word, the editors of the OED proposed that all words be tracked over time. The idea was that a kind of temporal trajectory for each word should be established. The trajectory would start with the first literary reference that contains the word under investigation followed by a series of references where the accepted meaning of the word has changed. Once the OED has been established, producing subsequent editions would simply involve updating each word trajectory based on changes in the language that may have occurred since the last edition. Of course, coming up with the original OED was an extremely laborious task.

The Professor in charge of the OED effort relied primarily on a large number of volunteers. Each volunteer was assigned a small number of words; they would then scour the literature for references to their assigned words and after a few years report back with appropriately referenced trajectories. Each volunteer was essentially following the sequential search approach that I previously described. After about 20 years, the OED effort was somewhere around the letter C. At this point, the Professor received a letter from an anonymous correspondent. The author of the letter announced that he admired the OED effort and that he wanted to lend a hand. Not overly optimistic, the Professor sent the next dozen words on his list to the would-be volunteer. He did not expect that he would hear back from the individual for the foreseeable future, if ever. A few weeks later, detailed reports for each of the twelve words were received. It turned out that all the reports were of the highest quality. The Professor was suspicious. Maybe this mysterious volunteer had antici-pated these words in advance and was attempting some sort of elaborate hoax. To test this hypothesis, the Professor selected another 12 words, this time at random from the remaining list of unresearched words, which were many. To his astonishment, a few weeks later full and detailed reports were delivered and once again they checked out. The Professor wrote a letter requesting a face-to-face meeting. The volunteer declined. After repeated entreaties, the volunteer eventually acquiesced and for-warded a place and time to meet.

It turns out that the volunteer was from a wealthy family but had been committed to an asylum for the mentally ill. However, this remarkable fellow did have access to one of the finest private literary collections in the country. It turns out that upon hearing of the OED efforts, this indi-vidual started on the following course of action:

1. He assigned an index card to each of the non-obsolete words in the English language.
2. He then organized his library in chronological order and started to read from the beginning.
3. Whenever he came across what looked like a new word or a change in meaning, he would write the book title, date of publica-tion, page number and line on the index card for that word.

Upon completion of this 20-year odyssey, he contacted the OED Professor and offered his services. When given a particular word (*X*), he simply went to the corresponding index card and — voila! — all the necessary references (Y) were at his disposal. This is a great example of a search strategy known as *indexing*.

Of course, the modern internet search engines, including both Altavista and Netscape, are based on this concept. Every night, web crawlers are sent out to process all known web pages. For every possible search word X, a list of web pages that contain that word is constructed. When you or I put together a query such as $X =$ 'What were the favourite pastimes of the British Aristocracy between 1797 and 1813?', keywords are extracted, and the crawler-produced lists of web pages for each word X are analyzed. If a webpage makes it onto one of these lists, it is now nominated for further consideration. Now, if a given webpage Y is on multiple lists, this means that it contains multiple key words. Each webpage can then be ranked based on the number of keywords that it contains. In terms of high-dimensional search spaces, each word can be thought of as a dimension and each webpage can be thought of as a point in this search space, where the coordinate Y_i of document Y is the number of times that the ith keyword is contained in that document. When I recently plunked our *Pride and Prejudice*-related X into such a search engine, I was returned webpages with titles such as:

- Royal Taste: Food, Power and Status at the European Courts ...
- The Peerage, Baronetage, and Knightage, of Great Britain and ...
- The British Cyclopedia of Literature, History, Geography, ...

The first time that I made use of this kind of indexing strategy was when I built a fingerprint identification system for latent prints found at crime scenes. Conceptually, this task is similar to the face identification problem that we previously discussed. The approach was based on the work of Andrea Califano (Califano *et al.* 1998). Fingerprints can be thought of as a collection of ridge lines. Features known as minutiae occur whenever a ridge line terminates or bifurcates. Like a star being described by its local constellation, a minutia can be described by its local neighbourhood. One such scheme may involve dividing the space around a minutia into eight regions or octants. For each octant, one can locate the closest neighbouring minutiae and then describe the relationship between these minutiae in terms of distance and relative orientation. Thresholding results in a kind of discrete binning process that produces what can be thought of as a dictionary of word-like descriptions. Thus, like a webpage, a fingerprint can be thought of as a collection of minutiae-based words. This allows for a similar indexing approach.

Two points should be made. First, once the minutia index cards have been constructed, the act of search no longer requires comparing a given fingerprint against all fingerprints in the database. In comparison to sequential search, indexing is practically instantaneous. Second, this approach views a document (or a fingerprint) as a kind of 'bag of words'. The bagging process neglects one key concept: the global arrangement or order of the words. In the case of fingerprint identification, fingerprints nominated via indexing must then be analyzed sequentially in order to ensure consistency with respect to global spatial structure. The next question then comes down to: what does one do when there is no obvious indexing scheme?

Distribution and Sampling

Let's consider the game of Chess. At any given point in time, one can describe the configuration X of the chessboard in terms of the location of the black and white pieces. When it is your turn to make a move, your goal is to decide which piece to move and where. One could start by considering all the possible moves that one could take, then consider all the *probable* responses that the opponent would take. This leads to a back-and-forth recursive scheme known as an Alpha-Beta search. Future configurations of the chessboard can be thought of as possible end states Y. If one can assess the advantage that one might hope to receive for a given end state Y, then one can compute the utility function $U(Y|X)$. With time constraints, one can only afford to perform a limited number of recursions. That is to say, the depth of one's search is constrained. What if the opponent understands such limitations and has gone just a little bit deeper? The opponent may have discovered that while a given state Y may look attractive to you, a few cunning moves later the tables will quickly turn, and the opponent will gain the upper hand. As Admiral Akbar would put it — 'It's a Trap!' Such manoeuvres are sometimes elevated to the lofty status of gambit.

For a given X, instead of a systematic Alpha-Beta search, what we really want is to have a kind of magic eight ball that, when shaken, will produce useful Ys (future board configurations) that one can analyze for traps and possible advantages. Every time one shakes the eight ball, one gets an uncorrelated but useful Y. The behaviour of this device can be described by a *distribution* $P(Y|X)$, such that likely instances of Y — values of Y where $P(Y|X)$ is high — are also instances of Y where $U(Y|X)$ is high. The process of plucking highly probable values of Y out of thin air is known as sampling the distribution. At this point, the attentive reader probably recalls my previous intervention on Variational Methods. Let's return briefly to this tantalizing topic by way of the famous Metropolis–Hastings (MH) (Hastings 1970) algorithm.

Given a distribution $P(Y|X)$, we hope to produce fair samples of Y such as would be produced by our magic eight ball. The algorithm assumes that we have access to a function $f(Y)$ which is proportional to $P(Y|X)$. We also have access to a function $g(Y^{(i)}|Y^{(i-1)})$, such that if $Y^{(i-1)}$ is a likely sample of $P(Y|X)$, then $Y^{(i)}$ is likely to be a likely sample of $P(Y|X)$. This function is known as a proposal distribution. A simple proposal distribution might be a Gaussian centred at Y_{i-1}. The key is that we know how to sample the proposal distribution. The algorithm starts with an arbitrary value $Y^{(0)}$, we sample the proposal distribution and generate a candidate for $Y^{(1)}$. We then compute the value $\alpha = \frac{f(Y^{(1)})}{f(Y^{(0)})}$. The larger the value of α, the more likely that Y_1 is a fair sample from $P(Y|X)$. Using a random number generator, we compute a threshold and if α is larger than the threshold, we accept the candidate Y_1 and go on to compute Y_2. This process continues iteratively. Eventually, samples generated in this way will resemble the workings of the magic eight ball. This type of algorithm is known as a Monte Carlo Markov Chain (MCMC). The Monte Carlo term comes from the fact that at each iteration we are spinning the wheel of the proposal distribution. The term Markov Chain comes from the idea that the proposal distribution only depends on the last sample. As you may recall, the Gibbs Sampler is another form of MCMC. The key to this formulation is access to the function $f(Y)$ that we can directly evaluate. What happens when we don't have access to such a function? We could consider some form of quantum computing, but since the human brain does not appear to have the facilities required to construct conditions of near absolute zero, we might instead turn our hopes to the idea of prior experience. While we might not know how to map our current X to a useful Y, we may in the past have observed how other Xs have been mapped to their useful Ys. Enter the Deep Learner ...

Policy

Suppose that there was a book that contained an analysis of every chess game ever played at the Grand Master level. Each game could be analyzed in terms of turning points, which can be described by initial conditions X that would be considered innocuous, followed by a series of moves by both players ending with a state Y, where it becomes evident that X turns out to be a dangerous state for one of the players. This book represents a set of (X, Y) pairs, which can be used to train a neural network. The neural network is essentially an approximation of the proposal distribution $P(Y|X)$. The hope is that with sufficient data, the resulting neural network is able to generalize beyond what it was trained on so that novel configurations of X not previously encountered will still produce valuable Ys. Armed with such a weapon, a player is no longer forced to consider all possibilities via Alpha-Beta search, she may instead plug the current configuration of her chessboard X into her neural network magic eight ball and receive samples Y that act as seeds for in-depth analysis and evaluation. If instead of mapping X to interesting future configurations Y for consideration, our neural network simply informs us regarding the best next move to take, such a system would be known as a *policy*.

At this point, I offer the following evidence that various forms of learned neural networks may be a component of this type of System 1 functionality. First, it has been observed that the best predictor of whether or not a given individual will become a champion chess player is not the amount of time spent playing chess. It is instead the amount of time spent studying previous chess games. This makes sense if you want to expose the learner to the largest collection of (X, Y) pairs as quickly as possible. Second, back in high school, I was the number two player of our five-person varsity chess team. Unlike myself, our captain, the number one, was a true chess phenomenon. His name was Henry and he was one of the highest-ranked international players under 16 in the world. So feared was Henry that all the other Toronto teams would regularly swap their top player out of the number 1 position so they would not have to face the unbeatable Henry. One day, as part of a high school fundraiser, Henry set up 10 chessboards so that he could play multiple people simultaneously for cash. All winnings to be donated to charity. Henry would go from board to board, in a matter of seconds make his move and then go to the next opponent. Hoping to make a name for himself, the second-string substitute, nicknamed 'The Hammer' (yes, high school chess can be rough), attempted subterfuge. While Henry was attending to another board, The Hammer discretely advanced the location of one of his pawns by one position, resulting in a slightly more favourable configuration. Upon his return Henry announced that the board had been tampered with, he moved the pawn back to its original position, made his move and continued on. This form of memory appears to be a distinguishing capability of highly accomplished chess players. A possible explanation is that the ability to map X to configurations Y may also result in the ability to map X to previous versions of X. Interestingly, this capacity does not seem to apply to completely random chess configurations that would not 'naturally' occur. It appears that this kind of memory does not extrapolate significantly beyond the manifold of its training data … Third, the ability to map current configurations X to valuable actions using neural network-based policies is the means by which the current AI engines are now routinely beating expert players in games ranging from Go to StarCraft.

The range of possible search spaces seems to have no bound:

- Every possible set Y of predicates such that each set is potentially useful with respect to circumstances X, while not being so large as to cause an inference explosion.
- Every possible Simpson Episode Y, where each episode can be indexed via societal framing devices allowing for efficient pop culture references.
- Every memory Y that you have ever had allowing for both recall (do you remember when we went to X?) and recognition (have you seen X before?).

Returning to your thoughts on frames and framing. One might argue that framing the current context in a certain way is a means for constructing an X which can then be transmitted to another via language. The receiver of such an X can then bring to the fore useful sets of knowledge Y as well as useful frames for representation and reasoning. When the AI-Assistant takes human form, is this not just another form of framing needed to coax the human into the right frame of mind? Before being accused of assuming my own set of can-openers, I will, of course, concede that sequential search, hierarchical organization, indexing, MCMC, the machine learning magic eight ball, and even quantum computing are by no means the be-all-and-end-all for a serviceable System 1. We need to understand how to acquire the books in the first place, how they are represented, how they can be encoded in a library made of meat, and how the earnest GAIE might hope to one day reproduce this remarkable phenomenon in our beloved AI-Assistant.

Part 2

Communication

Chapter 8

Conversation with a Friend

Suman Gupta

The Can Opener

Let me finish the True Story with which you started, Peter — about the Engineer, Physicist, and Economist on a desert island with a can of beans — since, inexplicably, you have left it incomplete.

... The Economist raised his hand. The other two looked at him sceptically, amazed that a mere Economist could have the temerity to address two geniuses. The Physicist knew she's a genius because by definition every Physicist is a genius; the Engineer was convinced she's a genius and regarded the Physicist with unrequited fellow-feeling. Both knew that the Economist must be quite dim because he's not a Physicist or even an Engineer. But politeness reluctantly prevailed, and the conversation then went as follows:

Economist: Why don't we just assume that we have a can-opener!
[A whole two minutes of silence followed while the other two absorbed this.]
Physicist [*reluctantly*]: I have to admit that that's a brilliant nudge. For some reason — silly me — we were trying to find a solution to our conundrum by starting from the first principles of mechanics and thermodynamics and working sequentially and somewhat randomly through various possible solutions with the resources at hand. I was sadly taken in by the reinvent-the-wheel syndrome to which Engineers

are typically prone. But of course, the solution to this problem exists already and all we have to do is emulate it with the resources at hand. We have the concept of the can-opener already, now the question is how to devise one here. A can-opener is an instrument made of a stronger material than the can which can penetrate and then shear the can, to which end the lever-principle might come in handy. The cutting force (CF) needed is: length of the cut (L) × thickness of the can (T) × the shear strength (MPa) of the metal the can is made of. I can see that this can is made of aluminium, so requires a shear strength of 207 MPa, with a thickness of probably around 5 μm. I perceive that there's dense igneous rock on this island, it should be possible to find a stone of 300 or more MPa with an edge of blade-like surface area, which can be honed by another stone if necessary. I notice that my colleague the Engineer's forearm development is satisfactory, no doubt due to many hours of tennis, so with such a stone, and using the edge of the can as a fulcrum, the necessary penetrative force and then CF is easily achieved with edifying results.

Engineer [*jealous*]: The can-opener principle is a fine one, I daresay, but the difficulty of locating a stone with the desired properties is detrimental to the can-opener suggestion — especially since I, for one, am starving. But now that we are going by pre-existing solutions, which rather inelegantly take recourse to short-cuts rather than rebuilding-the-wheel, why not focus on the sandpaper-principle? All we need to do is locate a stone surface with the appropriate grit size to enable mildly strenuous two-body abrasion applied in a controlled way on the can so as to achieve ...

Economist [*encouraging*]: I am so grateful I have such knowledgeable companions with me at this difficult time! Once you have sorted that out and we are full of beans, I suggest that we do a survey of other edible matter on this desert island. You [*with an approving nod to the Physicist*] very astutely observed that there may be clams around, and quite possibly, may I add, seaweed and maybe even fish. We need to do a survey and an inventory of all edible matter and utilizable materials that this island resource-base offers, and then establish a cycle of production with equitable input of labour, and agree on some principles for, so to speak, the division of the cake ...

Physicist [*awed*]: How come you are not a Physicist? How come I am not an Economist?

Economist [*modestly*]: Oh, you're infinitely cleverer than I and [*with an obsequious smile to the Engineer*] even you are so much brainier. It's just that I have some inherited knowledge of desert island scenarios, one of my ancestors was the great *homo economicus* Robinson Crusoe ...

Cooperative Acts

One has to admit that the Economist's suggestion was open to other constructions. The exchange might have gone thus:

Economist: Why don't we just assume that we have a can-opener!
[A whole two minutes of embarrassed silence follows.]
Engineer [*pityingly*]: And what do you propose we do after assuming this?
Physicist [*as to a child*]: We can't open that can with an assumed can-opener, you see?
Economist [*crushed*]: What I meant is ...
Engineer [*airily*]: Don't worry, we understand perfectly. [*To the Physicist*] When a solution is not readily conceived, we need to start looking for it. I suggest that you and I do a sequential search in two different directions with a view to spotting something that we may be inspired to convert into a tool or method to our purpose.
Economist [*agonized*]: I ...
Engineer [*heartily to the Economist*]: You have the most important task, you will stay here and guard that can of beans with your life!
Physicist [*petulantly*]: I don't want to go looking for ideas. If only I could lie down here and think long enough, the solution will come to me.

However, this is not what happened in the True Story. What happened was that the Physicist — and therefore the Engineer — were inclined to understand what the Economist said as being meaningful and relevant. They then made reasonable inferences about what that meaning and relevance are given their situation and proceeded from there. The Economist didn't have to explain and elaborate. And even if they had failed to make immediate sense of what he said, they would have probed patiently to determine whether there was good sense there — because they would have been inclined to assume that what the Economist said was meaningful and relevant.

They would, in fact, treat '*communication as a cooperative act, subject to constraints of maximizing a shared utility function*', as your friends Stephanie Stacy and Tao Gao have put it for what appears to be quite an idealized model. In fact, this is more a working hypothesis than an inference, but a strong hypothesis because, if assumed (taken as an assumption), it opens a lot of cans. It enables a rational structure to be put on various kinds of communicative practices (not all of which are, in fact, cooperative acts — e.g., the quite plausible conversation that didn't take place in the True Story is not wholly cooperative). Assumptions often are can-openers where lots of different and diverse observations are sealed in cans, and new ones are getting canned as we speak.

Let's pause awhile on the hypothesis of a cooperative principle in communication. Or rather, on certain kinds of communication, because *all* communication is a bit much to be covered by an Imagined-We framework (remember my notes on framing?) and rational action planning/ inverse action interpretation underpinned by a cooperative principle. In everyday communication, we can generally come up with plausible, even normative, real-world examples of communication or of significative acts which don't fit models with regular underpinning assumptions. Let's pause, in fact, on ordinary-language conversations, one kind of real-world communicative modality. For explaining many of the practices of ordinary-language conversations, as I had observed in an earlier intervention, a cooperative principle is a strong hypothesis.

It is worth pausing on this because it might have a bearing on your outlines, in your previous intervention, of sequential searching, indexing, distribution and sampling, and policy making by way of trying to get to an account of System 1. Those outlines don't quite account for System 1, as far as I can see, because System 1 involves short-cuts, working with *ad hoc* assumptions — which may or may not appear in automated policy making, and I don't yet see why they may or may not from what you say.

Conversations

The thing about explaining ordinary-language conversation practices is that the evidence bases — i.e., the obtainable conversation datasets — are necessarily fluid. One could go by recording snippets of such conversations with some context markers and put some convenient limits on the scale of recording (how long the snippet, how dense the context markers). But no such dataset contains all possible practices even within the limits on scales; new ones crop up and some become archaic while a dataset is being elicited and organized. Moreover, any set of convenient limits could be excessively delimiting. Alternatively, and this is more common, researchers go for plausible conversation snippets with some intuitive grasp of practices and principles, which seems reasonable in that researchers are as much normative conversation practitioners for a given cohort as anyone else. Between quantity and experience, the exemplifying data are seldom sufficient for proofs but often suffice for proposing strong hypotheses.

The practice in ordinary-language conversations which analysis often focuses on is: interlocutors seem to convey and grasp a lot more in their exchanges than is explicitly said by either. Conversations work efficiently and functionally both by saying explicitly and by implicitly not-saying (by implying, suggesting, etc.). Incidentally, when I say 'saying' I mean more than verbalizing; here 'saying' contains the whole panoply of explicit signs given by an interlocutor (words spoken, hand gestures, tone, raised eyebrows, grimaces, stance ...).

Here are three well-known hypotheses to explain this feature of ordinary-language conversations:

The Paul Grice Hypothesis (1989 [1975])

The effective conveying of the not-said in ordinary-language conversations is explicable if we assume a cooperative principle. The cooperative principle involves interlocutors *A* and *B* undertaking their exchanges with some pre-existing maxims in mind. Given that they share those maxims, they proceed to understand each other even when not everything they convey and grasp is explicitly stated. Here's a list of these maxims:

Maxim of Quantity: Information
- Make your contribution as informative as is required for the current purposes of the exchange.
- Do not make your contribution more informative than is required.

Maxim of Quality: Truth
- Do not say what you believe to be false.
- Do not say that for which you lack adequate evidence.

Maxim of Relation: Relevance
- Be relevant.

Maxim of Manner: Clarity ('be perspicuous')
- Avoid obscurity of expression.
- Avoid ambiguity.
- Be brief (avoid unnecessary prolixity).
- Be orderly.

These sound a bit school-teacherly, the sort of thing my English composition teacher or Moral Tutor might have drummed into me. But these are not meant to be good rules to follow in conversations; these are rather preconceived assumptions in terms of which conversational exchanges proceed, often by flouting or playing with them. The very fact that they are flouted or played with, and are understood as being flouted or played with, underpin their baseline function. The question then, of course, is: how is this baseline established? The answer might be that it is contained in the grammar of conversations, i.e., conversational language is pre-structured according to syntactical rules which take the principles and maxims as normative. This grammar might have evolved through usage and conventions and could to some degree be codifications of a process of cultural adaptations.

The Dan Sperber and Deirdre Wilson Hypothesis (*1995* [*1986*])

Insofar as the not-said aspect of ordinary-language conversations go, this hypothesis focuses on relevance as the key. The idea is that instead of a cooperative principle underpinned by a number of maxims, all of which seem to have a voluntaristic air about them, as if interlocutors have somehow subscribed to pre-made choices, necessity plays a more determinative role. That the not-said is conveyed and grasped in conversation is not because some precedent choices are dominant but because there are no other ways in which conversational exchanges can proceed functionally. Relevance, this hypothesis goes, is not something embedded in the relationship between what is said and not-said, but in the relationship between what is said and the cognitive environment or context shared by the interlocutors. This relationship works according to shared assumptions which are necessarily made by interlocutors given the context within which they converse, which then obviates the need to say everything that bears upon the exchange and understanding. The relationship could be articulated as following two 'extent conditions':

> *Extent condition* 1: An assumption is relevant in a context to the extent that its contextual effects in this context are large.
> *Extent condition* 2: An assumption is relevant in a context to the extent that the effort required to process it in this context is small. (Wilson and Sperber 1995: 125).

Definitions of effects and effort are proposed, but we don't need to go there — the rationale is self-evident. In some sense, these given conditions make conversation in the received sense possible. By this hypothesis, the baseline consists in a hardwired economy of effort and effect, in terms of which a mechanistic rationale structures ordinary-language conversation.

The Robert Stalnaker Hypothesis (1999 [1974])

This could be regarded as an alternative to Sperber and Wilson's. The idea is that insofar as the not-said in ordinary-language conversations go, a cooperative principle and a set of underpinning maxims may well be necessary conditions themselves rather than choices and conventions which have evolved and become embedded in the grammar. That is, the principle/maxims are shared assumptions which allow for testing. It is the result of interlocutors quickly testing these assumptions in the given conversational situation — even while conversing — which necessarily leads to functional saying and not-saying in exchanges. The mode of testing is of checking which possible worlds a shared assumption works in and thereby homing in on the degree to which that assumption applies in this world, i.e., the world of this conversation. The hypothesis is put succinctly thus:

> Communication, whether linguistic or not, normally takes place against a background of beliefs or assumptions which are shared by the speaker and his audience, and which are recognized by them to be shared. [...] Which facts or opinions we can reasonably take for granted in this way, as much as what further information either of us wants to convey, will

guide the direction of our conversation — will determine what is said. I will not say things that are already taken for granted, since that would be redundant. Nor will I assert things incompatible with the common background, since that would be self-defeating. My aim in making assertions is to distinguish among the possible situations which are compatible with all beliefs or assumptions that I assume that we share. Or it could be put the other way around: the common background is defined by the possible situations which I intend to distinguish among my assertions and other speech acts. Propositions true in all of them are propositions whose truth is taken for granted. (Stalnaker 1999: 48–9).

So, there is at least a cooperative principle at work insofar as each interlocutor assumes, and also assumes that the other assumes, some shared predicates and beliefs. But that is not sufficient to make the conversational logic function. At every step of exchanges, the extent to which predicates and beliefs need to be said or not-said is tested (very speedily) by each interlocutor by checking how they may work in other possible situations — other worlds. This process may depend upon the interlocutors' experience of other conversations (so, an inductive process), or may call upon an accruing pool of many interlocutors' collective tests (established patterns of usage, possibly also structured in the grammar).

System 1

System 1 does something before System 2 kicks in and indeed System 2 would be hard work if System 1 doesn't do something already. There are some shortcuts that System 1 enables so that System 2 can unfold without labouring intensively and for long. In a way, the sieving of what's said and what's not-said in an ordinary-language conversation is a System 1 thing which, so to speak, happens, so that the conversation itself can proceed progressively following System 2 apprehensions. If that didn't happen, and there was only System 2 to kick off with the conversation, we can imagine very long-winded exchanges where each interlocutor has to fully say everything for the other to follow, and the other would have to do the same, and posing any question at any point would be apt to lead into indefinite regression. In fact, such a conversation may just turn into one interlocutor's exhausting monologue — ergo not a conversation at all.

The three hypotheses are about what the ordinary-language conversational System 1 does as a *system*, i.e., not a set of random moves. The techniques for getting to such System 1 processes that you enumerated in the last intervention — sequential searching, indexing, distribution and sampling (especially the Gibbs sort), and policy making (deep learning) — could arise at two levels in contemplating those hypotheses:

- To test the robustness of the hypotheses by applying it to a given conversational dataset.
- To emulate an automated ordinary-language conversation which involves saying and not-saying by using a conversation dataset for training.

The techniques you lay out have a direction from simple to complex or from determinate to less determinate. Sequential searching and indexing cover all the ground available, all the variables on this ground, with less or more ordered thoroughness. In this case, the ground is distinct and well-defined. Distribution and sampling allow for more complicated determinations, especially MCMC sampling where not all variables are known or a dominant variable is difficult to pin down. The ground is indistinct in itself and has fuzzy margins. Policy making by seeking the most efficient pathway to get, let's say, some reward or maximize some expectation (like that really rare thing, a conversation without any misunderstanding) is useful, e.g., where the variables keep changing. The ground is not only indistinct but also mutable.

As I noted, the datasets for conversations are fluid. For the purpose of testing the robustness of the hypotheses, we will need to depend upon what sort of ordinary-language conversation dataset we have (of conversation snippets and contextual factors). If we firmly fix a given dataset of conversation snippets and contextual factors, we can do sequential searching enhanced by indexing with good effect. If we begin to vary the length of snippets according to what we are asking and bring in a larger number of variable contextual factors, distribution and sampling algorithms will come in very handy. If we have to track how any set of variable conversation snippets and multivariate contextual factors mutate with time, then some sort of deep learning follows as a recourse. Any of these could test the robustness of the three hypotheses to some precise extent (in the form: the hypothesis X holds in $n\%$ of conversational situations). That may help give a stronger sense of System 1 at work here, and it may help emulate an ordinary-language conversation through automated means. But it won't be explaining very much more than the explanations given with the hypotheses, such as: System 1 is grounded in grammar, in culture, in possible worlds, in cognitive environments, some combination of all those and maybe other unknown factors.

The possibility of emulating an ordinary-language conversation through automation is the point I am leading towards — which leads to a question.

The AI-Assistant Friend

We have so far been building upon the facial recognition — and recognition *per se* — capacities of our AI-Assistant, where you have impressed me with what can be done in problem-solving 'monkey' terms while I have put in a plea for thinking in everyday-life 'elephant' terms.

Let's shift to a somewhat different capacity of our AI-Assistant: communication.

What's the state of play in this regard?

Let me be clear about what I am asking. I am not asking whether our AI-Assistant can answer a question which involves reaching for relevant information from an existing pool of information. Nor am I asking whether our AI-Assistant can give the average response or most popular or well-tested response to a normative genre of proposition (like saying 'Clams are delicious' when the Economist says 'We can eat clams' and the Engineer declares 'I am starving'). I can sort of see how that kind of communication can be automatized reasonably efficiently (and dressed up to appeal to an interlocutor's tendency to project). I am setting the bar quite high: what is the state of play with regard to the horizon of ordinary-language conversations?

For this question, it is best to think of a genre of ordinary-language conversation as the horizon. Let's say, the kind of conversation that takes place between friends. This kind of conversation is often not purposive; it could be an end in itself. The conversation itself is the confirmation of friendship and friendship is satisfied in conversation. It could be something like a conversation where two friends:

- develop an idea together for the fun of it,
- engage in pleasant joshing, taking the piss,

- reassure each other, lend moral support, offer an arm to lean on,
- have an honest heart-to-heart, wear their hearts on their sleeves, spill their guts,
- build castles in the air, take a reality check ...

An AI-Assistant which can offer conversation could be a true friend, and a very lucrative commodity. Think of all the lonely, friendless, yearning souls out there.

Chapter 9

Alan Turing, Kurt Gödel, and David Hilbert Go to a Bar ...

Peter Tu

Suman, like your can-opener-wielding economist, thy wisdom and insight overflow once again. Your thoughts on human conversation sparked much conversation between James Kubricht, Stephanie Stacy, and myself. The following are some of the thoughts that Stephanie had based on your last intervention:

Suman, you argue that technology picks up on Signals Given Off (SGOs), and that current approaches only create a primitive linking to a small subset of the types of corresponding signals that could occur (e.g., as in deception detection). SGOs can be thought of as a type of 'context' that can greatly influence the interpretation of a signal, but are not help-ful without a richer link to the underlying signal. From your examples, it's a bit blurry about whether signals given off can be intentional (e.g., when adopting an annoyed tone of voice do I mean for you to know I am upset and respond accordingly or just speaking with unconscious annoy-ance), but I'm thinking about them as non-intentional. Given this, the interpretation of a signal using the context of SGOs is actually not even part of cooperative communication, which most communication is assumed to be.

In terms of our Imagined-We (IW) framework, because this is a signal the speaker does not mean to give off, it does not ever enter the public common ground used for inference. And given that it does not enter the common ground, an appropriate response does not ever have to address the SGO (it's irrelevant to this model). Instead, the IW draws from more basic perceptual features of the environment/shared knowledge that can be assumed to be public with high confidence.

So, given this, where might SGOs fit in? I'd imagine that this could go into some private model of the speaker (with a higher degree of uncertainty and maybe some recursion) that instead influences how the responder might seek information. For example, you could ask about it to explicitly bring it into your shared knowledge (if you deem it relevant).

On your closing idea about having the tools for a catalogue, but still needing to understand how to acquire books in the first place, etc. We might be able to begin tackling this through some sort of bootstrapping. In the same vein as some of our previous work on bootstrapping, a joint commitment under the IW framework, Tao and I are thinking about the possibility of bootstrapping some sort of agreement on signal-mapping to features using the IW. Obviously, the even harder question is how to scale up when the space is big and we are not even sure this will work, but I think it would be an interesting stab at the problem.

Conversation Starters

Let me now turn to your question regarding a friendly conversation, where an AI might be able to hold forth with small talk and a pleasant joke or two. Let me start by stating right off the bat that I do not believe that the current state of AI supports this level of communication and dare I say intimacy. I will now describe what currently passes for artificial conversation, followed by a discussion of what might or might not be possible.

I would argue that modern video games can give the illusion of conversation. I just finished playing *Last of Us: Part II* (LOUII). As you may recall from LOUI, Ellie and Joel fought their way across a zombie-ridden America with the hope of finding a cure for the pandemic. It turned out that the cost for such a cure was too great for Joel and so they decided to settle down somewhere near Seattle. Not too far, I guess, from where Deacon St James and his compadres had their own post-apocalyptic adventures. In LOUII, we find ourselves immersed in a terrible tail of revenge. Critics have argued the LOUII is a great example of ludonarrative dissonance, which is the conflict between a video game's narrative told through the story and the narrative told through the gameplay. The saga teaches us about the pointlessness of violence. However, without copious amounts of violence, the gameplay would be rather pointless. Peppered throughout this epic is the opportunity to initiate various conversational set pieces. Of course, this is all scripted and so is not quite what we are looking for.

Something that is a little less hard-wired in nature is automatic image captioning. Here a machine learning algorithm is given a large corpus of images with captions. Some sort of neural network embedding is used to transform any image into a large feature vector. This feature vector can be thought of as a sequence, which can be concatenated with the words of the associated caption resulting in a larger sequence. Mechanisms such as RNNs (Recurrent Neural Networks) and LSTMs (Long-Term Short-Term Memory networks) can be trained on such joint sequences. When a new image is presented, it is first processed by the neural network producing the first portion of the sequence. The trained RNN/ LSTM then produces a distribution over possible completions of the sequence, which can be sampled resulting in realistic and possibly unique captions. If the captions are more explanatory in nature, the output of such systems will have a more narrative quality. One could imagine being at a beach resort, sitting beside a comely robot which utters, in a somewhat nasal tone, 'Sun setting over palm trees' — not exactly riveting banter, but a start.

Mechanisms that might be a little bit more engaging are the chatbots. There are many ways of constructing these devices ranging from Eliza ('How does that make you feel?') to Alexa ('My, that Jeff Bezos is a snappy dresser'). One approach is to make use of a corpus of recorded conversations. Once again, such data can be viewed as sequences, which are amenable to analysis and syntheses by RNN/LSTM neural networks. Word embeddings can be used to represent a given utterance. The idea is that each word is assigned a point in a high-dimensional space such that the Euclidean distances between words are equivalent to some measure of semantic distance. Given what passes for conversation at the local Starbucks, a pair of chatbots might fit in nicely. However, I will agree that such machinations do not rise to your desired level of discourse.

Turing Machine

When you described an intimate conversation, what really caught my eye was the idea of a joke. In order to make a somewhat misogynistic argument, the late Christopher Hitchens made the assertion that jokes are like the feathers of a peacock — they are meant to demonstrate one's intelligence to the opposite sex. I guess that this is akin to the professor's penchant for sesquipedalian repartee. As I recall from my high school days, the alpha-males seemed to be constantly incensed with other alpha-males who had the audacity to steal one of their witticisms. This leads to the hypothesis that a new form of Turing test (Turing 1950), one that might address some of the issues raised by John Searle's Chinese Room analysis (Searle 1980), might be the ability to comprehend and construct a good joke in a contextually relevant manner.

Assertions for why this form of intelligence may be beyond the reach of AI usually comes down to some sort of argument regarding the limits of algorithms. If we are going to go down this path, then I fear we are going to have to turn back the pages (imagine the sound of a harp and maybe some clockwise swirling mist) and take a look at the spellbinding work of the great Alan Turing. Luckily for us, Charles Petzold has provided a guided tour (Petzold 2008) from which I will attempt to briefly summarize.

Let's start by considering various sets of numbers. The natural numbers are $\{0, 1, 2, 3, \ldots\}$. The Integers are $\{\ldots, -3, -2, -1, 0, 1, 2, 3, \ldots\}$. The rational numbers are the ratio of any pair of integers, with the exception that you cannot divide by zero. The irrational numbers are those that are not rational. Irrational numbers can be thought of as an infinite sequence of non-repeating digits such as the square root of 2. The rational numbers plus the irrational numbers make up the real numbers. You can also break up the real numbers into the algebraic and the transcendental, where algebraic numbers are the roots of polynomials. Examples of transcendental numbers are π and e.

One of the interesting concepts of number theory is the idea of countability. If you can put the members of a set of numbers into correspondence with the natural numbers, then you can say that the set is countable or enumerable. Clearly, the natural numbers are enumerable. Without too much imagination you could see how the integers are enumerable. Since the integers are enumerable, with a little bit more ingenuity one could see how the rational numbers are also enumerable. It turns out that the algebraic numbers too are enumerable. So, what about the transcendentals and hence the reals? Let's assume that the real numbers are enumerable. One could then make a list of all real numbers between 0 and 1. It should be noted that all such numbers have an infinite number of digits. Even rational numbers such as ½ have an infinite number of digits: 0.5000000 ... We now use a trick known as diagonalization. The idea is that we can construct a new number b by setting the nth digit of b equal to the nth digit of the nth number in the list of real numbers and then add 1 to that digit. What is odd about b is that it is clearly different from every number in the list and is hence not part of the list. This is because the nth number will be guaranteed to be different from b by 1 on the nth digit. We can then conclude that the real numbers are not countable. Not only are they not countable, it turns out that there are far more transcendental numbers than there are algebraic numbers. Alan Turing starts by trying to define a new set of numbers, those that are computable.

To begin this quest, we start with what is now known as a Turing Machine (TM) (cf. Turing 1937). A TM is assumed to have access to an infinite length of tape, the ability to move the tape to the left or to the right, the ability to read a symbol from the current location of the tape, and the ability to write a symbol onto the current location of the tape. Turing then defines the idea of a state, which has: (i) a state number, (ii) a set of instructions that are issued depending on the current symbol on the tape (a kind of branching function), followed by (iii) a new state that the machine jumps to after the instructions have been carried out. One constraint on a TM is that the number of states must be finite. The goal of a TM is to produce a number in binary form (0s and 1s) between 0 and 1. Remember that all such numbers are an infinite sequence of 0s and 1s even if after some point all the digits are zero. If for some reason a TM gets stuck and is unable to produce an infinite sequence of numbers, it is referred to as being circular. One might consider a non-circular TM as a bug-free TM. It turns out that all devices that can implement a TM can be viewed as being equivalent to one another and that all modern-day digital computers are essentially TM devices — so by starting to consider the limits of the TMs, we may gain insights into the limits of AI and as a consequence algorithmic humour. Let's get back to the question of computable numbers.

Turing shows that every possible TM can be represented by a finite natural number. In one of the great intellectual feats of our time, Turing constructs a TM called U (the universal machine) that can take a natural number that defines a specific TM and then produce the number that TM would have produced. He then shows how the rational and algebraic numbers can be produced by a TM. He also shows how certain transcendentals like π and e can also be produced using power series representations. When you think about it, it is quite remarkable that a number which is a non-repeating infinite sequence, such as π, is equivalent to a TM which is defined by a finite number. Since each TM is associated with a natural number, the TMs are hence enumerable. However, we know that the reals are not enumerable, which means that not every real number is computable. This makes sense if you think that most real numbers are essentially an infinite sequence of random digits with no inherent structure.

For reasons that will soon be clear, Turing then asks the question regarding whether it is possible for a TM to determine if any given TM is non-circular. This is similar but not quite the same as the halting problem, which is an attempt to define a generic method for determining whether a functional algorithm will terminate with an answer. Turing starts by assuming that there is a TM called D that can take any finite number that is used to represent a TM and output an s (satisfactory) for those that represent non-circular TMs and a u (unsatisfactory) for those that are circular or ill-defined (while every properly defined TM can be described by a finite natural number, not every finite natural number defines a properly defined TM). He then considers the concerns of a sceptic.

Since each TM can be represented by a natural number, the number that is produced by a TM can also be associated with a natural number. This means that the computable numbers must be countable. However, if we use our diagonalization trick again, one could then take this list of computable numbers and produce a new number that is not on the list. This would lead one to believe that, like the reals, the set of computable numbers is not countable. A contradiction! Following this logic, let's assume that B is the TM that is in charge of computing the number that does not reside on the list of computable numbers. The algorithm for B would look something like the following:

1. Set k equal to 0.
2. Set n equal to 0.
3. Apply D to the TM defined by k to determine if it is a non-circular TM
   a. If the output of D is s (satisfactory)
   {(i) Use U to compute the number produced by the TM defined by k up to the nth digit.

    (ii) Add 1 to this digit and output this value as the nth digit that is produced by B.

    (iii) Increment n by 1}.

4. Increment k by 1.

5. Go to Step 3.

On the face of it, this looks pretty tractable. However, let us consider what happens when $k = k_B$, where k_B is the natural number that defines the TM for B. If D determines that k_B is satisfactory, then it will ask U to compute the number produced by the TM defined by k_B (which is B). This, of course, starts that whole process over again which will itself lead to the same point where once again we need to start the whole process over again. This is known as an infinite recursion — it never ends. Yikes! This means that B is circular so that the number that is not on the list can't actually be computed. This is consistent with our argument that the computable numbers remain countable. This also implies that D cannot exist, which means that there is no general algorithm for deciding whether a TM is non-circular. At the heart of this analysis we come to the conclusion that while the non-circular TMs are enumerable, they cannot in reality be enumerated. While computable numbers and Turing Machines are all very interesting, Alan Turing really had his sights set on what is known as David Hilbert's Entscheidungsproblem (Hilbert and Ackermann 1950 [1928]). To go down this path, we need some familiarity with entities known as propositions and predicates.

Entscheidungsproblem

Propositions: A proposition is a logical statement that is either true or false. For example, the statement 'My car is blue'. Logical operations such as and/or/not can be used to combine propositions resulting in new propositions. A proposition that is true regardless of the values of its component propositions is known as a tautology, i.e., A or not(A).

Predicates: A predicate is a parameterized proposition where the parameter is often associated with a class instance. For example, IsBlue(i) is true if the object referred to by the index i is in fact blue. Once the parameter of the predicate has been defined, the predicate is reduced to a proposition. For example, IsBlue(my-car) is a proposition. A predicate can also take on multiple parameters such as IsNear(*i,j*), where *i* and *j* might refer to two different objects. The evaluation of logical statements such as 'there exists an element *n* belonging to the set *N*, such that the predicate *p*(*n*) is true' is the topic known as first-order predicate calculus.

A theorem is basically a mathematical statement or formula made up of propositions and predicates that is either true or false. Mathematicians employ all sorts of tactics in order to construct proofs for such theorems. For example, if one wants to prove that a given formula is true, one can start by assuming that it is false, investigate the logical implications that result, and hopefully find some form of contradiction. This process is known by the Harry Potteresque phrase *reductio ad absurdum*. Another approach is to attempt to derive the formula based on a set of accepted axioms. An axiom is assumed to be true. Various inference rules can be used to manipulate the axioms resulting in new statements. If one can apply a sequence of manipulations to the axioms and arrive at the proposed formula, then one has derived the theorem and can thus conclude that it is true. To this end, David Hilbert was in search of a set of axioms that could be used to prove logical statements defined using first-order predicate calculus. He was hoping that these axioms would have the following properties:

- *Independence*: No axiom could be derived from the other axioms.
- *Consistency*: It must not be possible to derive two theorems that contradict each other.
- *Completeness*: The ability to derive all true formulas from the axioms.
- *Decidability*: A general method to determine the provability of any given well-formed formulae (not that it was true or false, but whether one could produce a proof one way or the other).

While starting off with high hopes, Kurt Gödel was the first to crash the party (Gödel 1986 [1931]). His inconsistency theorem showed that axioms added to first-order predicate logic that allowed for the derivation of arithmetic rendered the system incomplete. He had derived from within this system a formula and its negation. Gödel associated every formula and every proof with a number. He was then able to develop a formula that asserted its own unprovability.

OK, so consistency is off the table; it might still be possible to construct a general method to determine if a formula was provable (decidability). This is the Entscheidungsproblem. Well, the math gets a little bit hairy here, so I will make a long story short. Using much of the machinery used to demonstrate that a TM could not decide whether or not a TM is non-circular, Turing showed that no general algorithm could be used to determine if a formula is provable or not. Turing showed that the British Museum-like algorithm, which involved computing a list of every possible derivation and simply comparing it to the formula at hand, was not possible.

Quantum Mind

Alan Turing was a gentle soul and died well before his time. This was mainly due to the barbarism of his era. But the ideas that his work unleashed reverberate to this day. It was soon shown that a neural network could be used to implement a TM. Norbert Weiner started the field of Cybernetics. John Von Neuman delved into experiments on cellular automata. Claude Shannon developed information theory. Researchers then started to question if the mind is more than a TM. Roger Penrose and others have put forth the idea of a quantum mind (cf. Penrose 1989). The following are various takeaways from such contemplations:

- A quantum mind would allow for infinite parallelism.
- A quantum mind could produce truly random numbers.
- Devotees of free will who believe that the mind is just a TM cling to decidability as a source of comfort. If the decisions we make are due to a TM, there does not seem to be a way to predict what our 'free will' will do.
- The quantum mind enthusiasts might hold forth on 'free will' using the 'many worlds' argument. The idea is that at every decision point, the universe simply splits to accommodate all eventualities. So, from our perspective as free agents, we appear to be sitting at the end of a sequence of well-considered decisions. Oops, having just decided to have a pastrami sandwich for my lunch, I fear I may have caused another universe to come into existence. I hope that the other Peter enjoys his ham and swiss.
- Penrose argues that even if we cannot derive a formula from axioms, we still may know the truth of such a thing. As Turing has

shown a TM does not in general have the means for arriving at such knowledge. Might it be the case that a good joke tickles our uncanny sense of truthfulness?

Flash forward to today ... imagine harps playing in reverse and receding mist. The profundity of Turing's work is evidenced by the fact that AI's highest honour is the Turing Award. Yoshua Bengio, Geoffrey Hinton, and Yann LeCun were recipients of the 2018 ASM A.M Turing Award for their ground-breaking work on deep neural networks (see Bengio's Turing Lecture 2019). Highlights from his talk include general adversarial networks, attention networks, word embeddings, sparsity and causality, the need for training using multiple reward criteria, as well as System 1 vs. System 2 capabilities. It is still too early to know whether such investigations will result in a usable artificial sense of humour for our AI-Assistant. If not, we may yet require a quantum mind or at the very least a usable theory for situation comedies.

So, Suman, have you heard any good jokes lately and if so what made you laugh?

Chapter 10

Helpfully, Seriously, Ambiguously

Suman Gupta

Cooperation

Far be it from me to aspire to emulate an Economist. The Economist's wisdom is ineffable. Mine is a humble calling.

To begin with, let me try and think through Stephanie's interesting notes about Signals Given Off (SGO) and Signals Given (SG), and the idea of cooperation in the Imagined-We framework (in the way that I understand it), and the respective roles of speaker and responder.

If SGO is non-intentional as opposed to SG which is intentional, should SGO be left outside the frame of cooperation which is structured through the Imagined We? Ergo, is cooperation necessarily intentional in communication?

Let's take a very simple account of an ordinary-language communication act.

Speaker X and responder Y engage in a communication act with the mutual expectation that they will understand each other, i.e., they know they will cooperate in understanding each other. This expectation is not so much because they are well-disposed to each other but because of collective preconditions/knowledge/experience for engaging in communication. Those include having the same language, having conventions and histories in common, sharing a cognitive habitus and socio-cultural context, etc. For the purposes of this argument, let's call the totality of all these collective preconditions/knowledge/experience the Imagined We.

Speaker X intends to convey to responder Y a message $[z]$ by producing a set of verbal and non-verbal signals $s1$ (X's intention is narrowly defined by the target of conveying $[z]$ to Y). Some of the signals in $s1$ are knowingly produced (SG) and some unknowingly (SGO) by X, so $s1 =$ SG + SGO. We may say, X intended to convey $[z]$ to Y by SG, and the SGO were unintentional by-products. But that doesn't put SGO outside the frame of the communication act.

Responder Y receives $s1$ but does not necessarily know how much of the set is SG and how much SGO. Y has to infer what the $[z]$ that X intended to convey is from $s1$. Several possibilities open up:

1. Y correctly sieves out the SG that X intended from the $s1$ received, disregards the SGO therein, and infers $[z]$ as X intended — perfect communication.
2. Y takes the breakdown of SG and SGO somewhat differently from what X intended, and infers that $s1 = (SG + x) + (SGO - x)$, or some such variation, and infers that in fact X intended to convey a slightly different message $[z']$ – modified communication.
3. Y receives the SG as intended by X and therefore $[z]$, but doesn't disregard the SGO and takes those as having a bearing $[b]$ on $[z]$, and thus receives more than X intended, such as $[z] + [b][z]$.

Further possibilities can be listed. The only way in which X can know whether Y received $[z]$ as intended is if Y confirms it in response, i.e., through a message $R[z]$ to X. This involves Y sending a set of signals $s2$ consisting of its own proportions of SG and SGO to convey $R[z]$ to X – which repeats the cycle.

What is evident is that intentionality is only one dimension of the multidimensional communication act. Intentionality is not determinedly *what* is communicated by a speaker and can't simply be pegged by what X intended. Intentionality functions somewhere between X's $s1$ and Y's $s2$, or between the intended $[z]$ and the inferred $R[z]$. To limit the content of communication only to X's SG and to disregard the SGO in any framework for grounding communication — i.e., to focus exclusively on perfect communication — is so idealistic as to be of doubtful use.

Nevertheless, we could argue that generally the intentions of two interlocutors like X and Y seem to be reasonably negotiated through communication acts. We function on the basis that communication is functional even if there isn't perfect communication. It would be misdirected, it seems to me, to think of cooperation as tied rigidly to intentionality in communication. That takes me to the concept of the Imagined We as I briefly outlined it above (which might be different from what Stephenie refers to).

So, the Imagined We is a complete set of all collective preconditions/ knowledge/experience that enable all Xs and Ys who are part of the collective to engage in communication. The Imagined We is taken as the basis of cooperation which is materialized in communication between X and Y. By this account, all communication acts by any in the collective are necessarily cooperative acts, however friendly or unfriendly their tenor.

Let's focus on just the linguistic quotient within the Imagined We, which is narrower than my broad indicators above (having the same language, shared conventions and histories, common cognitive habitus and socio-cultural context, etc.). This linguistic quotient would include shared vocabulary, rules of grammar, Gricean maxims, Sperber and Wilsonian extent conditions for relevance, Stalnakerian 'other-worlds' tests, etc. The cooperative principle works something like this: in communicating, X knows that Y knows and Y knows that X knows and both know that others know that they are within Imagined We already.

But that doesn't necessarily mean that the Imagined We itself intends or cooperates at any level or in any sense. Imagined We is not an agent but collective preconditions/knowledge/experiences. There's a prevailing tendency, it seems to me, to think of Imagined We as a sort of meta-agent rather than as the grounding in terms of which agents X and Y communicate. I am not sure why such confusion arises.

Insofar as the linguistic quotient goes, for instance, Imagined We consists in some rules — like a syntactical code. Through this code X and Y can enter a cooperative process of issuing and inferring from SG and SGO. But that doesn't mean that the communicative intent of either is necessarily perfectly communicated. The syntactical code that is a quotient of Imagined We allows for processing of both the intentional and the non-intentional to a functional extent for communication to work — or, to proceed. Cooperation in the frame of Imagined We includes intended and not-intended signals to be processed in communication acts. Nothing more. Neither intending nor cooperation need apply in a consistent and continuous way from the Imagined-We framework to SG/SGO in a specific communication act.

But what might the antithesis of such cooperation mean, what is non-cooperation in this context? By the cooperative principle, any possible communication based on Imagined We is *per se* cooperative, even if a specific communicative act is non-cooperative (such as Y refusing to understand X or actively misunderstanding X). In this context, it is difficult to understand why the counterpoint of 'cooperation' is sometimes taken as 'competition' — why 'cooperation' and 'competition' are considered complementary. The complementarity of 'cooperation' and 'competition' might make sense insofar as X and Y both strive for a common goal; but 'competition' has no meaning insofar as X and Y communicate in terms of the cooperative principle of Imagined We. Cooperation in communication in Imagined-We terms may enable communicative acts whereby agents X and Y can express/perform both active cooperation and active competition. In Imagined-We terms, there is only cooperation or failure of communication — competition is meaningless.

Insofar as the grounding problem in emergent languages goes, that would be the base to reckon from.

I have put this chain of reasoning in an abstract way, and it really could use concrete examples of communication acts to be tested, demonstrated, and clarified — which I would very much like to offer. But let me leave that there and see what comes back. I have spent longer on this than I intended (or didn't intend) and want to spend a bit of time on the substantial other points you made in the last intervention, Peter. Among other things, so far not only is this intervention lacking in jokes, it is dull as ditch water.

Ambiguities and Metaphors

If by a joke you mean a little story or anecdote which one has memorized and delivers at an apt juncture to make people laugh — I have almost never been able to deliver one without it falling flat. If by a joke you mean a spur-of-the-moment response to a situation or comment, with an absurd or quixotic turn, which makes people laugh — I have occasionally come up with those more successfully. More often I have said things with great earnestness which, to my astonishment, have made people roll around slapping their thighs and wiping tears of merriment — which is to say, instead of making a joke I have sometimes been a joke. Not a joker, but a joke embodied.

It seems to me you are chewing upon something way more complex than the shortcuts of everyday conversation which I was recommending pausing on. Philosophers, linguists, literary critics, anthropologists, and the like have occasionally — nervously — ventured into working out the mechanics of jokes. There are theories and hypotheses. These mainly impress by wringing every drop of joy out of any given joke. Here's a joke that Immanuel Kant (I am unable to imagine him as a light-hearted sort) cited to make some philosophical observations:

> An Indian at the table of an Englishman in Surat, when he saw a bottle of ale opened and all the beer turned into froth and overflowing, testified his great astonishment with many exclamations. When the Englishman asked him, "What is there in this to astonish you so much?" he answered, "I am not at all astonished that it should flow out, but I do wonder how you ever got it in." (Kant 1892 [1790]: Part 1, section 54).

I hope that cracked a smile rather than a sneer, Peter; if you want to clutch your brow and think hard about it, go to *Critique of Judgement* (1892 [1790]). And no, Kant wasn't chortling at the expense of the simple-minded Indian in Surat, quite the contrary. For much of human history, philosophy has had a standoffish relationship with jokes.

Joking aside, I admired your summaries of Turing's, Hilbert's, and Gödel's mental gymnastics and struggled a bit to pin down your overall argument. By your account, these demonstrate the 'limits of algorithms' which might explain why they can't be harnessed to deal with some of the trickier aspects of everyday communication, like the simple business of using ellipses or the very complex business of telling a joke. That would suggest that ordinary-language communication somehow doesn't have such limits. But is that a meaningful juxtaposition? Are the limits of algorithms really comparable or contrastable to or differentiable from what ordinary-language communication does? What is the link which will allow a meaningful juxtaposition of how algorithms work in terms of communicative capacities and how ordinary-language systems work for communicative practice?

The examples of the limits of algorithms you outline so well — the countability/uncountability nexus of real numbers in terms of TM circularity or non-circularity, Hilbert's quest for axioms to prove first-order predicate calculus hitting the wall of Gödel's undecidability theory — remind me of William Byers's thoughtful book *How Mathematicians Think* (2007). Byers argues that far from being a practice for generating consistent schema of proofs, mathematics is a system that is built to logically hold together ambiguities by delving into them. Ambiguities are the focal points of mathematical system building. Byers employs a well-defined sense of ambiguity: 'Ambiguity involves a single situation or idea that is perceived in two self-consistent but mutually incompatible frames of reference' (Byers 2007: 28). In fact, what his examples describe are exactly what you describe as countability/uncountability of real numbers or Gödel's inconsistency. In Byers's account, the whole business of mathematics is suffused with ambiguity, from such elementary significations as the equal sign (=) or decimal numbers ($1/3 = 0.333 \ldots$) or the square root of 2 to such complex operations as proving Fermat's Last Theorem or proving the unsolvability of Hilbert's Tenth Problem.

But how does all that bear upon ordinary-language communication? It is not quite clear. There is that old equivalence that Galileo had drawn, 'Mathematics is the language of science' (usefully discussed in Fletcher 2007: Ch. 1). It is evident that rather than mapping two systems — linguistic and mathematical — side by side, Galileo was using 'language' as a metaphor for describing the relationship between mathematics and the natural sciences. As it happens, the metaphor is suspected of being the link that may throw light upon how ordinary language and mathematics bear upon each other. This is not just a matter of scientists taking recourse to metaphor consistently in elaborating inferences obtained mathematically, or of mathematics teaching being crucially dependent on the use of metaphors (a richly researched area), but of something more seminal to mathematical thinking itself. Byers has this to say about it:

> Metaphors are ambiguous. […] In fact, they have the following characteristics: (a) duality — there is always a comparison involved; (b) incompatibility — a metaphor is of the form *A* equals *B* (or *A is B*) when it is obvious that A does not equal B; and (c) creative dynamism — a metaphor must be grasped, it requires an insight.
>
> […]
>
> When mathematics is seen as a metaphor, it brings to the fore the central role of understanding on the part of both the learner and the expert. Metaphors are not purely 'logical' entities. Speaking or reading a metaphor doesn't make that metaphor come alive for you. Grasping a metaphor requires a discontinuous leap. […] A metaphoric description of mathematics will inevitably include a discussion of 'doing' mathematics. Sfard includes the following fascinating quote from a mathematician: 'To understand a new concept I must create an appropriate

metaphor. A personification. Or a spatial metaphor. A metaphor of structure. Only then can I answer questions, solve problems. I may even be able to perform some manipulations on the concept. Only when I have the metaphor. Without the metaphor I just can't do it.' (Byers 2007: 70–1; the quotation within is from Sfard 1994).

Byers was fond of numinous terms like 'creative dynamism', 'creativity', 'insight' (not unlike some AI Engineers). But they are not really needed to contemplate this point. A more mundane sense of how metaphors in language work can convey the point (the literature on metaphor is gigantic, I base the following roughly on Max Black 1962).

A metaphor involves an analogy, but a specific kind of analogy. Consider these two sentences:

(1) The ship was buffeted by waves as high as mountains.
(2) Mountainous waves buffeted the ship.

Example (1) is simile: the analogy is specific. There are two domains, 'waves' and 'mountains', and they are explicitly compared along one parameter, 'height' — the two domains are held side by side and overlap at that one parameter. Example (2) is a metaphor: the analogy is less specific. Again, there are two domains, 'waves' and 'mountains', but instead of being held side by side with one overlapping parameter, there's a switch or substitution. 'Mountain' is substituted as an adjective for 'waves' whereby it is not necessary to clarify in terms of what parameter its adjectival form should be understood. It is left to the respondent to decide what parameters are relevant here in bringing the two domains together. The respondent might think the parameter is 'height' (as in the simile), but might also think it is 'shape', or perhaps more affectively 'feeling small' or 'feeling threatened', or perhaps all those together. At the same time, the respondent might register the difference between 'mountain' and 'wave' as being meaningful, one solid and the other liquid, one permanent and the other temporary, etc. The work of the metaphor then is richer than that of the simile, and the domain matching is more than mapping analogues. Rather than being *comparative*, the metaphor's work could be regarded as *constitutive*. So, because the metaphor of the 'mountain' was used, we understand the 'wave' in a particular and complex way, as compacting a set of connotations and nuances. Had a different metaphor been used (e.g., 'towering waves'), we might have understood the waves in a somewhat different way, compacting a distinct set of connotations and nuances. The metaphor does more than simply describe the 'wave', it confers a tangible quality to the 'wave' — it, so to speak, constitutes our sense of the wave and its place in this/our cognitive universe.

Just as metaphors play a constitutive part in linguistic expression, ambiguities play a constitutive part in mathematical expression. That, I think, is what Byers argues, citing others who have pursued this idea. So, to understand the thought process of mathematics we have to understand ambiguity, just as to understand the thought process of ordinary language we have to understand metaphor. Or, in your terms, Peter: as ambiguity is to the limits of algorithms so metaphor is to the limits of ordinary language. Contemplating these two limits may bring us closer to the grounding problem in communication.

But that reminds me: in the final chapter of Byers's book (Ch. 9), he takes a rather dim view of what he calls 'algorithmic thinking'. He regards functionalizing AI systems through algorithms as taking recourse to the more trivial elements of mathematics, and accordingly decides that no AI system can really *do* mathematics. I think he would peg the ambiguities you have pointed to via Turing, Hilbert, and Gödel as within the sphere of mathematics rather than algorithmic thinking. Turing works through mathematical ambiguity to come up with algorithms about which he comes up with more mathematical ambiguities. He then set up his Machine, and his Machine will then slavishly work according to those algorithms, and eventually, that may well include churning out more algorithms — but the Machine will never get to either mathematics or ordinary language in the way Turing can. Well, that's what Byers argues, not I — I am just saying.

Perhaps our AI-friend can be programmed to convert mathematical ambiguities into ordinary-language metaphors.

Chapter 11

Getting It: The Joke and the Gist

Peter Tu and Stephanie Stacy

Suman, my colleague Stephanie Stacy graciously offered to craft a response to your comments and questions on the Imagined We and related matters — see what follows. I follow this by returning to your thoughts on jokes, metaphors, and ambiguities.

Imagined We

Suman, you describe the Imagined We (IW) as a set of collective preconditions, knowledge, and experience; however, this is only the starting point. This collective knowledge serves as the common ground shared between communicators. This then serves as the platform upon which more complex inferences are drawn. The IW explicitly models agency through Theory of Mind (ToM) modelling. Traditionally, ToM can be used to model actions as the rational product of an individual's underlying mental states — beliefs, desires, and intentions. Here, the available common ground helps constrain the scope of the probable mental states. The IW takes this ToM modelling one step further, shifting the problem from the individual point of view to a shared 'view from nowhere'. Under this shared agency model, the mental states are treated as joint. What do we believe? What do we want? What do we want to do?

From this standpoint, it is not wrong then to conceptualize the scene from above, similar to a meta-agent's point of view. This agent with joint mental states, able to control all cooperators, could make rational, utility-maximizing decisions about how to coordinate everyone. However, in reality of course, the 'We' agent does not actually exist; instead, each individual agent imagines it. Communication helps different simulated versions of this 'Imagined We' to converge since individually simulating a joint mind can lead to misalignment.

You also argue that defining intentionality as the meaning a speaker is trying to convey is inadequate because a receiver can never perfectly distinguish between that speaker's SGs and SGOs. Any confirmation of this signaller's meaning must be explicitly asked, leading to a recursive cycle. I agree that the entanglement of SGs and SGOs is worth careful consideration and there are many avenues here that are wide open for further work. However, the IW can gain some traction on this problem when we consider how it handles meaning and expectation.

Under this framework, a signal's meaning can be understood as a target mind that the signaller is trying to convey. The ontology of ToM automatically serves as an ontology of meaning in everyday activities. When we want to interpret a signal, we can interpret it in terms of its beliefs: what information it is trying to provide, desires: what is the motivation it is trying to describe, and intentions: what is the deliberative action. Second, because the IW is a model of joint agency, each agent forms a set of predictions for the expected joint action. Of course, an agent can only take its own action, but just by forming an expectation about your partner, you gain insight into whether there is a misunderstanding (and are able to derive interesting properties such as re-engagement in a task and punishment for failing to do your part). Hence, I do not need to explicitly ask your meaning, I need only to compare my actual observations of you to those simulated in the IW to recognize a misunderstanding. Of course, there is no way to eliminate the uncertainty entirely, but that is true of human communication as well. It is exactly when these breakdowns in understanding occur that we can use communication as a tool to clarify and try to re-align ourselves.

From this explanation, it is evident that our starting point for the IW is not a direct model of language, but a model grounded in our understanding of both the perceptual physical world — intuitive physics — and the social minds of others — intuitive psychology, both of which use an underlying backbone of cooperation. This starting point is inspired by Michael Tomasello's view on the origins of human communication:

That there must be some fairly specific connections between the fundamentally cooperative structure of human communication, as initially discovered by Grice, and the especially cooperative structure of human, as opposed to other primate, social interaction and culture in general. (Tomasello 2008: xi).

To understand human communication from an evolutionary perspective, we can look at its similarities and differences to chimpanzee communication and cooperation in empirical studies. Specifically, Tomasello focuses on communicative gestures instead of vocal communication. This is because chimpanzee vocal communication is highly tied to emotion, does not often consider the listener, and lacks flexibility (Tomasello 2007). In contrast, chimpanzee gesture is capable of producing flexible, intention-directed actions that are ritualized and individually learned (Tomasello *et al.* 1989). Moreover, gesture is likely to have been the precursor to vocal communication — many gestures can be visually grounded in their meaning whereas vocal language is an arbitrary code mapping.

One key example of gestural communication is pointing, a seemingly simple gesture which chimpanzees do not do in natural settings (Tomasello 2007). Yet, somehow it is trivial for even an infant who cannot speak to understand a pointing hand provides information relevant to them (Behne *et al.* 2005). In contrast, chimpanzees fail at this task, not able to understand a helpful human's pointing at hidden food (Tomasello *et al.* 1997). However, when re-framed as a competitive task, chimpanzees are able to use similar human-reaching behaviour to infer food location (Hare and Tomasello 2004). Chimpanzees do have some of the underlying cognitive processes such as understanding of others' goals, perception, and knowledge (Call and Tomasello 2008); however, they still fail to grasp informative pointing, either because they do not believe others have the motivation to help them or are not equipped with the proper skills to correctly interpret the behaviour as helpful.

In fact, chimpanzee gesture is entirely imperative, without, e.g., the human unique interpretations of declarative (informing) or expressive (sharing emotions) pointing. Furthermore, Tomasello maintains that the reasons chimpanzees do not point (and fail to understand informative pointing) boil down to a fundamental lack of *shared intentionality* (Tomasello 2006). Philosophers have described shared intentionality as involving shared goals that cooperators pursue in a coordinated manner

(Bratman 1992; Clark 1996; Searle 1995). This seems to be a uniquely human trait as there are, as of yet, no examples of this behaviour in nonhuman animals (Tomasello 2006). Thus, the IW follows this same train of logic by focusing on a shared intentionality perspective — the joint beliefs, joint desires, and joint intentions modelled in the IW.

Finally, in response to the complementary nature of cooperation and competition, I do not see it as a problem that competition is outside of the scope of the IW. In fact, there are not many cases that are truly zero-sum (outside of an idealistic game theory world). Complete competition can be treated as qualitatively different from any degree of cooperation. This is because in zero-sum cases, one can act according to a minimax policy. Here, an agent prepares for the worst-case scenario and takes the best action under that assumption. Because the agent assumes the worst, it does not need to develop a strategy targeted towards the behaviours of the other agent. As a result, there is no need to model other agents' mental states.

Anything other than zero-sum scenarios necessitates signalling intent and inferring others' minds and goals to find a solution that is mutually advantageous (Schelling 1980). As a result, strategies develop to support reaching a mutually beneficial end, such as negotiation and bargaining. Even in war, which might be considered the extreme of human competition, there are spaces to signal intent and opportunities for some mutual gain. For example, there may be a particular front one side is determined to hold — no matter the cost. Signalling intent to defend that land may lead the other side to concede, realizing it is mutually beneficial to avoid many deaths, and fight more aggressively on a different front (Schelling 1980). In order for these mutually advantageous situations to be actualized, agents must make inferences about others states of minds to cooperate.

Jokes, Metaphors, Ambiguities

Let's now turn to the topic of jokes, metaphors, and ambiguities. Suman, to capture many of the intriguing concepts that you outlined in your previous intervention, I have taken the liberty of summarizing your thoughts in bullet form:

- From time to time philosophers have attempted to work out the mechanics of both humour and jokes (e.g., Kant's *Critique of Judgement*).

- It may be the case that the 'limits of algorithms', as explored by Turing and Gödel, might explain why algorithms may have limits when it comes to the complex business of telling jokes.
- It appears that linguistic communication does not have such limitations.
- In Byers's *How Mathematicians Think*, we take the following points:
    - Math is not about collecting proofs.
    - Mathematics is a system for delving into ambiguities so that they can be logically held together.
    - We define an ambiguity as 'an idea that is perceived to be true by two self-consistent but mutually incompatible frames of reference'.
    - Mathematics is suffused with ambiguities.
- Galileo: 'Mathematics is the language of science.'
- Language is a metaphor for describing the relationship between the natural sciences — does this metaphor provide a link between language and mathematics?
- Byers: Metaphors are like ambiguities:
    - Duality: A comparison between two things.
    - Incompatibility: A = B when it is obvious that A ≠ B.
    - Creative dynamism: A metaphor must be grasped; it requires an insight.
- Metaphors are not purely logical (they cannot be derived).
- Grasping a metaphor requires a discontinuous leap.
- Mathematician: To understand a new concept, I must create an appropriate metaphor.
- Max Black: A metaphor involves a specific kind of analogy.
    - Similes: A specific analogy, where there is an explicit mapping between concepts (e.g., the waves were as tall as mountains).
    - Metaphor: 'Mountainous waves', confers a tangible quality to the wave. It gives a sense of the wave and its place in our cognitive universe.
- The role of metaphors in linguistic expression is similar to the role of ambiguities in mathematics.
- To understand the thought process of mathematics, we have to understand ambiguities.
- To understand the thought process of ordinary language, we have to understand metaphors.

- Ambiguity is at the limits of algorithms.
- Metaphor is at the limits of ordinary language.
- Contemplating these limits may bring us closer to the grounding problem of communication.
- Byers: AI cannot do mathematics.
- Can AI be programmed to convert ambiguities into metaphors?

I like the idea of ambiguities and metaphors. In this context, one might argue that both metaphors and ambiguities are associated with conceptual measures of distance which may sometimes result in a form equivalence coupled with misgiving. I would argue that at the heart of many a joke lies an ambiguous metaphor. In this way, humour might be viewed as a form of compression. Like a wormhole in space–time, they may reveal that two seemingly disparate concepts are far closer than one might have thought. As you describe, such acts of compression may require various forms of creativity — both when constructing a joke and getting it. The getting-it part feels reminiscent of the description of attainment as given by Sayre (1965) in his work on recognition. If we view humour in this way, then 'getting a joke' may be like discovering a proof. One of my motivations for describing the Turing work was to consider the possibility of developing an argument for the limits of an algorithm's ability to 'get a joke'. This would be similar to the analysis of the limits of an algorithm's ability to determine the provability of a logical statement. It might have involved some sort of British Museum approach whereby all possible jokes are first borrowed from the library of Babel (that fictitious construct, where everything that ever has, can, or will be written, resides). Through clever trickery, one might find that the set of all jokes is countable but alas not enumerable. While this path is certainly tempting, let's take a different fork in the road by considering the ideas of familiarity and meaning.

When you describe the mathematician's modus operandi for gaining intellectual dominion over a new and daunting domain, it seems to involve the construction of metaphorical bridges between what she knows and what she hopes to know. In Terrance Deacon's *Symbolic Species* (1997), we see the argument that the meaning of a concept may emerge from its connections with other concepts. Such linkages may be statistical or physical but also metaphorical. Seen in this light, conceptual grounding seems to involve connecting ungrounded concepts with those that already have meaning. Douglas Hofstadter and Emmanuel Sander (2013) have made the argument that metaphors and analogies are 'the currency of thought' and that this has led to their description of intelligence as involving the ability to 'get the gist of things'. This seems to bring another concept into the mix and that is the idea of attention.

So why, might you ask, am I interested in mixing the ideas of metaphors and attention? Just roll with me on this for a bit ... One of the recent breakthroughs in machine translation (the ability to take a sentence from one language and translate it into another language) has been achieved through the incorporation of attention modules into the translation process. Initial formulations for the translation problem involve the use of some sort of recurrent neural network that takes as input a sentence X from the input language and then produces the corresponding sentence Y from the target language. It turns out that the accuracy of estimating Y_i (the ith word in sentence Y) increases significantly if the algorithm can accurately estimate which words in X to prioritize. It turns out that this form of attention can be learned and thus incorporated into the machine translation process (Bahdanau 2016). Visual question and answer problems (VQ&A) focus on images and text-based queries. The image could be a collection of random objects and the text-based query might be something like: 'What is the colour of the object found to the bottom left of the orange square?' In this paradigm, the image can be viewed as a form of knowledge. Based on the structure of the question, the algorithm must first attend to orange objects that are square, it must then refocus to regions that are at the bottom left of the orange square. Like the machine translation problem, this can be viewed as a form of dynamic attention, which can be learned (Hudson 2018). If one combines the idea of attention plus instructions for how one should process the information garnering attention, one can then view such sequences of combined attention and action as a form of programming. Going a step further, we see how the VQ&A problem has been recast via the 'Child as Programmer' paradigm (Yi 2018). The idea is that in order to solve problems such as VQ&A, children are essentially learning how to construct programs. Given sufficient training data (images, text-based queries, and manually defined programs that result in the correct answer), it was shown that architectures which transform the image into a high-dimensional embedding and then use the resulting feature representation as input to a recurrent neural network can be trained to produce the desired programs.

Motivated by Michael Tomasello's (2010) hypothesis that much of our early forms of communication were based on physical gestures and pantomime, where the body was used to represent physical objects, my colleagues and I used the 'Child as Programmer' paradigm to automatically construct metaphors between physical objects and the human body. The metaphor construction programs were used to first segment the image of an object into its constituent parts. These are then labelled using the analogous names of human body parts. For example, a table would be transformed into a person kneeling on all fours. The legs of the table being mapped to human arms and legs and the flat surface of the table being analogous to the human back. I would argue that constructing such an isomorphism allows a human agent to not only refer to a table but also convey a sense of 'tableness' by virtue of the fact that one could imagine what it feels like to have weight placed on one's back as well as the sense of weight-bearing pressure experienced by the arms and legs. In this way, the pantomime becomes not just an analogy but maybe even a true metaphor. Such metaphors are all well and fine for you and me, but it is not clear that our AI-Assistant is going to find much satisfaction from all this cleverness.

It seems that we are at a bit of a chicken-and-egg moment. For a concept to be meaningful, it must be connected via metaphor to something that already has meaning. This, of course, implies that somewhere along the line there is a concept that our AI-Assistant will find intrinsically meaningful. It can be argued that humans have access to various forms of visceral metaphor. The idea is that our ancestors have spent most of history scratching out an existence on the plains of Africa. This would have involved catching, growing, or scavenging for food as well as avoiding death at least until the time when they could pass on the genetic torch to their children. It can thus be argued that certain concepts are 'bred in the bone'. When we say things like 'The economy went right over the cliff', a complex construct such as the economy takes on a form with visceral meaning. With this argument, we might say that the egg in our chicken-and-egg problem comes to us from the mists of time. But this still feels like we are just kicking the can down the ancestral road. We still need to find that golden egg.

In *Rhythms of the Brain*, Gyorgy Buzsaki (2006) takes us on a fascinating tour of modern neuroscience and hints at what meaning might really mean. Much of the brain's architecture can be thought of as a massive collection of neural oscillators. In general, oscillation occurs in the presence of opposing forces. Consider an assembly of neurons composed of excitatory and inhibitory elements. Once activated by an external stimulus, the excitatory neurons start to produce impulses which in turn activate the inhibitory neurons. Activated inhibitory neurons force the excitatory neurons to stop firing. Without input, the inhibitory neurons eventually stop deactivating the excitatory neurons. If the initial external stimulus is still present, the whole cycle simply starts again.

Oscillators have a number of intriguing properties. They are predictive in the sense that if one knows the phase of an oscillator at time t, then the state of the oscillator at time $t + \Delta t$ can be predicted. Oscillators can also be synchronized with relatively little effort or energy. This is illustrated by a couple walking down a path hand in hand. By simply touching hands, their gaits quickly fall in synch. Other properties include resonance, phase locking, cross-frequency coupling, damping, and inhibition. Like the ocean, a vast collection of oscillators can also support a wide variety of waves. Waves can carry information, and this allows for interaction between neural assemblies across large distances without the need for direct neural connectivity.

The brain can be seen as a system whose output is also its input. Instead of operating like a function, where external stimuli are processed in order to produce specific outcomes, the brain should be viewed as a system that is perturbed by external stimuli. Thus, its future state is a function of both external stimuli and more importantly its current state. The resulting perturbations manifest in transient self-organization of the brain in the form of various wave phenomena as well as temporary synchronization between both neighbouring and distant oscillators. Observations support the assertion that such self-organizing behaviour can be described as complex, where complexity is defined as the transition between predictable and chaotic behaviour. Typical of complex systems is the existence of attractor states which have often been credited with allowing for a sense of free will. Given this system-level description of the brain, let us now consider the binding problem.

The ability to combine sensed visual features, such as colour, texture, and edges, in order to perceive semantic objects, such as birds, trees, and elephants, is known as binding. Two competing hypotheses exist: the connectionist or gnostic nerve and the synchrony hypotheses. The connectionist approach consists of a feed-forward network, where low-level features are combined into increasingly complex features culminating in a single neuron that is activated if an instance of a specific object class has been observed. These are known as gnostic nerves. The connectionist approach is the inspiration for modern deep learning methods such as convolutional neural networks. It is surely the case that connectionist architectures are used by the brain. However, complete reliance on the connectionist hypotheses can be criticized at various levels. Given the number of possible object classes and their variety of states, space limitations would preclude the maintenance of a comprehensive set of gnostic nerves. In contrast, the synchrony hypothesis assumes that features derived from external stimuli activate specific oscillators primarily found in the cortex region of the brain. If multiple oscillators are consistently observed to be simultaneously active, it can be hypothesized that these triggering features can be associated with a specific object class. This form of learning can then be consolidated during the sleep process. It has been argued that during sleep, key observations are 'replayed' in the form of dreams allowing for solidification of the concept. This is achieved via plastic neural growth that loosely connects the simultaneously active oscillators so that, in the future, they will not only be active in the presence of their associated object class stimuli but will also be temporarily synchronized. Thus, for future encounters with the target object class, the brain enters a state of temporary synchronized self-organization. An advantage of the synchrony framework is that a modest set of feature-driven oscillators can be wired to recognize a combinatorically large number of object classes and associated instances.

The ability to produce self-organizing behaviour associated with observed objects can be extended to additional concepts such as actions and interactions. This sets the stage for the ability to produce self-organizing behaviour over time. As previously stated, the brain should be viewed as an evolving system, where future states are governed by external stimuli as well as the current state. An experienced episode can be described as a series of events $(e_1, e_2, ..., e_T)$. The brain can be configured to produce self-organizing behaviour for each event e_t. However, the resulting brain state associated with event e_t sets the stage for self-organizing behaviour associated with event e_{t+1}. If the stimuli for e_{t+1} is subsequently encountered, the brain will naturally enter into the self-organizing behaviour associated with e_{t+1}. If the associated stimuli for event e_{t+1} is not encountered, the brain will not enter into the self-organizing behaviour associated with e_{t+1}. More importantly, if the brain is not experiencing the self-organizing behaviour associated with event e_t, then even if stimuli associated with e_{t+1} is encountered, the brain cannot enter into the self-organizing behaviour associated with e_{t+1}. In this way, the brain can be viewed as a prediction machine. This form of constrained state transition is achieved via neural wiring that results in previously described oscilla-tory effects such as damping, resonance, and synchronization. It can thus be argued that the brain's experience of learned temporal events can be thought of as a form of system-level resonance. As will be discussed, it is hypothesized that the original purpose for developing this form of tempo-ral experience was movement and navigation.

The brain is composed of a number of diverse sub-systems such as the cerebellum and the basal ganglia. These regions appear to serve different purposes and thus have different architectures. These regions are con-nected to each other bidirectionally. Thus, the concept of top-down con-trol does not seem to apply. While the neocortex is composed of a large set of oscillators associated with physical stimuli that are primarily bound by local connections, the hippocampus can be viewed as a set of neural oscillators or assemblies that can directly connect with any other assembly in the hippocampus. In this way, the hippocampus can be seen as a con-figurable random graph. It is hypothesized that the hippocampus plays a significant role with respect to physical mapping/navigation as well as the more general task of declarative memory.

There are two forms of basic navigation: dead-reckoning and land-mark recognition. Dead-reckoning involves measuring a direction or bear-ing followed by an estimate of distance travelled. In this way, the agent can keep track of where it is in space. It has been observed that if an agent explores the same path over and over again, a set of neural assemblies known as directional place neurons are established in the hippocampus. Directional place neurons are associated with a specific location along the path. They are known as directional since place neurons can only be acti-vated if the place neurons associated with the previous location on the path have been activated. This form of dead-reckoning-based map construction is illustrative of the brain's experience of time that was previ-ously described. Eventually, multiple paths will be formed with intersec-tions at various place neurons. Over time, directional place neurons can become omnidirectional place neurons. They will become active if the agent arrives at the associated location independent of path taken. The agent now recognizes a location based on local features as opposed to the path taken. This is the basis for landmark navigation.

It has been hypothesized that mechanisms used for feature analysis (cortex) and mapping (hippocampus) may form the basis for declarative memory, both episodic and semantic. A suitable metaphor might be that the cortex should be viewed as the library and the hippocampus as the librarian. Structures used for dead reckoning become candidates for indexing elements of episodic memory, while landmark-based mechanisms could be used to maintain semantic memory. In this way, the hippocampus can serve as an auto-associative mechanism allowing for rapid recall and recognition. Given such mapping capabilities, we can now address the question of what might be intrinsically meaningful to the brain.

The only thing that the brain can both control and measure is its body. The brain can send motion instructions to various body parts. The brain will then receive sensations of the resulting motions. The time between sending a motion instruction and receiving a motion sensation then becomes a measure of distance. Using dead reckoning methods, the brain can essentially construct a map of its body. Evidence for this hypothesis is that during infancy almost all animals spend a considerable amount of time simply twitching their muscles. The brain's body then becomes the fundamental calibration object by which all other objects can be subsequently understood. It can be argued that this may be one of the reasons why we perceive space and time in linear as opposed to alternative scales such as logarithmic. Having previously described how methods such as the 'Child as Programmer' approach could be used to map objects in the world to the body, along with the hundreds of thousands of years spent using gestures and pantomime as our main means of communication, we might have a glimpse of how meaning may have taken root and blossomed. The question then comes down to whether or not such mechanisms can be grafted on to our AI-Assistant, thus bestowing it with the gift of meaning.

Chapter 12

The Tomasello Assumption and Virtuous Cooperation

Suman Gupta

The Assumption

The two parts of the last intervention could lead us down numerous meandering bypaths of the Theory of Mind into the Elysian Fields where our AI-Assistant may come to frolic. But I was schooled at the Look-Before-You-Leap Academy. Should I leap where you have leapt already? Or should I pause on: *where* have they leapt and *why* have they leapt there and …? Twiddling my thumbs thus while others are charging purposefully ahead comes easily to me. So, while you gallop away sorting out the mechanics of communication, I want to dig back a bit and contemplate the hobbyhorse you are riding.

In the first part of that intervention, Stephanie makes her argument by focusing on the pre-conceptual development of human communication *à la* Michael Tomasello: gestures (pointing and pantomiming) precede words; great apes and infants offer clues which can be glued together to obtain the grounding of the human communication system. In the second, Peter infers the meaning of meaning by looking closely at the operating system of human communication, input to neural processing to output. Somehow, the pre-conceptual is wedded to this too with the 'Child as Programmer' paradigm — again *à la* Tomasello. The two parts are not too different. Whether looking to the pre-conceptual development or the operating system itself, the idea is to discover the primary principles and primitive components of human communication so as to model it and let it develop towards a complex analogue ... perhaps eventually to program it into our AI-Assistant, which will then join our all-too-human babble.

In brief, in both parts there's a reaching towards some stable *preliminary* (in the sense of preceding and primary) bases for human communication — whether inferred from its evolutionary/biogenetic origins or from observing the seat of its operating system closely. The idea is: you need the first principles and primitive components before you can model the thing and let it grow. Let me call this the *Tomasello Assumption*, not because it really is his, but because you have been leaning so heavily on (some of) his work. Let me pause on this assumption as if it is his, in his terms.

This assumption has much to do with our perpetual fascination with *origins*. It goes something like this. To understand the prevailing human *communication system* we need to get to its origins from a pre-conceptual mode of communication, in terms of an evolutionary pragmatics that precedes and then leads into human communication. Analogously, to understand a specific human *communication act* we need to chart its origin in and passage from the operational system of brain/neural network. Once understood, we are a step or two away from modelling–programming it, act-by-act and system *in toto*.

Philology

In communication studies, such an expectation has been more or less constitutive of the field itself. As a scientific study of language, 18th- and 19th-century comparative philology (or historical linguistics) — via William Jones, Wilhelm von Humboldt, Franz Bopp, Jacob and Wilhelm Grimm, Max Müller, and others — was largely an enterprise of tracing diversification of language formations from common (or pure) origins, basically following a phylogenetic-tree model backwards. Its field of evidence was naturally confined to human linguistic practice in the present and the textual record, which allowed for considerable interference of social preconceptions into their seemingly disinterested scientific methods. One element therein was the notion that the development of specific languages was genetically linked to human groups or nationalities, to which a racial turn could be and was given with unfortunate consequences. Through the late 19th and early 20th centuries, linguistics focused decisively on living usage with historical (textual) linguistics remaining an ancillary pursuit; description and ordering of practices rather than proposing teleological frameworks took methodological centre-stage. Searches for the origins of language in that philological vein became increasingly unfashionable as the troubled 20th century unfolded.

I understand, of course, that such lessons of history have no immediate bearing on the current search for the origins of language, where the Tomasello Assumption comes up. Here the interference of the social is seemingly removed from the search for origins. The pre-conceptual rationale of communication inferred from animals/infants, evolutionary pragmatics and its evidence (e.g., with the fossil record of communicative organs), observation of neural processing ... — these seem to seal inroads for social convictions, desires, and prejudices. These offer clarification for those seeking knowledge-in-itself and these offer functional application for technicians of practical knowledge: an unideological model to draw upon in programming the AI-Assistant. Maybe. But contemplation of origins is ever a tricky business, and history may seep in where most systematically extirpated.

Why Tomasello?

The current state of research into the origins of human communication presents an immensely complex interdisciplinary field. This generally refuses Noam Chomsky's generative grammar approach, i.e., that universal syntactic structures are genetically embedded (as Tomasello 1992 and 2003 on language acquisition systematically did), and recommends an evolutionary pragmatic process instead, usually drawing upon ape/infant communication (as in Tomasello 2008). In this direction, Tomasello's contribution is a limited and quite specific one.

Overarching accounts of the field, such as Jean-Louis Dessalles (2007 [2000]) or, later, Dor, Knight, and Lewis (2014), draw attention to a range of other approaches. Quite a lot of arguments which take issue with what I have dubbed the Tomasello Assumption and his inferences are found. Particularly important here are Dorothy Cheney and Robert Seyfarth's investigations. To the purpose of the current exchanges, Seyfarth and Cheney (2018) is useful. This volume gives a summary of their investigations, stressing that despite obvious differences in vocal signal-ling between apes (limited hard-wired range) and humans (a fluidly intentional–cooperative combinatorial system), 'continuities are more apparent': (a) 'when one considers the neural and cognitive mechanisms that underlie call perception, and the social function of language and com-munication in the daily lives of individuals (10); (b) recognition of indi-vidual faces and voices; (c) the multimodal processing of audial signals; (d) the recognition of objects; (e) the recognition of call meanings. Also helpfully, in this volume there are a series of responses to these investiga-tions by linguistics researchers working on the existing human communi-cation system, based on sound signals. These responses both underline the overlaps and the discontinuities between Seyfarth and Cheney's investiga-tions and directions of linguistics research. Seyfarth and Cheney conclude with a response to those.

So, I find myself wondering why you have chosen to focus on Tomasello's formulations to model (approximate) human communication with an 'Imaginary We' construct. What advantage does his specific approach offer to your search for first principles and primitive compo-nents, of originary structures, to model communication — rather than, say, Cheney and Seyfarth, i.e., factoring in pre-conceptual sound communica-tion input in a multimodal system?

The only answer that I can think of is: *you go for it precisely because Tomasello is determined to find those originary structures of the human oral–audial combinatorial communication system without reference to that system. He purports to say something about its structures by asserting that its origins are outside it — in pre-conceptual gestures — thus seem-ingly bypassing the social subscriptions implicit in that system. The obser-vations made on the human system are after the fact, i.e., they are made to fit in.*

This position seems friendly for your efforts towards developing machine–human communication. Putatively your efforts are then safely outside the social underpinnings of language, bereft of ideological import, ahistorical. The two parts of your previous intervention follow accordingly. You seem to say something about the intention–cooperation principle and meaning/neurological processing of the human communi-cation system without any substantial reference to it. You assert it is like 'this' in advance, and then fit your illustrations selectively from the human communication system into 'this'. This is a risky thing to do, but does it work?

Soundless/Unsound?

There are some long-standing objections to Tomasello's (2008) approach, i.e., to the assertion that gestures articulate the grounding for human oral–audial communication in a continuous rationale. In Tomasello's words:

> The main point ... is that most of what makes human communication so powerful is the psychological infrastructure that is present already in species-unique forms of gesturing such as pointing or pantomiming, and language is built upon, and relies totally upon, this infrastructure. Without this infrastructure, communicative contentions, like *gavagai* [referring Quine], are only sounds, signifying nothing. (218–219).

Such confidence, however, doesn't quite overcome those objections. This assumption goes back a while (e.g., Corballis 1991), and the objections were succinctly summarized somewhat earlier than Tomasello's book in Dessalles (2007 [2000]: 143–144).

- First, for a communicative system in relation to a cognitive environment, there is a distinction to reckon with between one based on gestures alone and one based on combined sounds-cum-gestures. There is no internal rationale in the former to push for a switch to the latter. The difference is similar to conversations in Deaf sign languages and in spoken–gestural languages. There is no obvious internal reason for the former to adopt the latter (except social reasons, that the latter are institutionalized and present advantages for the Hearing).
- Second, in terms of evolutionary pragmatics, it is difficult to imagine 'selective pressures that could transfer the *abstract* capability of one motor system, such as the sequencing capability independent of what is being sequenced, from one brain loci to another'. (144).

You will no doubt argue that all this doesn't matter. The point is not whether Tomasello hit upon an empirical truth of evolution, but that he offers a rationale which can be put to the functional end of evolving machine–human communication. The point is, in other words, that if we go along with Tomasello's account, we have quite a useful set of first principles and primitive components to play with.

Of course, the more distant these principles and components are from the actuality of the human communication system, the more sceptical one might feel about their eventual functionality with regard to that system ... but nevertheless. Let's go along with this optimistic step. It seems to me that there are some further quibbles to consider though.

The Virtue of Cooperation?

This brings us to the heart of the 'Imagined We' as a non-material collective agent mediating/regulating all communicative acts. This is essentially a crystallization of the intentional–cooperative principle which is putatively imbued equally in all human communication and therefore can be given an independent agentic status (a bit like a mathematical constant).

Scholars have ever sought to see human activity as not only dominant over other species, but also as reaching a pinnacle of complexity and moral consciousness over other species. Tomasello seems an unlikely candidate for such a move, but his concept of 'cooperation' does come with an unmistakable moral quotient. Its operation is given as unique to humans and higher primates (no problem there if cooperation is non-normatively understood), and cooperation is intrinsically good (which is normative and problematic). Having described what intentionality in a signal is, he thus goes on to say:

> To qualify as *cooperative* communication, among other things the communicator's proximate goal must be somehow to help or share with the recipient — even though, of course, evolutionarily there must be some benefit to the communicator for being so helpful as well. (Tomasello 2008: 15).

There's an interesting turn of phrase: cooperation (sharing, helping) seems to be almost independent or fortuitously attached to evolutionary species/self-interest (which is 'even though' and 'as well'). Tomasello repeatedly understands pointing as being exclusively understandable as being helpful (it seems pointing can't be intended as hostile warning or repudiation). The elaboration of the cooperative mode in three parts follows accordingly with those nice upbeat values of helping and sharing centred (73–96); and that is taken with moral verve as the shared ground of ape–human gestural and linguistic modalities: 'the recipient's search for relevance is guided equally in both cases by mutual assumptions of helpfulness' (107); and ultimately, it is maintained that cooperation preceded 'non-cooperative purposes such as lying' (170).

What does remain unclear is whether such helpfulness is coterminous with evolutionary species/self-interest or whether it is grounded in communication even when it is not necessarily consistent with evolutionary interest? Does such an account of cooperation-as-helpfulness gel with evolutionary pragmatics?

Maybe that doesn't matter insofar as we are thinking of the AI-Assistant to come. We want this entity to subscribe to that sort of understanding of the cooperative principle, whether we actually do so ourselves in our communication system or not. And yet, is our cooperative principle in communication intrinsically good, helpful, beneficial, altruistic, or is it more complex and less normatively charged? Could the cooperative principle be predicated on non-cooperation as well, could its helpfulness be accommodative of unhelpfulness/conflict and *vice versa*? Should the 'Imagined We' be constructed as a crystallization of helpfulness?

Some curious turns of thinking appear with that implicit moral investment in the grounding framework for human and proximate primate communication. One of Tomasello's weakest arguments appears when he considers the division of human communication into different language codes (systems of oral–audial signs, different languages). He seems to argue that gestures are transferred to codes in the human communicative system according to the constraints of human cognition, and a diversity of codes (different languages) appear because of 'the need for groups of humans to differentiate themselves from other groups' (Tomasello 2008: 314). One might get the impression that gestures unify while codes divide — that gesture-centred primate species are large happy families while the human species overcomes its natural cooperativeness and turns arbitrarily into bickering factions because of its propensity to speak. In a contrary direction, elsewhere one finds this odd statement in introducing research in the field: 'Needless to say, humans are capable of violence, just as apes and monkeys are. In certain contexts, violence pays. But in the case of many non-human primates, dominance asserted through violence or threat is the *internal principle* of social organization, a situation which humans would find psychologically intolerable' (Dor, Knight, and Lewis 2014: 4). It carries on to suggest that violent/conflict situations are literally a 'breakdown' of human communication. This seems to take the cooperative principle of human communication to mean that conflict is not an 'internal principle' for humans and, as the British Telecom advertisement recently had it, 'it is good to talk'.

A Different Hypothesis

Tomasello (2008) has an alluringly scientific way of presenting his argument. He offers hypotheses, gives his evidence, and the hypotheses are then declared conclusions. Much depends on how evidence is sought or selected to support hypotheses. When a researcher is enthusiastic about his hypotheses, the evidence can sometimes be readily found (perhaps the hypotheses were inferences to begin with) — possibly, so to speak, the tail wags the dog at times.

Let me suggest a different 'pure' hypothesis by way of a principle for human (or ape) intentional communication: 'pure' in that it is based on a conceptual rationale, but not in the least on observation, evidence, testing — it may become a conclusion if those were done and supported it.

Some terms: As I have argued in an earlier intervention, 'competition' is not really a counterpoint of 'cooperation'. Let's say instead, the counterpoint of 'cooperation' is 'non-cooperation'. Where 'cooperation' is coterminous with 'helpfulness'/'sharing', 'non-cooperation' is coterminous with 'hostility'/'conflict'/'selfishness'.

Hypothesis: Intentional communication is cooperative insofar as it is not non-cooperative, and non-cooperative insofar as it is not cooperative. Whether it is one or the other, which is premised on the possibility of both, depends upon the intentional constraints and cognitive environment in terms of which signalling happens. Intentional signalling is premised on the priority of one or the other in relation to both cooperation and non-cooperation, which are mutually definitive. So, the underlying principle should, more aptly, be regarded as intentionality *and* a cooperation/non-cooperation principle (let's call this the C/NC principle). That way we don't have to drag in any moral baggage with stating the cooperation principle, and nor do we have to go in circles saying 'but to signal non-cooperation we need to have the cooperation principle first' or 'but for *a priori* cooperation in intentional communication we need a concept of intentional non-cooperation' ... and so on, in circles. Most importantly, we can avoid our love of tacit moral input and other such social interferences.

Conceptual rationale: Rather than a cooperation principle shouldering the pragmatics of evolutionary species/self-interest uncomfortably, a C/NC principle may gel more easily with that pragmatics. Even for gestures. Pointing can be helpful ('that's the way to go') or hostile ('don't dare go there'). Importantly, either way it works *because* it serves evolutionary species/self-interest. If helpfully, that's because the signal allows for mutual self-interest to be served for issuer and recipient. If with hostility, that's because the signal serves the non-mutual individual self-interests of the issuer. The non-cooperative gesture may mean: 'I pointed to signal that if you disobey, we will fight, but my body is better preserved if I don't have to fight. But make no mistake ...' This is not intended as helpful; it is based on an implicit logic of self-preservation. A non-cooperative gesture might absorb conflict into communicative performance in preference to actual bodily harm without being any the less conflictually intended by the one issuing the signal.

So, if we started looking for evidence of intentionality in terms of a C/NC principle — rather than a morally loaded cooperative principle — in human (or ape) communication, might we find it? May it come down to 'seek and ye shall find'?

And what does it mean for the 'Imaginary We' if it is understood as a crystallization of intentionality with a C/NC principle? How does C/NC work in terms of apes/infants pointing and pantomiming? Does C/NC work in the same way in the human oral–audial combinatorial communication system?

Chapter 13

As Long as It Catches Mice ...

Peter Tu, Stephanie Stacy, and Federico Rossano

In 1866, the French Academy of Sciences banned all publications on the origins of human language. This was in response to the fact that just about any individual with an academic posting could posit almost any arbitrary thought on this topic. The problem was that there was no real way of judging the merit, or lack thereof, of such conjectures. In the absence of a historical record, argument and logic alone did not suffice. With this said, I would argue that instead of focusing on whether or not a model of language accurately informs us regarding how human speech actually came into being, we can consider the utility that such theories afford us as we attempt to construct computational entities that emulate various sophisticated human capabilities. To this end, I will describe some recent work that my colleague Tao Gao (and to a modest degree I) have been pursuing with respect to multi-agent cooperation. But before providing such details, my colleagues Stephanie Stacy and Federico Rossano have put together an interesting response to some of the questions that you raised in your last intervention.

Rebuttal and Response

Why Not Tomasello?

Suman, you seem to take no issue with trying to build models of communication by emulating the first principle-type origin story of human communication. Instead, you discredit Tomasello's version because it is not the only one out there and you feel Tomasello is 'determined to find [the] originary structures of the human oral–audial combinatorial communication system without reference to that system'.

To the first point, describing an 'origin' is not a known truth, it's an accumulation of clues from the long distant past that leave their residue on the observable, measurable evidence of the present. In this case, there may always be multiple versions of an origin story, which, to some degree, all rely on a bit of bio-poetry to connect the dots. What is important, then, is to distinguish what can give credibility to a version. We focus on Tomasello and his work not because he is the only scientist we can cite who supports this perspective, but because he is an incredibly prolific and highly cited researcher with hundreds of research papers under his belt, well-developed ideas, and a wide range of supporting experimental evidence from young children, non-human primates, and several other animal species (including dogs). His work has been highly impactful in Linguistics, Psychology, and Biological Anthropology. Tomasello's work has been inspired by and built upon other established psychologists, namely Lev Vygotsky and Jerome Bruner, who argue that language relies on its interaction with action and attention. Furthermore, he draws from philosophers such as Paul Grice, John Searle, and John L. Austin to explain the connection between cooperation and communication through a shared intentionality hypothesis. We cannot know that Tomasello's origin of communication is the true origin, but it is built in the context of a well-established body of research and ideas that lend credence to his own hypotheses.

Notably — and this is the critical feature of science that scholars from other fields do not have to adhere to — we know that scientific theories are, indeed, theories and have to be falsifiable, at least in principle. But it is too easy to come up with a theory on a whim and recommend somebody else go out and test it for you. At the very least, Tomasello has not only developed the theory, but has also focused much of his life's work on trying to falsify it through hundreds of experiments on several species and populations.

You argue that Tomasello is able to push the burden of language origins to something outside of language — gesture — bypassing the social aspect of it and never referencing that system. This argument seems to largely ignore the empirical studies that Tomasello and many others conduct to situate this theory with its evolutionary and social context, using the available evidence of the present. Tomasello contrasts cognitive capacity and motivation of human infants and toddlers against non-human primates, finding cooperation to be the distinguishing factor. From this perspective, the key point is that language is an evolutionary adaptation we've developed as support for complex underlying social cognition. Language is the tool to help us coordinate and do things together. Gesture and spoken language are simply the modalities that allow us to coordinate to achieve complex goals that can now even occur on a large, institutional level. This emphasizes rather than ignores the social aspect of communication.

Bruner (1975) in particular emphasizes the importance of examining language from its use. And that use is, at its most primitive level, tied back to instrumental actions in the environment: to tasks and interactions. To explain the process of developing a communication system from scratch, we require some way to ground communicative exchanges — at least at first — in something shared. Our shared perceptual experiences from interacting in the environment together serve as a natural platform for this. Then, we can use language as a tool to achieve things we want, starting from this interaction. The Imagined-We modelling approach reflects this by deriving the utility of a signal from an evaluation of the rational instrumental actions we expect a listener to take upon hearing the signal.

The underlying 'system' bearing the burden, and indeed a large portion of Tomasello's focus, is social cognition. Tomasello gives an evolutionary account of human thinking as the development of an individual's ability to simulate and evaluate personal beliefs, desires, and intentions as well as understanding others as intentional agents. Tomasello pushes this further, arguing that humans, unlike other non-human primates, form a special type of shared intentionality, joint goals, and attention to facilitate small-scale collaboration (Tomasello 2014).

Gesture and Vocalizations

Delving deeper into the specific argument of moving from gesture to vocalization, the objections are that there seems to be no incentive to make the shift. However, something that Tomasello does well is to focus on the bigger picture: to look at history from an evolutionary angle. There is much discussion about whether language originates from the vocal modality, but humans are the only primates that are wholly considered to be vocal learners. Non-human primates are flexible in the gestural domain, but their vocal abilities are very constrained, tied tightly to emotion, and largely ignore their audience, with few exceptions (Arbib *et al.* 2008). The question that we need to consider then is why is it that this modality — sound — is most prominent for humans and not other primates? From this point of view, a more parsimonious story suggests that all primates were originally communicating through gesture and humans then shifted towards vocal learning. So, what can explain this shift? If we frame this question in terms of the earlier proposed purpose of language: a social tool to support underlying cognition, increasingly flexible and complex cognition requires a medium that can support it. Sound offers a good solution because it is extremely flexible and abstract. Even within infant language development, we can see the same pattern on a small scale: infants begin to gesture to communicate before vocalizing and there is correlative evidence strongly linking these phenomena together (Carpenter *et al.* 1998; Colonnesi *et al.* 2010). Thus, both in terms of ontogeny and phylogeny, the evidence supports this shift.

You mention that the shift in modality would require a shift in brain areas responsible for communication that would not make sense. But this is a misunderstanding of Tomasello's theory. It would not be the case that there is a creature that only makes gestures and all of a sudden starts producing flexible vocalizations. There is no blank slate in evolution. In Tomasello's version of language evolution, our common ancestor with chimpanzees and bonobos would most certainly be vocalizing, just as chimpanzees and bonobos do. The key difference here is whether they could use their vocalizations flexibly and whether they could learn new ones. In other words, this common ancestor would not need to turn on vocalizations all of a sudden and rely on them. Rather, it would need to be able to learn new ones and have full control of their delivery. That flexibility is already in place for great apes when we look at their gestures and one could reasonably assume it was in place in our common ancestor with them. If we believe that *natura non facit saltum*, then we might consider it more plausible to see a shift towards flexibility from gestures to vocalizations rather than having vocalizations go suddenly from 1 to 100 and only then extending this new flexibility to the visual/gestural modality. The failure in understanding the gesture origins comes from our obsession with auditory signals and the false belief that human communication is mono modal. Human communication is naturally multimodal, as any face-to-face interaction would remind us. In a multimodal setting, all modalities contribute to the meaning-making process, but we do not have equal control of all of them. Flexible control is what differentiates theories about origins. If you believe that minor control over the intensity and duration of vocalizations is very close to speaking, then look at your dog and ask her when she is going to talk. It takes a brain capable of processing contextual information in a certain way, control over different modalities, and ultimately the motivation to produce a signal for a recipient expecting that the recipient will do something about it.

Cooperative/Non-Cooperative

This leads us to your comment about the issue with the assumption that communication has to be cooperative while there are several instances of non-cooperativeness in human communication. The claim is not that human communication is motivationally prosocial (i.e., aimed at helping others), but rather that in every communicative act we start with an assumption of cooperation. This is to say that when somebody tells us that it is cold outside, we start with the assumption that they are telling the truth and we put on a coat. This is why lies can succeed: because they are relatively rare and build on an assumption of truth. Cooperativeness, in this sense, means that the assumption is that people will be truthful in their communications until proven wrong. When this fails, we stop trusting that individual, but we do not change our assumptions about the truthfulness of communication of other people. If we did not have the tendency to assume truth, why would we even bother to ask people for directions? It starts from infancy, when a child is exposed to parents naming things for them. There would be no point in learning the name of any object or animal or person if the child assumed that her parents were being non-cooperative while communicating with her. So, cooperation is the assumption, not the motivation.

When we look at the motivation for communication, we can certainly agree that often humans aim to manipulate, rather than help. But this fits with the model of animal communication put forward by Dawkins and Krebs (1978), e.g., claiming that the individual producing a signal aims to manipulate the recipient to maximize their own benefits. Funnily enough, your beloved Seyfarth and Cheney (e.g., 2003) are among the main proponents of the opposite theory that the main motivation for animal communication is transferring information and therefore that reliable, trustworthy, signals are privileged. Accordingly, even baring your teeth or raising your fists becomes a cooperative signal in that it displays a warning and prevents further harm. We agree with you that Tomasello at times seems to conflate the prosocial helpfulness of young children with the cooperative assumption of human communication, where one is a motivation to act and the other an expectation of truth. It is totally possible to engage in cooperative communication while being manipulative. I might tell you that we are running out of milk right before you are ready to get to the store just so that you do the purchase and pay for it. I am not lying. We are running out of milk. The assumption of truth is respected. I am just controlling the timing of my delivery because I can predict your behaviour well enough to know what you will do next. We now have evidence that non-human primates have to some degree the ability to manipulate others' conduct (see, e.g., Voelter *et al.* 2017), but humans can most certainly take it to the next level.

So, cooperation (here meant as truthfulness) is the assumption in human communication, not its individual motivation (prosociality and/or altruism is not a requirement, and manipulation is most certainly an option; see, e.g., Rossano, 2018).

The Imagined We

Returning to the question of assessing the merit of a cognitive theory based on the utility and affordance that it provides, I would like to describe some recent investigations into the tantalizing topic of cooperation.

Tao and I have been working on the question of how, in the absence of a centralized controller and direct communication channels, multiple agents are able to cooperate in order to solve various tasks. To this end, one of the classical multi-agent AI problems is the predator–prey scenario. In this work, the predators are modelled as wolves and the prey are modelled as sheep. At every time step, each wolf and sheep may elect to move one space either horizontally, vertically, or diagonally. There can be multiple wolves and multiple sheep. Each animal (both wolves and sheep) can observe the location of all the other animals; however, since there is no direct communication, the animals do not know what the other animals are *thinking*. The wolves are driven to catch sheep, while the sheep wish to avoid capture. However, the sheep are faster than the wolves. So, if the wolves are to be successful, they must learn how to cooperate.

Our fundamental argument is that in order to be successful, the wolves must discover various tactics and strategies, but that the learning framework in which the wolves are immersed will place limits regarding which tactics are available for discovery. Let us start by considering what many believe to be the state of the art in cooperative teamwork: Multi-Agent Reinforcement Learning (MARL). A recent implementation of this paradigm can be found in Lowe *et al.* (2017). In the MARL approach, all wolves and sheep are modelled as independent agents. Each agent has access to the state representation of the environment which is the 2D location of every wolf and every sheep. During the learning phase, each agent must attempt to construct a policy which dictates which action it should take based on the current state of the environment. Note that each policy is specific for each agent and so should not be confused with the idea of a joint policy. A reward function is used to drive the learning process. The sheep are rewarded if they remain alive and so their policies tend to result in evasive behaviour. In order to encourage cooperation, all wolves are equally rewarded if any of the wolves capture a sheep. This can be viewed as a form of shared reward. Since the learning process is performed jointly, sheep develop new skills in order to compensate for advances made by the wolves and vice versa. A policy can be graded based on the expected long-term reward that will be received if a given policy is followed. The learning process terminates when the wolves and sheep arrive at a point where neither wolves nor sheep can develop a better policy — this is known as the Nash equilibrium.

The first scenario to consider is the situation where there are multiple wolves and a single sheep. The resulting behaviour of the wolves appears to be remarkably cooperative. The wolves have learnt various tactics, such as how to surround the sheep as well as corner a sheep. Depending on the situation, some wolves appear to take on the role of chaser while others appear to attempt to block an escaping sheep. The learning process is made more challenging by introducing physical obstacles that are randomly placed during each iteration of learning. Note that since the locations of the obstacles are always changing, the animals cannot develop a policy that is tuned to a specific obstacle configuration. In short, the MARL method is quite impressive. However, in the next scenario, instead of a single sheep, we now introduce multiple sheep into the environment. For a given number of sheep and wolves, the animals are allowed to develop a specific policy for that configuration. Initially, one might think that with additional sheep, there comes additional opportunity. Thus, as the number of sheep increases, the expected reward for the wolves should also increase. This is not the case. In fact, as the number of sheep increases, the performance of the wolves decreases.

Observation of the behaviours induced via MARL under crowded conditions demonstrates that the wolves are unable to focus their attentions on a specific target. Their efforts become divided, and they are thus less successful. In essence, the concept of group-level commitment appears to be beyond the grasp of the MARL paradigm. This provides new meaning to the proverb that there is safety in numbers. Not that the probability of being the sole victim is $1/N$, and thus with larger N, the odds of being the victim decreases, but rather that the predators become less effective as N increases. At this point, Tao and his team started to question the role of shared reward. Maybe a more direct attribution of reward to actions taken will result in more effective policies. It turns out that by converting to an individual reward strategy, where the wolf that captures the sheep is the one that gets all the reward (winner takes all), the expected reward of each wolf increases when compared to the shared reward scheme. However, even under individual reward, as the number of sheep increases, the performance of the wolves continues to decrease but not as much as with the shared reward scheme (see Minglu Zhao *et al.* 2021 for details). The next change in scenario is based on including a cost for actions taken. With this modification, each wolf must pay a small price for every step that it takes. It was observed that this change exacerbates the performance gap between shared and individual reward. That is to say, the difference between individual and shared reward performances increases as the action cost increases. Under individual reward the wolves pretty much behave the same. However, under shared reward, the wolves appear to be more inclined to what appears to be a form of laziness. This is an example of what is known as the free rider problem.

So, what does all this experimentation and analysis have to say about cooperation? For one thing, we can argue that cooperation may be more complex than one might think and that what may at first glance appear to be a manifestation of cooperative behaviour might be just a craftier form of opportunism. It has been hypothesized that cooperation in the animal kingdom might be limited to a form of MARL and thus unable to take advantage of tactics such as group-level commitment.

In the MARL paradigm, agents do not seem to develop a concept of the agency of others. From an individual wolf's perspective, the other wolves can be thought of as furniture-like objects that simply exhibit certain behaviours. The wolf then crafts its behaviour based on its observations of the behaviours of others. However, if the wolves can construct a mental model of the other wolves, such a paradigm shift may open the door to new possibilities.

One of the most basic mental models for agents is the idea that each agent maintains a set of desires, beliefs, and intentions. Beliefs are based on observations of the world. The agent's beliefs and desires are used to construct its intentions. Intentions dictate the actions that the agent will take. Given such a construct, one could imagine a scenario by which each wolf attempts to estimate the desires, beliefs, and intentions of all the other wolves and then use this information to inform its intentions regarding which actions it should take. This would be considered to be a form of hard Theory of Mind. One difficulty with this formulation is that each wolf must realize that all other wolves are attempting to infer the cognitive state of all other wolves, including itself. This results in a complicated and possibly infinite recursive mind-reading problem. As the number of wolves increases, so too does the complexity of this form of analysis. At the end of the day, it is not clear how such forms of clairvoyance would directly result in a joint plan. Michael Tomasello's work provides a path out of this predicament. Motivated by such guidance, Tao and his colleagues developed the idea of the Imagined We (IW).

We start by positing the existence of an IW construct. The IW would have its own desires, beliefs, and intentions. We can then introduce the concept of commitment to the IW intentions. That is to say, let's assume that the IW knows which sheep the group should focus on. The task of each wolf now comes down to inferring what the IW wants it to do and then doing it. The problem, of course, is that this is a form of latent variable inference for an entity that does not really exist! However, if all other wolves are doing the same thing, each wolf can base its analysis on not only the current locations of each wolf and sheep but also on the actions taken by all the other wolves. This results in a form of iterative estimation as opposed to recursive mind reading. In this way, the joint inference of the IW actually constructs a distributed form of the IW (see Ning *et al.* 2020 for details).

Once commitment has been established, the problem reduces to the single-sheep scenario which we know can be solved using MARL. Experiments with this formulation reveal that the IW paradigm outperforms both the independent and joint reward versions of MARL for two or more sheep and more importantly as the number of sheep increases so too does the expected reward of the IW wolves.

I hope that this exciting investigation illustrates the point that I am trying to make regarding how we might assess the merit of hypotheses proposed by luminaries such as Tomasello. While pure logic and argument will always have their place, we know that there are limits to such forms of discourse and analysis. By taking a more *the-proof-is-in-the-pudding* approach, we may consider additional metrics such as the utility and affordances that are enabled by such theories.

The following table illustrates the hypothesis that as we incorporate additional constructs into the learning formulation, new tactics, strategies, and capabilities may become available to the cooperating agents. This represents possible next steps for this research agenda.

Constructs	Potential tactics, strategies, and capabilities
Role-based hierarchies	Gambits and traps
Communal memory and experience	Metaphors and reasoning by analogy
Respect and shame	Insurance schemes, sacrifice
Communal wisdom	Risk analysis, best practices
Altruism	Trade, tragedy of the commons (avoidance)
Communal and individual narratives	Intention, subterfuge, deceit

A Bend in the Road

Suman, to date we have discussed how our AI-Assistant might be capable of both physical and social awareness as well as how it might elect to take actions and even communicate with its subject. I would now like to turn the page and consider what it will take for the AI-Assistant to become a source of explainable knowledge. That is to say, in addition to awareness, I want the AI-Assistant to also have a deeper understanding of its environment. David Deutsch (2011) contrasts explainable knowledge with the idea of biological knowledge. Our DNA essentially encodes a recipe for constructing eyeballs. This is a very useful piece of biological knowledge.

However, our DNA does not provide teachings regarding the properties of light and hence our DNA does not provide the means for constructing cameras, microscopes, or telescopes. Nor does it inform us as to why the sky is blue at midday and yet red at sunset. Explainable knowledge in the form of a theory of light is needed for such tasks.

To this end, I want to consider not just how the AI-Assistant might tap into explainable knowledge but more importantly how it might be capable of producing explainable knowledge. As we explore this facet of the AI-Assistant's cognitive existence, we may revisit topics such as the grounding problem and creativity. I also anticipate discussion of new topics, such as causality, the scientific method, knowledge representation, complex systems, and the wisdom of societies. Like the captain of a ship staring off into a foggy night, my capacity to predict where your thoughts on this topic might take us is limited at best. I thus continue to be both excited and intrigued regarding where this conversation will take us.

Part 3

Explanation

Chapter 14

Parables and Explanations

Suman Gupta

It is a good idea to turn to the part played by explanations in knowledge construction and where our AI-Assistant may come in there. This intervention is mainly devoted to some preliminary thoughts on that. But first, a few quick notes on your last intervention.

Animal Parables

I really enjoyed the defence of Tomasello's work. Let me say straightaway that I have the greatest respect for Tomasello's achievements.

Why Not Tomasello?

Here's an animal parable. My good friend Peter finds that he has mice infestation in his domestic man cave. He toys with the idea of designing an AI-Assistant which will locate mice in real time within a defined space, take out said mice with a laser weapon, collect and instantly convert the carcasses into chicken feed. He has visions of resigning, filing for yet another patent, and establishing Peter's Mouse Buster PLC. After daydreaming for a while, he decides that it's easier to get a fierce and voracious cat instead.

In the local pet shop No Napping, Peter is offered a choice between two deadly cats. One is called The-Great-Tomasello and the other

147

My-Beloved-Seyfarth-&-Cheney. The-Great-Tomasello is really quick and sharp but has a limited appetite, can kill a respectable number of mice quickly but will then take a longish holiday before doing it again. My-Beloved-Seyfarth-&-Cheney is ponderous and steady, keeps relentlessly killing mice in slow motion till none can be detected, but it takes a longish while.

Faced with this choice, Peter pulls out his pocket calculator and asks the friendly No-Napping Slave for some specifications and makes a quick calculation of mice casualties for each cat over period P, that being the period over which Peter is willing to leave a cat in charge of his domestic man cave, puts in a limit R according to the mice-reproduction rate, throws in a pleasing-to-the-eye factor X in his calculations … and makes his decision.

Message: The-Great-Tomasello and My-Beloved-Seyfarth-&-Cheney are not better or worse cats than each other. They are equally formidable in their own ways. Neither had honed their mouse-killing skills with a view to serving Peter's interests in the future. It is up to Peter to choose which cat serves his interests best after the fact, and his choice is no reflection on the status and standing of either of these feline heroes.

[Ergo: Purpose — to get AI-Assistant to converse with humans. Human communication involves a combination of sounds and gestures with an emphasis on sounds. We could approach the task of understanding such communication, before designing it as an AI-Assistant capacity, by beginning with the origins of communication inferred from apes and tracking some process towards human communication thereafter. There are two models of the origins of communication to be inferred from apes, and one can be chosen for the given purpose. Model 1 focuses on ape gestures alone. Model 2 focuses on the combination of ape gestures and sounds, such as they are. Both models have some persuasive advantages and evidence attached to them; neither is falsifiable. So, it is the purpose that determines whether to go with Model 1 or Model 2.]

Gesture and Vocalizations

I didn't suggest there had to be a move from gestures to vocalizations from 1 to 100 overnight and I certainly do not subscribe to *natura facit salit* as a general principle; for some inexplicable reason, you assumed otherwise. But an incremental evolutionary shift needs to be hypothesized in terms of a functional logic and I don't see anything along those lines in your intervention.

You say: 'The failure in understanding the gesture origins comes from our obsession with auditory signals and the false belief that human communication is mono modal.' That's not the view I took. How do you know that it is *only* gesture origins and not gesture-and-sound origins?

Cooperative/Non-Cooperative

You seem to be saying: 'an assumption of cooperation' = 'an assumption of truth'. I would be very cautious about going along with that.

Here's an animal parable based on Real-World Observation. A cat Brave and a dog Bold are facing up to each other in An Alley. Brave hisses threateningly at Bold, and Bold cooperates with Brave in receiving this signal as Brave's genuine intention to scratch Bold to shreds if he doesn't retreat immediately. Bold growls menacingly at Brave, and Brave cooperates with Bold in receiving this message as Bold's genuine intention to savage Brave to bits if she doesn't give way pronto. Then Brave charges at Bold with sharp claws outstretched and Bold yelps and runs off with tail between legs before Brave even touches him.

Message: Where was the truth? Perceptions of intentions are discernible, cooperation therein inferable, but manifestations of truths are a somewhat different matter.

Let's not mix up signalling intentions and meaningfully receiving signals of intentions as being the same as conveying and receiving truths: this is a category mix-up. Issuing/receiving signals have to do with intentions and not with precedent or consequential truth claims or confirmations. Now we can go back to Square One and ask: how do we know that cooperation in individual signalling and understanding individual intentions translates into consequent cooperative behaviour as a collective tenet underpinning all communication? For this Tomasello gives a reasonable answer which does not involve truths, but it does contain some misleading normative content (cooperation is good). I was suggesting that we can get rid of that normative content by understanding cooperation in a more nuanced way, as mutually activated cooperation/non-cooperation in signalling intentions and in responsively acting — cooperation is always in it, but not such that agreement or beneficence is implied.

The Exciting Research

It is exciting to have a beautiful logical structure for conceiving research methods and then sticking the findings on that so as to either confirm or adjust that structure, and thereby come up with formulations which seem to explain observations and might be functionalizable for given purposes.

I am not sure you needed Tomasello to come up with the Imagined We. It seems arguable that you could have come up with the Imagined We straight from Paul Grice's conversational maxims. The main advantage of having Tomasello mediate the Imagined We is that it allows for unleashing a lot of animal parables based on Real-World Observations. I was taken by the parable of the wolves.

Explanatory Knowledge

Let me start with a narrowly common-sense notion of explanation: it has to do with answering 'why' questions.

Tom asks, 'why X?' and Jerry says 'Because Y'. Tom may then be satisfied with Jerry's answer and say, 'Y explains X'. But Tom may not be satisfied with this and ask Jerry 'Why Y?' and Jerry will say 'Because N' ... This could carry on for a considerable time if Tom really wants to get to the bottom of things, assuming that there's a bottom. When X can be considered as explained here would depend on how deep Tom wants to get and how deep Jerry can get. So, there's a slippery quality to the notion of explanation: it depends not only on what is explained and how, but who is asking whom for an explanation ... and why.

Famously, in an interview Richard Feynman (1983) had once paused wittily on the issue of asking 'why'. By way of illustrating what that may involve, he traced the following paths of *why*-questions, starting from the proposition 'Aunt Minnie is in the hospital'.

- Why? Because she went out, slipped on the ice, and broke her hip.
- Why did she slip on the ice? Well, ice is slippery. Everybody knows that, no problem.
- Why is ice slippery? That's kinda curious. Ice is extremely slippery. It's very interesting [...] because there aren't many things as slippery as ice. It's not very hard to get greasy stuff, but that's sort of wet and slimy. But a solid that's so slippery? Because it is, in the

case of ice, when you stand on it (they say) momentarily the pressure melts the ice a little bit, so you get a sort of instantaneous water surface on which you're slipping.

- Why on ice and not on other things? Because water expands when it freezes, so the pressure tries to undo the expansion and melts it. It's capable of melting, but other substances get cracked when they're freezing, and when you push them, they're satisfied to be solid.
- Why does water expand when it freezes and other substances don't? I'm not answering your question, but I'm telling you how difficult the *why*-question is. You have to know what it is that you're permitted to understand and allow to be understood and known, and what it is you're not. You'll notice, in this example, that the more I ask why, the deeper a thing is, the more interesting it gets.
- We could even go further and say, 'Why did she fall down when she slipped?' It has to do with gravity, involves all the planets and everything else. Nevermind! It goes on and on.

Feynman's reflections on 'why' questions are really useful because they show how close, in some respects, everyday explanations are to scientific explanations, and, in some respects, how distant. That's worth getting out there because it seemed possible to me that when you say 'explanatory knowledge' you really mean scientific explanations rather than various levels of context-dependent everyday explanations. But is it only scientific explanatory knowledge that we want our AI-Assistant to acquire? That would be helpful for all scientists (or make the lot redundant), but would do little insofar as we want, for instance, our AI-Assistant to be our familiar, to talk to us ordinary people, and be generally supportive in everyday life.

You may say: to understand explanatory knowledge at any level it is best to start with scientific explanation because that is the deepest level. That is to say, if we get on top of scientific explanation, we can easily get to the relatively shallower levels of everyday explanation. But that is not, as Feynman says, quite the case. The answer to the question 'Why is ice slippery?' has a direct bearing on the question 'Why is Aunt Minnie in hospital?', but, at the same time, the latter question did not necessarily implicate the former. What is likely to be regarded as a sufficient explanation for the latter question does not necessarily imply giving an explanation for the former question. *There is no necessarily continuous relationship for explanations at deeper and shallower levels; explanations are according to what suffices at particular levels.* In fact, and again as Feynman notes, even scientific explanations do not necessarily go deeper and deeper into one direction of 'all the planets and everything else'. If the questioner were more focused on the condition of Aunt Minnie's hip, it could take a different direction: 'Why did her hip break?'; 'Because she has osteoporosis'; 'Why does she have osteoporosis?' ... could lead into 'life, the world, and everything'. Maybe ultimately that *is* the same direction, or maybe it isn't. Certainly though, the immediate explanation for Aunt Minnie's hospitalization is not tantamount to explaining everything.

What we need then is an account of *explanation* which doesn't immediately privilege scientific explanation as the only sort worth considering and nor particularly fixates on some level of everyday explanation. Such an account needs to apply to *all* levels of explanation, at various depths of knowledge, and for various purposes of informing.

One way to go about that would be to define what a 'level' is for explanatory purposes. Let's say: *persons belong to an explanatory level insofar as they share first principles from which they can make inferences to obtain what they understand as sufficient explanations for 'why' questions.*

I have thrown in the phrase 'first principles' there without quite explaining it, but it is key to the definition of an explanatory level. In a common-sense way, we could say: 'First principles are ideas on which *A* and *B* agree, which they can draw upon to explain a phenomenon or observation of which they are uncertain such that their uncertainty is sufficiently dispelled. Insofar as *A* and *B* have such first principles and those suffice for obtaining explanations, *A* and *B* are on the same explanatory level.' A mathematician may call them 'axioms'. How, we may ask, are first principles appointed for *A* and *B* at a specific level, so that they can be called upon for making explanatory inferences sufficient for that level? The first principles may be appointed in anticipation of the kinds of 'why' questions that *A* and *B* need explanations for (which courts some circularity); or, what 'why' questions *A* and *B* choose to seek explanations for depends upon the first principles they already have (which still begs the question of how they had them to begin with). I suspect the slipperiness of explanatory knowledge lies at this juncture.

At this point, we may need to look into how explanatory levels relate to concepts of induction and deduction, proof and falsification, paradigmatic reasoning and paradigm shifts, and so on ... but then we are already *within* a particular explanatory level. But that's okay, so long as it takes in all levels.

But let me pause there. I am not sure that this is the sort of thing you had in mind in raising the issue of explanatory knowledge.

Chapter 15

Nonlinear Explanations

Peter Tu and Alfredo Gabaldon

Suman, your questions regarding what constitutes an explanation and more importantly what we mean by a good explanation are a nice way to start this conversation. As an engineer, my first inclination is to state that an explanation is useful if it affords us something. For example, the unfortunate lady that broke her hip teaches us that one must tread lightly on ice. One of our great gifts as a species is our capacity to use tools with only the shallowest of understandings. In contrast, most animals seem to require relatively deep knowledge of how an instrument works before they can make use of it. If asked to explain the basic principles that govern how modern-day toilets operate, most will be hard-pressed to produce a valid explanation. Yet, the act of flushing is a common part of just about all of our repertoires. Another example of a useful explanation is what David Deutsch (2011) calls creative copying. We may observe a capability such as a bird's ability to fly. We can then explain how this phenomenon works so that we can first deduce that we cannot fly the way that birds do and, second, that we can devise an alternative solution such as hot air balloons or jet propulsion. Dan Kahneman (2011) warns that we tend to view the world with a causal eye, when in fact the world is actually very random. This tendency leads to his idea of success bias. We assume that the winners of our time have achieved greatness due to judicious decision-making, acumen, and skill, whereas in reality, they were more often just in the right place at the right time.

It seems that explanation and causality go hand in hand. To this end, a discussion of Judea Pearl's thoughts on this subject is warranted (Pearl 2009). My colleague Alfredo Gabaldon graciously offers the following summary of *The Book of Why* (Pearl and Mackenzie 2019) which helps guide us through this thorny topic.

The Book of Why

Pearl makes a number of interesting claims in his book. Starting from the fact that we all have the ability to think about things we observe, things we do, and things we imagine, his first claim is that these three abilities are fundamentally different. Each requires a higher level of cognition than the previous one: thinking about imaginary things (that don't exist or haven't happened in the real world) is harder than thinking about doing things, which is harder than thinking about what we simply observe. He calls this the Ladder of Causation. In level 1 (Association) of the ladder, one is an observer looking for regularities or associations in what we see in order to answer questions of the form 'What do I believe about Y given that I observe X?' Level 2 (Intervention) involves reasoning about what will happen if we do something that changes the world instead of just observing it. In level 3 (Counterfactuals), we ask questions about what the world would be like if we had acted differently. To illustrate the three levels of reasoning, Pearl uses the firing squad example. A court order (CO) to execute a prisoner is given. Upon receiving the court order, the firing squad captain (C) signals the squad to fire. The two soldiers (A and B) in the squad fire their weapons upon receiving the signal from the captain, and finally, the prisoner dies (D). It is assumed that the captain and the soldiers follow their orders, the causal model has a link from CO to C, from C to A and from C to B, from A to D and from B to D. With this model in hand, an observation that the prisoner is dead would lead to the conclusion that a court order was issued, which led to the captain signalling to fire, which led to the soldiers firing. Using this model one would also conclude that B fired after observing that A fired. These are examples of level 1 reasoning. A level 2 question would be: if A decides, of his own volition, to fire, would the prisoner be dead? Put another way, instead of observing A, we are changing the scenario through an intervention that makes A true. To solve this problem, Pearl argues, we need to modify the model by removing all causal arrows pointing at A. Once we do this, we can answer the question: is the prisoner dead? Yes, because the arrow from A to D is still there. Did B fire? Probably not. The arrow from C to A is no longer there, so we can't conclude anything about C, CO, or B. Finally, a level 3 counterfactual question would be: the court order was issued, everyone followed their orders, and the prisoner is dead. Would the prisoner be alive if A had decided, on his own, not to fire his weapon? To answer this question, we remove the arrow from C to A as before since A again acts on his own. Then, since the model still has a causal path from CO to C to B to D, we conclude that the prisoner would not be saved by A's decision not to shoot.

The second claim Pearl makes is that statistics and conditional probability formulations can only answer level 1 questions. They don't even have the mathematical language to express level 2 and 3 questions. This is true of any attempts there have been to capture causal relationships in terms of conditional probabilities. For example, interpreting 'X causes Y' as 'X raises the probability of Y' and expressing it as $P(Y|X) > P(Y)$. This fails, since the inequality is true whether X causes Y, Y causes X, or a third variable causes both X and Y. Conditional probability statements like $P(Y|X)$ are about observations and hence can only answer level 1 questions. For the same reason, formalisms based on conditional probabilities such as Bayes Nets can only support level 1 reasoning. The whole field of statistics, Pearl argues, lacks a mathematical language to pose level 2 and 3 problems directly. In order to bring probabilities to the higher levels of the Ladder of Causation, one must extend the language with a construct for *doing* (as opposed to observing): $P(Y|\mathrm{do}(X))$.

Pearl's third claim is that it is not possible to answer level 2 and 3 questions only from observational data. To answer level 2 questions, one must either perform an experiment (an intervention in the world) or supplement the observational data with a causal model. A sufficiently good causal model, Pearl says, lets us answer level 2 queries using level 1 data. To answer level 3 questions, even experiments don't help, since one cannot go back in time and take a different action (can't go back in time and tell a patient not to take the drug). Simpson's Paradox is one of many examples used to illustrate why models are necessary. In a nutshell, the data in Simpson's Paradox show that a drug increases the risk of a heart attack in men and in women, but when one looks at the general population, the data indicate that the drug results in a lower risk of a heart attack. To solve the puzzle, Pearl argues, one must consider the process that generated the data. In other words, we need a causal model that spells out the reality of our assumptions about the process that produced the observed data. In this example, the causal model captures that gender has a causal effect on the risk of a heart attack (men are more susceptible than women) and gender also has an effect on the decision to take the drug (women are more likely to take the drug). While in this example the correct answer is to look at the data partitioned by gender and not the aggregated data, there are similar examples where the correct answer is the opposite, and there is no way to tell from the data what is the right way to look at it.

There are other highly interesting parts of the book I didn't summarize here. Pearl goes over the history of how causality was removed from statistics. He explains that statistics has the tool of Randomized Controlled Trials to find answers to $P(Y|do(X))$, but still lacks the language and tools to systematically determine which variables should or should not be controlled for. Another chapter is devoted to recounting the struggle of statistics during the 1950s and 1960s to solve the problem of whether smoking causes lung cancer. Lacking a language to pose the question as P(lung-cancer|do(smoke)) and unable to carry out a randomized controlled trial, statisticians and scientists spent 15 years debating the question, often filling rooms full of smoke while doing so. There are also a number of chapters that are devoted to the algorithms for level 2 and 3 causal reasoning.

In the last chapter, Pearl comes to the topic of Big Data and AI. He asserts again that no matter how big one's Big Data is, without a model one will not be able to answer causal questions. Pearl then turns to AI and Free Will. He says that whether one believes that we truly have free will or that free will is an illusion, free will gives us the ability to think and speak about our intentions and giving the same ability to a team of robots will enable them to perform better. Pearl believes that the development of counterfactual (level 3) reasoning algorithms is a major step towards answering questions about consciousness and agency and towards endowing machines with them. Having spent quite a few years studying AI formalisms for common-sense reasoning about actions, which are all about causes and effects, I'm very sympathetic to Pearl's arguments. I did find odd his dismissal of, almost contempt for, 'rule-based systems'. I find it odd because his causal diagrams are essentially drawings of rules and because I know of at least one 'rule-based system' in which it is possible to express and reason about questions at all three levels of the Ladder of Causation. We can assume that by 'rule-based system' Pearl means the early systems that used simple forward or backward chaining mechanisms for reasoning and had very simple or no formal semantics. It is also preferable that Pearl continue pushing the Causal Revolution and not waste time learning the newest developments in 'rule-based systems'.

Deduction and Abduction

Having gotten a taste of Pearl's many pearls of wisdom, let's further explore the concept of explanation. Murray Shanahan's (1989) paper 'Prediction is Deduction, but Explanation is Abduction' sets the stage for how explanations are constructed. A summary of this paper is as follows:

- Causal laws are captured in a theory T.
- Each law has the intuitive form: effect if cause.
- A set of events is represented by a set of sentences Δ.
- Prediction: Find the causal consequences of Δ by finding the logical consequences G such that $T \cup \Delta \vDash G$.
- For explanation, events and properties are represented by G, and the task is to find sets of events Δ which could have caused G, in other words, to find Δ's such that $T \cup \Delta \vDash G$.
- The same theory T is used for both prediction and explanation.
- The author points out that the frame problem requires that properties persist and offers the idea of negation as failure:
  - hold-at(P, T) if
    happens(E) and $E < T$ and
    initiates(E, P) and not clipped(E, P, T)
  - clipped(E, P, T) if
    happens(E') and terminated(E', P) and
    not $T <= E'$ and not $E' < E$

The last bit about the frame problem is important for those who are concerned with the difficulties associated with implementation of this form of reasoning. From our perspective, the key takeaway is that our ability to predict what will happen vs. explain why something has happened is based on a set of cause-and-effect statements T. The difference being that prediction is the act of following the logical consequences of a series of events Δ to arrive at a final state G, while explanation is the act of discovering the set of events Δ that will result in the state G. Assuming that all the causal knowledge that is needed is at our fingertips, the act of abduction then comes down to a question of search. That is to say, how do we manage to find the events Δ that satisfy the equation $T \cup \Delta \vDash G$? At this juncture, we could and should consider a myriad of questions. How does one represent causal knowledge? As you have rightly asked, at what granularity does such reasoning have to take place? Atoms hitting atoms, $F = MA$, or the fact that the Joker's penchant for mayhem mirrors the events depicted in *The King of Comedy*.

With your indulgence, I would like to start by taking us on a bit of a tangential direction by first considering the question of the search for Δ and our experience of it. As you may recall, in a previous intervention, I described Gyorgy Buzsaki's (2006) description of the hippocampus as being first designed for the task of navigation and then used for the binding problem and maybe even memory. Determining one's location, recognizing a ripe banana, or plucking a memory comes down to some sort of search through a random graph. Might it be the case that solving for Δ is also tantamount to searching for a path through one of the hippocampus's many random graphs?

One quality of the way we seem to explain things is that it does not feel like a search. On the contrary, solutions often seem to arrive in their entirety. This is not too dissimilar from the binding problem. When we see a face, we don't start piecing together parts and then eventually conclude that it is indeed a face — the face just pops out at us. The act of recognition seems to simply emerge. This leads to the idea that we are somehow attracted to familiar locations, acts of recognition, memories, and maybe explanations. As you recall, Buzsaki describes the brain as a complex entity at the boundary between predictable and chaotic. Such mechanisms are known as nonlinear dynamic systems, and they can be characterized by what are known as attractor states. Let's pause here for half a tic and quickly review what we mean by nonlinear dynamic systems and their mysterious attractor states.

Nonlinear Dynamic Systems

As described by Jeffrey Goldstein (2011), dynamical systems evolve over time. Nonlinearity refers to a disproportional relationship among variables, e.g., mutual interaction or feedback loops. The butterfly effect of chaotic systems argues that the motion of a Brazilian butterfly could have a disproportional effect on weather patterns over the Midwestern United States.

A time series representation often plots the value of system variable(s) on the *y*- and/or *z*-axis against time on the *x*-axis. Whole industries attempt to glean insight from such representations. Another approach to gaining insight with regard to a dynamic system is to construct a phase or state space diagram/portrait. In this case, each axis represents a system variable. For each point in time, one can then plot a point in the phase portrait based on the values of these variables. In this way, time is implicitly represented by trajectories in the phase portrait.

It is often the case that once a transient phenomenon has terminated, the remaining phase portrait points tend to occupy a minimal region of the phase space. This could be a single point if the system has flatlined. It could be a contiguous locus of points such as an oval, which is associated with periodic behaviour. This is known as a limit cycle. Such regions are known as attractors and represent the long-term dynamics of a system.

An attractor may have a basin of attraction such that if the initial conditions of a dynamic system fall within this region, it will end up at the attractor — kind of like a black hole. There can be multiple attractors and so people may intuit that the behaviour of a system is governed by its attractors. One might even go as far as arguing that the attractors act in a causal manner much like Aristotle's telos or final cause. However, this is going too far; one must remember that phase portraits represent and do not cause system dynamics. Attractors do not have to be a single point or limit cycle. They can be fractals that never intersect and can be chaotic or strange attractors. A seemingly random process can be found to be a deterministic and lawful system if a set of complex attractor states can be identified. A truly random process would result in a phase portrait that is completely black.

Nonlinear Explanations

The physical laws that govern a dynamical system are responsible for the existence of attractor states. A change in the physical laws can result in what is known as a bifurcation, where the shape of the attractor state(s) transforms into a new configuration(s). Returning to the brain, given external stimuli, the self-organizing nature of the brain will often lead to various stable interpretations of the world. The system stabilizes into various configurations of temporary synchronization. This is governed by the neural connections that allow for synchronization. Could we view such a stable state of oscillation as an attractor state? Thus, different attractor states can be associated with different stable configurations and hence different interpretations of the world. This may be true for the same stimuli or slight changes in the stimuli. The classic example of this is the ambiguous figure that can be perceived as both a young and an old woman (see Boring 1930: 444).

AN AMBIGUOUS FIGURE

From time to time, key knowledge or insights might be found. This might cause a plastic change in neural architecture that governs the dynamics of the brain. Could this be viewed as a bifurcation event? A drastic change in an attractor would constitute a radical change in interpretation of observations — could this be an act of creation? The eureka moment? This may explain why sleep seems to be such an important part of creativity — the brain needs time to rewire itself.

It can be argued that the sense of free will might be based on the mind having to weave its way through a continuum of what are known as ghost attractors. Various stimuli and other inputs gently nudge the mind out of a given basin of attraction into another. Multiple attractor states may then come into contention. Much of the arguments behind Roger Penrose's (1989) *Emperor's New Mind* is based on the work of Turing and Gödel, which basically states that there are logical statements that, while true, may not be provable based on a set of axioms. Thus, a Turing machine would not be able to 'know' the truth of such things. Yet, we humans seem to be able to come to grips with such statements. As we have previously discussed, a definition of mathematical ambiguity is a statement that can be true for two mathematical systems that are mutually contradictory. The role of the mathematician is to come to grips with such contradictions. Might it be the case that the proof of the unprovable is essentially jumping between attractor states that have different theories T? Maybe coming to grips with mathematical ambiguity is equivalent to having each foot firmly planted in two different attractor states.

So, I am painting a picture of our capacity to produce explanations Δ as being the output of a nonlinear dynamic system. Changes in the neural circuitry represent the emergence of new attractor states. Part of our deliberative process seems to be akin to wandering through an endless field of ghost attractors. Sometimes these attractors are strange or even exotic. One could imagine, that like a binary star or maybe a Siamese twin, multiple attractors might be connected in ways that allow for contradictory explanations to exist in a state of harmony. Maybe that is how our AI-Assistant will explain the particle and wave nature of light. Will the jokes of our AI-Assistant be tantamount to a wormhole between two seemingly disparate attractor states? Maybe poetry itself will simply be viewed as a contraction of the phase space. One day the AI-Assistant may come to the sneaking suspicion that the laws of the universe might themselves be governed by attractor states ...

Chapter 16

Unsystematic Notes

Suman Gupta

Peter and Alfredo — Many thanks for your splendidly helpful summary of Judea Pearl's arguments. I also admired Pearl and Mackenzie's lucid step-by-step exposition of *do*-calculus in *The Book of Why* (2018). At one point there, Pearl magnanimously observes:

> I usually pay a great deal of attention to what philosophers have to say about slippery concepts such as causation, induction, and the logic of scientific inference. Philosophers have the advantage of standing apart from the hurly-burly of scientific debate and the practical realities of dealing with data. They have been less contaminated than other scientists by the anticausal biases of statistics. They can call upon a tradition of thought about causation that goes back at least to Aristotle, and they can talk about causation without blushing or hiding it behind the label of 'association'. However, in their effort to mathematize the concept of causation — itself a laudable idea — philosophers were too quick to commit to the only uncertainty-handling language they knew, the language of probability. (45).

In the following, I will try to sneak into the space allowed to philosophers here without the laudable mathematizing ambition. The following offers some unsystematic notes on Pearl's arguments; that is to say, using Pearl's arguments as a springboard. These notes bear upon your glibly made initial assumptions: 'As an engineer, my first inclination is to state that an explanation is useful if it affords us something'; 'It seems that explanation and causality go hand in hand'. They also have some bearing on the careful questions you raise later about nonlinear explanation.

Algorithmic Reasoning

The power of Pearl's account of the language for signifying causality lies, I feel, in seeming instinctively meaningful once it is proposed. Ingenious though it was to arrive at, once put there, the *do* notation — such that '*X* causes *Y*' is expressed as $P(Y|\text{do}(X))$, as opposed to the conditional probability that '*X* raises the chance of *Y*' or $P(Y|X)$ — brings about an immediately obvious sharpness where a certain murkiness prevailed. The delinking of causality from statistical correlation, it appears to me, follows from as much as leads into this wonderfully expressive device. Sieving Bayesian networks of mapping conditional probabilities through the *do*-notation system follows as a crystallizing step out of somewhat obfuscating complexity. Inserting counterfactuals — more or less like controlling what-if or why-not questions, $P(Y|\sim\text{do}(X))$ — broadens the scope of analysis whereby causality can be pinned down. Setting out rules according to chain/fork/collider junctions in the resulting models, neutralizing lurking variables through Randomized Controlled Trials, and finally having a decision-making move of removing the *do*-notation in $P(Y|\text{do}(X))$ in terms of data like $P(Y|X,A,B,Z)$ — all these are remarkably neat as an argument. One can see why data, however large scale, without such a causality mapping model would be slippery: that the model can't be inferred from the data, and that the model and data tested with each other would ensure functional outcomes. It *works*, is the sealing claim in the argument: for such-and-such 'why'-questions we can make observations, run them with *do*-calculus, and make interventions which function. Moreover, doing these allow us to conceive of the world in intentional ways which may become machine replicated. The bottom-line claim (an assertion) is that the human brain is constructed to work like that already, it's all given.

- 'Considering the extreme ease with which people can communicate their knowledge with dot-and-arrow diagrams, I believe that our brains indeed use a representation like this.' (Pearl and Mackenzie 2018: 37).
- 'Our brains are endowed with special machinery for comprehending cause-effect relationships.' (Pearl and Mackenzie 2018: 101).

- 'Our brains are not wired to do probability problems, but they are wired to do causal problems. And this causal wiring produces systematic probabilistic mistakes, like optical illusions.' (Pearl and Mackenzie 2018: 174).
- 'Our brains are not prepared to accept causeless correlations, and we need special training.' (Pearl and Mackenzie 2018: 221).
- 'The mistake was particularly illuminating because it pinpoints the exact flaw in the wiring of our brains. We live our lives as if the common cause principle were true.' (Pearl and Mackenzie 2018: 176).
- 'Causal diagrams, with their simple rules of following and erasing arrows, must be close to the way that our brains represent counterfactuals. This assertion must remain unproven for the time being ...' (Pearl and Mackenzie 2018: 236).

Pearl imbues his argument with a kind of prior confirmation from the way 'our brains' *are*: 'our brains', so to speak, testify to his argument as a disembodied organ. Voilà!

Let's put these assertions on how-our-brains-are-made aside. The impression of neatness rests in an adherence to sequential (not linear) reasoning, which allows for satisfactorily dealing with certain kinds of *why*-questions: those that can be dealt with via data/models towards interventions for desired outcomes (*why*-answered). Pearl's various clarifying examples — shooting squad, factors in epidemiological determination, smoking and disease, etc. — are a selection of this kind of *why*-questions. These are questions which comply with your initial assumption, made as an engineer, that explanations lead to 'affordances'. These are *why*-questions where it is totally clear why we are asking *why*-questions: to make successful interventions. It reminds me of one of our past discussions on 'recognition': the face-recognition technology works because we know the answer to 'why recognize?', which is the affordance of 'making an identification' or 'matching an indexed category'. But this kind of *why*-question may not exhaust the scope of *why*-questions, and therefore also not the scope of what we do by way of explanation. Just as we may do more by way of recognition in real life than identifying or indexical matching, we may ask quite a lot of *why*-questions which do not anticipate 'affordances' like lessons and solutions.

The kind of sequential reasoning displayed here, of which Pearl gives a particularly admirable account, works neatly to deal with such *why*-questions. Let me pause on what I mean by sequential reasoning. Basically, it's what's pegged as algorithmic reasoning. Such reasoning leads to the articulation of a set of steps (not necessarily one after the other, not necessarily consecutive or linear) which elicits a clearly anticipated *why*-answer: an (or a set of) algorithm. In how that articulation is arrived at by an engineer, the process may or may not be sequential — the conceptual practice of getting to the algorithm may be more complicated than that. Admittedly, I am speculating. I am thinking back to our earlier discussion of metaphor and mathematics *á la* William Byers. I suspect this sequential reasoning is not entirely mathematical; rather, mathematics is made subject to the algorithmic reasoning's sequential imperative. In bare bones, it ultimately breaks down to sequences of yes/no, on/off steps conducive to digital processing. Pearl's dot-and-arrow models — where marking causality involves switching off some dot-and-arrows in a conditional probability model — is a fine representation of this sequentialization. The orders of sequencing are also evident in the stepping-up of *why*-answering (seeing/association $\rightarrow$ doing/intervention $\rightarrow$ imagining/counterfactuals); and in the breakdown of three nodes (or n-nodes) of networks into chains (A→B→C), forks (A←B→C), colliders (A→B←C). The maths kicks in with setting some axioms and shortcuts for sequential processing, such as for those nodes, and negotiating dependent probabilities and controlling variables. Such sequential reasoning could be regarded as grounded in a digital grammar which precedes and determines how mathematical equations are expressed. Perhaps in a grammar of analogue reasoning, mathematical expression could find fuller play — but I am speculating again, and, in any case, that's outside the scope of these notes.

The point is that such algorithmic reasoning offers a neat argument for engaging with causal models and data for certain kinds of *why*-questions, a limited range of explanation: i.e., where the *why*-question has a determinate *why*-answered for the objective of making interventions and ensuring they are successful. These are *why*-questions that solve practical problems. In a simplistic analogy: the sequential reasoning to make answering such *why*-questions possible is akin to a criminal prosecutor establishing the motive of a crime by asking questions of the accused which the accused can only answer with 'yes' or 'no'. It takes admirable ingenuity from the prosecutor, and the revelation of the motive seems logically unquestionable when the prosecutor pulls things together.

But there are a great many *why*-questions posed in everyday life which are not of this sort. Those are arguably squarely within the range of processes which we commonly understand as explanatory.

Moreover, they may well have a bearing on the *why*-questions which are of the above sort.

First Causes and Final Conditions

A great many *why*-questions we ask are normative and have indeterminate answers but nevertheless nudge explanatory efforts one way or another. Why do we exist? Why do the innocent suffer? Why do you love/hate me? Why do people seek happiness? Why are some people great? Why is that painting beautiful? Why am I lonely? Why is freedom important? Why was I born here? Why does life matter? Why am I so stupid? Why am I so wise? [Well, I filched that last one from Nietzsche, though he had it as a categorical statement, *Why I Am So Wise* — not a *why*-question but *why*-answered.] And so on.

It is possible that by pinning such questions to specific interlocutors in particular contexts, an engineer can come up with some sequential processing towards *why*-answered so as to have an 'affordance'. The engineer could go into environmental conditions, evolutionary processes, the mechanics of competition and collaboration, etc. to come up with a sequentially reasoned *why*-answered explanation that offers a lesson or a solution. However, it seems very possible that those who ask such questions are not looking for that sort of 'affordance', i.e., lesson or solution. They might well be put off by the good engineer's efforts ('But that's not what I was asking!'). Sometimes, such questions are rhetorical, not looking for explanations at all. That's not of interest here. Sometimes, such questions are seriously posed for explanations but in anticipation of sufficient answers which raise no direct 'affordance'. That is to say, the indeterminate but seemingly sufficient answers that are offered and happily received might be an indirect 'affordance', at a tangent. If the satisfying answer given by a wise man, like Nietzsche, was 'Because God is dead' or 'Because we are being fooled by powerful agencies to be sheep', that may not be strictly reasoned, mathematized, or algorithmized, and may not lead to such a straightforward affordance as an intervention. The answer may nevertheless serve a necessary social function like confirming some pre-conceived conviction or affirming some pre-appointed purpose for a like-minded group. There's the affordance of simply establishing like-minded groupness which allows people to speak to each other as if they understand each other. The explanation is in reiterating pre-conceived convictions and pre-appointed purposes in this prevailing context so that a common structure of causality can be consensually recognized.

Of course, none of those indeterminate *why*-questions interests the engineer as an engineer: why bother with these sorts of waffly *why*-questions? But they are the stuff of much philosophy. A philosopher might argue: the confirmations of pre-conceived convictions and the affirmations of pre-appointed purposes that are organized around such *why*-questions structure the very possibility of asking *any why*-question, including the sort calling for direct affordances and interventions. In philosophical terms, the argument goes, asking any *why*-question implies a regressive and progressive possibility of *why*-questions towards some abstract limit of First Causes and Final Conditions. All the *why*-questions that appear between those — including the ones that *do*-calculus can effectively deal with — are posed meaningfully by setting those abstract limits and having some *ad hoc* answers implied in them, at least to start us off. Ludwig Wittgenstein (1958: 88e, passage 241) would call those the boundaries of a 'form of life'. The answers to those First-Causes-and-Final-Conditions kind of *why*-questions are notional, simply agreed, taken for granted, so as to be able to express *all* consequent *why*-questions and have their *whys*-answered with serious intent. Theology provides some obviously familiar kinds of First Cause and Final Condition boundaries, albeit soon to be done away with (one hopes).

I am taking the argument back, Peter, to where we began our conversation from a few years back in asking 'what is intelligence?' (Gupta and Tu 2020: Ch. 3). Something about explanation and causality is being missed out — not being explained — if those indeterminate and normative sorts of *why*-questions are not in the picture. Without those, the prospects of our AI-Assistant look hopelessly tool-like and not promising for the joys of being a familiar.

Within the limits of Pearl's exposition of why *do*-calculus works, 'because our brains are like that' seems to be close to a First Cause. No doubt he can be pushed further with 'why are our brains like that?', and a few more steps ... that might end up with the Origin of Life or the Big Bang.

Within the limits of Pearl's exposition of why *do*-calculus works, 'the emergence of Strong AI' seems close to a Final Condition. That too can be pushed further with 'why have Strong AI?' and a few more steps ... that might end up with the Technocratic Utopia or something like that.

Lock-In

Jaron Lanier's manifesto, *You Are Not a Gadget* (2010), offering advice to save humanity from pervasive algorithmic reasoning embedded in applications, much is made of the concept of lock-in:

> The brittle character of maturing computer programs can cause digital designs to get frozen into place by a process known as lock-in. This happens when many software programs are designed to work with an existing one. The process of significantly changing software in a situation in which a lot of other software is dependent on it is the hardest thing to do. So, it almost never happens. (7).

His main examples are the long-term design fallout of operating systems like MIDI and UNIX. Lock-in, he observes, 'turns thoughts into facts' and gradually narrows down and restricts the possibilities of interventions. Another way of saying that would be that the conception of causality and the scope of explanation for *why*-questions become increasingly limited by the accrual of technological infrastructures, effectively restricting the logical parameters of explanatory logic.

What Lanier puts his finger on could be regarded as the technological concretization of a process which has a conceptual equivalent in the scientific method — but in the latter conceptual level, there are ways of deconcretizing. I have in mind Thomas Kuhn's *The Structure of Scientific Revolutions* (1970 [1962]), the following points about which I have made in a book (Gupta 2022: 100–1).

Kuhn describes scientific method in terms of 'normal science' and 'revolutionary science'. The practice of 'normal science' is described with reference to a specific understanding of *paradigms*, which could be thought of, in imperfect summary, as fundamental principles that hold together a rational system for describing and explaining the natural world (as opposed to the social world) at a given juncture of knowledge acquisition. Kuhn made an important distinction in using the term 'paradigm' from its standard usage. His argument goes as follows:

> In [...] standard application, the paradigm functions by permitting the replication of examples any one of which could in principle serve to replace it. In a science, on the other hand, a paradigm is rarely an object for replication. Instead, like an accepted judicial decision in the common

law, it is an object for further articulation and specification under new or more stringent conditions. (23).

This distinction is important for understanding both what Kuhn meant by 'normal' and by 'science', and therefore the phrase 'normal science'. This sense of 'paradigm' holds for the purpose of describing and explaining the natural world in a rational system, whereas the standard application is relevant to the social world and sociological analysis.

Given this scientific sense of 'paradigm', which is constantly being further articulated and specified in scientific practice, the idea of 'normal' appears in relation to some contradistinctive terms. Kuhn offered, in fact, several terms with different degrees of contradistinction to the 'normal' in 'normal science'. Two of these were within the broad area of normal scientific practice, but they suggest an increasing pressure being put upon its paradigms, testing the limits of description and explanation on their basis. Thus, there's the term 'anomaly', such as an observation which seems not to fit into the descriptions and explanations offered by scientific paradigms of the prevailing rational system. These call for intensive analysis in terms of the existing paradigms and may lead to some adjustment therein, but still within the precincts of 'normal science'. Somewhat more forcefully, there's the term 'crisis': i.e., a growing number of observations which seem to be out of synch with the paradigms of the prevailing rational system. These are still addressed insofar as possible through the prevailing paradigms, so still within 'normal science', but it is felt that the latter are now not quite sufficient for or equal to describing and explaining. Nevertheless, feeling that insufficiency, Kuhn observed, is not enough to give up on 'normal science' — the latter is still the basis of ongoing practice even though its limitations are admitted and troubling. The prevailing scientific paradigms of a rational system are only abandoned when they can be replaced by another set of paradigms erecting a distinct rational system, which has superior descriptive and explanatory powers and can overcome the growing 'crisis'. A paradigm shift takes place. The new paradigms then become the basis of an updated 'normal science'. This shift is designated by the principal contradistinctive term for 'normal science': 'revolutionary science' or 'extraordinary science' (Kuhn used both).

We could say, returning to lock-in, that in 'normal science' paradigms are locked in. But anomalies and crises, which the scientific method actively looks for, enable moments of 'revolutionary science' whereby paradigms are reset. Then, for a while, the new paradigms are locked-in, till the next accrual of anomalies and crises. With a modesty typical of AI engineers, Pearl often tells his readers how 'exciting' and 'revolutionary' his research into causality is. In fact, within the precincts of the kind of *why*-questions Pearl is interested in, he describes a paradigm shift which complies fairly well with Kuhn's account of 'revolutionary science': from conditional probability modelling to causality modelling. The difficulty he testifies to in conceptually moving from Bayesian networks to *Do*-calculus could be thought of as the difficulty of making a paradigm shift. Outside scientific precincts, the continuing hold of religious explanations in everyday and social discourse could perhaps be understood as a solidly locked-in set of paradigms from a pre-scientific mode of reasoning (in the modern sense of 'science').

Obviously, these are less than half-baked thoughts. But there is a key question in there: what role does lock-in play in posing and engaging with *why*-questions? Is it possible to have purely responsive explanations, free of lock-in? These questions, I think, have something to do with what you call 'attractor states' in your outline of nonlinear explanation.

Listening and Attracting

In Pearl's explanation of causality for *do*-calculus there's the metaphor for 'listening'. If *A* causes *B*, that's not because there's simply a probabilistically correlated description of *A* and of *B*, but because *B* in some sense 'listens' to *A*. In your stimulating sketch of nonlinear explanations, the processing of an explanation of *x* in a dynamic system *X* involves the possibility of various 'attractor states' which enable the explanatory processing of *x* according to the limit cycle of *X*.

I find myself quite interested in the part metaphors like 'listening' and 'attractor' play in these explanations of explanations. I have a feeling such metaphors do a lot of metatheoretical work for the theory delineated, and may have something to do with the parameters of First Causes and Final Conditions. But I need to think about this further and perhaps it's a blind alley.

Chapter 17

Intentional Explanations

Peter Tu

Suman, the other day I found myself wandering through Daniel Dennett's *Kinds of Minds* (1996). I thought it could be stimulating to try and address your latest thoughts on explanation through the lens of Dennett's interesting hypothesis regarding how our brand of sentience might have come into being. So, as is my wont, I will start by providing a somewhat Gatling-gunesque and meandering summary of one account of the journey that we *might* have taken. I will get to your points eventually, but be patient and let me muster my thoughts via Dennett.

What Kinds of Minds Are There?

Dennett starts by posing the following questions: Do dogs have a better understanding of dogs than we do, or might it be the case that such organisms may be attuned to the environment and to each other in very apt ways without having the slightest appreciation of their attunement? Can a mind without language and unable to communicate really exist, or is communication just a periphery? What about us? We do clever things without thinking at all. For example, optical flow at our periphery causes us to change the length of our stride. One can't say what it is like to have one's stride controlled in this manner, because it is not like anything. Can mindless creatures just do everything unconsciously? Is the line knowable?

While somewhat unfashionable by today's standards, Dennett places language at the centre of our capacity for thought. Ludwig Wittgenstein (1958: IIxi) had remarked, 'If a lion could talk, we could not understand him'. Dennett suggests that the act of giving language to a mind might in fact be giving it a mind. He argues that the assumption that languageless minds are like our minds must be questioned. In the influential paper 'What Is It Like To Be a Bat', Thomas Nagel offers a definition of consciousness: an entity possesses some form of consciousness if it is aware of what it is like to be that entity. Obviously, it is not possible to attribute consciousness in this way to, say, a glass of water. Dennett argues that similarly consciousness cannot be attributed to habitual behaviours, like automatic stride control. Thus, it is possible that we have no basis for attributing consciousness to animals. It might be the case that we have no basis for saying that a lion is aware of being like a lion.

Our moral code seems to be something to the effect of 'Whatever you do is OK as long as nobody minds'. This makes the question of what a mind is that much more important. Dennett suggests that such questions require that we consider our historical evolutionary path, which innovations occurred, and in what order.

The Intentional Systems Approach

In this section, Dennett considers the birth of agency and then lays the groundwork for how we might analyze such agency. This is in the form of the intentional stance. The following are some of his thoughts on this topic.

The birth of agency had simple beginnings. Through molecular biology, we witness our humble starting point in the form of macromolecules that are complex enough to perform actions instead of just lying around having effects. They, of course, know not what they do. DNA, RNA, and viruses are mindless replicators. We, in contrast, know well what we do, we can perform intentional actions after deliberating consciously about the reasons for and against. There are reasons for what macromolecules do, but they are unaware of those reasons. They, nevertheless, are the seeds of agency. These impersonal, unreflective, robotic, mindless little scraps of molecular machinery are the ultimate basis of all the agency and hence meaning and hence consciousness in the world. We are the descendants of self-replicating robots. Just because we are descended from robots does not make us robots. Unless, as is held by dualists and vitalists, there is some secret ingredient in us, the material world is all that we have to work with.

Plants, animals, and thermostats act as if they were simple-minded agents. We call them *intentional systems*. The perspective from which their pseudo or genuine agenthood is made visible is the *intentional stance*. The intentional stance is the strategy of interpreting the behaviour of an entity (person, animal, artefact, ...) by treating it as if it were a rational agent that governs its *choice* of *actions* by a consideration of its *beliefs* and *desires*.

Is anthropomorphizing a bad idea? If done carefully, it is not just a good idea but may be the key to unravelling the mysteries of the mind. This form of analysis will exploit similarities in order to discern differences. The basic strategy is to treat the entity in question as an agent in order to predict and thereby explain its actions. In contrast to the intentional stance, there are the physical and design stances. Physical stance: Use physics to predict the future. When I drop a stone, I do not attribute a desire to reach the ground, I attribute the action to the effects of gravity. For some things, the physical stance is all that we have. Design stance: we can predict how an alarm clock works based on design knowledge. This is a low-cost, low-risk shortcut enabling us to finesse our limited knowledge of physics. This works well on Mother Nature's artefacts.

When things are more complex, the intentional stance becomes a necessity. For example, predicting the behaviour of a chess program. You anticipate its behaviour as if it were a rational agent. The intentional stance works irrespective of whether the goals are appreciated by the so-called agent. One can implement the intentional stance by considering the question, 'If I were in its shoes, what would I do?' We treat intentional systems as if they are just like us, which they are not. This was a default approach taken by our ancestors (not to mention some of our mutual and close acquaintances) in the form of animism, with the assumption that each moving thing has a mind or a soul. Do tigers want to eat us? Do rivers want to reach the sea? What do clouds want in return for rain? We assume that the agent will make smart moves, which allows for prediction. We describe its perspective by attributing beliefs and desires to the agent. Since predictions are sensitive to the particular way that beliefs and desires are expressed (by us of the system), these systems are intentional systems — they exhibit intentionality.

Dennett then focuses on the concept of intentionality. In ordinary parlance, someone's actions may be intentional or not. Intentionality in the philosophical sense is just *aboutness*. Something exhibits intentionality if its competence is in some way about something else. Something that exhibits intentionality contains a representation of something else. A lock may have a representation of a key. A thermostat has a representation of temperature and desired temperature. This embodiment contributes to the competence of this simple intentional system. Medieval philosophers viewed intentionality as being similar to the act of aiming a metaphorical arrow at something (*intendo arcum in*). Intentional phenomena are equipped with metaphorical arrows aimed at whatever the phenomenon is about.

States of emotion or memory can be intentional but not in the ordinary sense. You can be intentional without doing anything intentionally. There is nothing intentional about recognizing a horse, but your state of recognition exhibits very particular aboutness. You recognize it as a horse. In order to think about something, you must have a way (one among many possible ways) of thinking about it. Any intentional system is dependent on its particular ways of thinking about whatever it is that its thoughts are about.

To understand a system's take on its circumstances, we must have an accurate picture of its particular capacities for distinguishing between things — its way of thinking about things. We overdo it by assuming our version of intentionality is the hallmark of intentionality. Logic is the capacity of language for making indefinitely fine-grained discriminations. This is known as *intensionality* (note the letter s). Predicates are a set of terms that define a logical statement. The set of things to which the term refers to is called the extension of the predicate. The Intension (with an s) of a statement is the particular way that the set of things is picked out or determined. The predicates 'Chelsea Clinton's father' and 'President of the United States in 1995' have the same extension (Bill Clinton), but they zero in on Bill Clinton in different ways, hence different intensions. The terms Equilateral Triangle and Equiangular Triangle refer to the same extension but with different intensions (sides vs. angles). The statement 'a rose by any other name smells as sweet' illustrates the concept of referential transparency. The mathematical terms 4×4 and 16 are an example of referential transparency. But when the topic is not roses but thinking about roses or talking about thinking about roses, differences in intension can matter. Such discourse exhibits referential opacity. The terms interfere with the topic.

Do dogs think? If so, they must think particular thoughts. A thought couldn't exist without being a particular thought. A thought must be composed of particular concepts. You can't think the thought 'that my dish is full of beef' without the concepts of dish and beef. These concepts need other concepts: bucket, plate, cow, flesh ... because these thoughts are different from 'that the bucket is full of beef'. Just which thought is the dog thinking? How can we express in English exactly the thought that the dog is thinking? Surely dogs have concepts, whatever they are. When we apply the intentional stance, we risk importing too much clarity. We are believe-alls, there is no limit to what we can believe. In between macromolecules and us, there is a story to be told.

Shortly after birth, the baby cuckoo eliminates all other eggs in the nest. The rationale is clear and has shaped the innate behaviours of the cuckoo. We can see it, even if the cuckoo can't. The rationale is 'Free Floating', it is not represented in the cuckoo but is operative in shaping and refining its behaviour.

John Searle (1980) argues that intentionality comes in two variants, original and derived. Original intentionality is the aboutness of our thoughts (beliefs, desires, and intentions (ordinary sense)). Original intentionality is the source of derived intentionality exhibited by some of our artefacts (words, sentences, books, maps, pictures, computer programs, ...). The phrase 'Our mothers bore us' is ambiguous and so gets its meaning from the author. What endows the states of mind of the author with intentionality?

Answer 1: They are composed of the language of thought — mentalese. How do you know what the sentences of the language of thought mean?

Answer 2: Picture theory of idea: They are about what they are about because they resemble their objects. My idea of a duck looks like a duck. How do you know what a duck looks like? It depends on the understanding that it is supposed to explain — this goes around in circles.

Answer 3: A memory or mental image is created by the brain much like a photo — they are both examples of derived intentionality. Where did the brain get its intentionality? From its creator, Mother Nature and the process of natural selection.

The intentionality of brain states is derived from the intentionality of the systems or processes that derived them. A robot's intentionality is derived from its developer. Derived intentionality can be derived from derived intentionality. Is chasing original intentionality a will-of-the-wisp adventure? We are descended from robots, composed of robots, all the intentionality that we enjoy is derived from the more fundamental intentionality of these billions of crude intentional systems.

The Body and Its Minds

Dennett offers the following thoughts regarding embodiment and the idea of *interoception*. Mother Nature has no foresight but has built things with foresight. Paul Valéry (1919) notes that the task of the mind is to produce the future. The mind is fundamentally an anticipator and an experience generator. It mines the present for clues and in combination with material saved from the past produces anticipations of the future. It then acts rationally on the basis of these hard-won anticipations. We are the first to appreciate Mother Nature's free-floating rationales and their designs. Does sentience differentiate between sensitivity and genuine minds? If so, what is it? Is sentience the lowest grade of consciousness?

By distributing the huge task of appreciation back into the body, we break the story that the nervous system is a pure information processing system. Nature appears to have built the apparatus of rationality not just on top of biological regulation, but from it and with it. You cannot tear me apart from my body leaving a nice clean edge. My body contains as much of me as my nervous system does. Once we abandon the crisp identification of mind with brain, we can see the body as a reservoir of wisdom that we exploit on a daily basis. Evolution embodies information in every part of every organism. This information does not have to be copied into the brain or represented by data structures but can be exploited by the nervous system. There is wisdom, particularly about preferences, in the rest of the body. The central nervous system can use the body as a sounding board, audience, or critic. Brain and body can build a farther-seeing mind, one that can produce more and a better future.

How Intentionality Came into Focus

In this regard, Dennett offers his vision of the tower of generate-and-test, which represents a progression of intentional creatures. The goal of such entities is to determine which actions to take throughout the course of their existence. Each floor of the tower empowers an organism to find better and better moves. We now start at the basement and head towards the penthouse.

Darwinian Creatures: Blindly generated by random mutation, different hard-wired phenotypes — they do what they do.

Skinnerian Creatures: Plasticity with wired reinforcers, actions based on feedback. David Hume's Associationism, B.F. Skinner's Behaviourism, and the Connectionism of today all reflect this form of learning. Together they represent the ABC learners. Trial and error is great unless it kills you first and one-shot-learning is hard for ABC learners.

Popperian Creatures: Karl Popper argued that science permits our hypothesis to die in our stead. Popperian creatures use a filter or inner environment to try things out allowing for better pre-selection. The inner environment contains information about the outer environment and its regularities. They need information about the world, by inheritance or acquisition, so as to achieve pre-selective effects. The body itself could be a way of vetting possible options. This allows for latent learning, where knowledge is gained without being specifically rewarded by detectable reinforcement. Perception of the world allows for better models of it and hence better action selection.

Gregorian Creatures: Richard Gregory provides a theory on the role of information and potential intelligence. A pair of scissors is not just the result of intelligence but the endower of intelligence. Gregorian Creatures can use tools to better model the environment and hence make better selections. The preeminent tools are mind tools — words. Mind tools are inherited from culture and permit the construction of more subtle action testers. Mind tools allow for the exploitation of the experience of others.

Dennett goes on to discuss how we might have evolved to a state where we could collect and make use of various mind tools.

The Creation of Thinking

Dennett then offers a tantalizing vision for how we might have stumbled into our capacity for thought. The following are Dennett's thoughts on thought.

The breakthrough comes from systems that themselves adopt the intentional stance with others and themselves. You need to think in order to think about thinking. Might thinking bootstrap itself into existence? Either we used ourselves as a testing environment for the thoughts of others, or we got used to thinking about others (intentional stance) and noticed that one can subject oneself to the same treatment.

First-Order Intentional Systems have beliefs and desires about many things but not about beliefs and desires. Second-Order Intentional Systems have beliefs and desires about others' beliefs and desires or their own. The big step was going from first to second-order intentionality. Most animals are not mind-readers but use vast lookup tables in the form of conjunctions of conditionals (if you see x, do a). Mind reading arises when lookup tables get too large. Explicit generalization permits lists to be broken down and rebuilt on demand from first principles as new cases arise.

In the arms race of producing the future, an agent has a tremendous advantage if it can produce more of and a better future about other agents than they can produce about itself. At some point, an agent may need to communicate its behaviours to others. At such times it has to carve up its behaviour into clear-cut alternatives. By creating an explicit menu of options from which to choose, our agent has to some degree be taken in by its own creation.

Unless we need to communicate our reasons there is no selective pressure to represent those reasons. So opaquely is such knowledge hidden in our connectionist meshes that it is knowledge in the system but is not knowledge to the system. We are looking for rationales that can be represented in the nervous system, not just be governed by their design. What does a cuckoo need in order to exploit the wisdom in its neural networks? The popular answer is symbols. To anchor a free-floating rationale the agent must make a representation of its reason. How does an agent learn to do this?

Dennett offers a hypothesis for how language acquisition is achieved with an emphasis on spoken language. The argument is that a form of self-narration allows for the ability to first recognize a spoken word which acts as a placeholder for a concept. This concept can then be associated with the deep cognitive processes that are synchronous with these concepts (remember our previous discussion on the synchrony principle of binding). In this way, the agent can extract ancient knowledge trapped in its connectionist meshes in the form of symbols, which can then be used to model the behaviour of other agents and the agent itself.

Our Minds and Other Minds

Dennett now considers the last step in our journey, which is the transition of thought to the awareness of thought. He argues that agents may have been making and using representations but did not know they were doing so. They may have been thinking without knowing that they were thinking. Mental content becomes conscious by winning the competition against other mental content for domination in the control of behaviour. Since we are talkers, talking to ourselves is one of our most influential activities; one of the most effective ways for mental content to become influential is for it to get into a position to drive the language using parts of our controls.

What you are is just an organization of competitive activity between a host of competencies that your body has developed. You can talk about acts, events, and reasons, because you made them and they made you. You are the agent whose life you can talk about. You can tell us and you can tell yourself. Fantasy and self-description are what we do — it is what we are. Without a natural language, we have no way of wresting concepts from their interwoven connectionist nests and manipulating them. The polar bear has snow-how but that is not a wieldable concept.

But What Do Others Think?

Well, Dennett's arguments certainly leave one a tad short of breath. But before considering how such musings might be relevant to our beloved AI-Assistant's capacity for explanation, I would like to consider what Dennett's peers have to say on this topic. Legendary podcaster Sam Harris (https://www.samharris.org/podcasts) has recently published 14 of his most memorable interviews (Harris 2020). Conveniently, many of these conversations focus directly on the topic at hand. The following are a few takeaways that I think may help bring valuable context.

David Chalmers (#34 podcast — The Light of the Mind) resists Dennett's argument that our sense of consciousness is in many ways just an illusion. He agrees with Nagel's suggestion that a being is conscious if there is something that it is like to be that being. He makes the distinction between the easy problems (computer vision, machine learning, natural language processing …) and the hard problems — how the phenomenon of awareness of self and subjective experience can exist. He raises the possibility of pan-psychism, which is the idea that all things may pose some form of subjective experience at different levels and that this might simply be a property of the physical world. One such framework is Tononi's Integrated Information Theory (IIT) (Tononi 2004), which proposes that the capacity for subjective experience is a result of the integration of information. An example of such integration is the fact that certain parts of the mind appear to model other parts of the mind. Chalmers fears that consciousness might be epiphenomenal. That is to say, subjective experience might exist but may have no bearing on the actions taken by the agent.

David Deutsch (#52 podcast — Finding Our Way in the Cosmos) makes the argument that science is more than just empiricism and that sound argument is critical to the scientific method. One can argue that this has a direct bearing on an agent's ability to construct the free-floating rationale that explains the behaviour of an evolved agent such as the cuckoo bird. When confronted with the fear that our AI systems may one day achieve such epistemological superiority that they will know things that we cannot know, Deutsch argues that Turing's work on universal computation will be our salvation. Since all Turing machines are equivalent, there is nothing that is knowable by one Turing machine that cannot be known by another Turing machine.

Anil Seth (#113 podcast — Consciousness and the Self) argues that there are many aspects of self. Our experience of a volitional self might result from the perception of volition. This seems to be consistent with the argument that, at some point, the mind will apply the intentional stance not just to other agents but to itself. The act of modelling and hence predicting one's own behaviour provides a perception of volition and hence the experience of volition.

Thomas Metzinger (#96 podcast — The Nature of Consciousness) argues that the experience of self (phenomenology) is grounded in embodiment, which is a form of interoception. This seems to be consistent with Dennett's convictions that the mind is a construct of both brain and body. It may be the case that the embodiment defines what can be intrinsically meaningful and that all other meaning is established via analogy to such experience. This is similar to the intentional stance in Gibson's affordance theory, where the mind perceives objects in terms of what it can do with them. This leads to Metzinger's concept of an affordance landscape, where ideas emerge and are perceived in terms of what the mind can do with such thoughts. As we have previously discussed, a picture emerges of the mind wandering through a field of affording thoughts or ghost attractors.

David Krakauer (#40 podcast — Complexity and Stupidity) offers a down-to-earth definition of intelligence: the capacity to make a hard task look easy. For example, the AI Engineer can solve differential equations and, at a pinch, construct a bridge that can be used to ford a fearsome river. Similarly, at a cocktail party, the humanities researcher can readily come up with a witty Oscar Wilde reference or suggest the perfect chardonnay for an evening of fine dining. Krakauer makes note of a culture's ability to accumulate cognitive artefacts. For example, those who learn to use an abacus are not only able to perform complex calculations, but their brains can become rewired so that at some point they don't even need the abacus itself to perform these computational gymnastics. He noted how up until the 15th century, western Europe used Roman numerals, which were adequate for counting but useless for multiplication and division. Of course, base 10 systems such as those used in India and Persia since the 4th century make such tasks look easy. Cognitive artefacts seem to be the lifeblood of Dennett's Gregorian creatures.

Max Tegmark (#94 podcast — Frontiers of Intelligence) suggests that mathematicians are fundamentally in the business of studying the properties of mathematical structures. He notes the remarkable relationship between the physical world and mathematics and argues that the properties of physical structures are essentially mathematical in nature. Instead of inventing mathematical constructs, he argues that we discover them, leading to the idea that such entities have their own form of existence. He makes the point that like string theory, our understanding of consciousness remains elusive primarily because we don't yet have the mathematics for it.

To the Matter at Hand

Algorithmic Reasoning

Suman, you make the argument that the *do*-calculus is limited to mapping out the mechanisms associated with mechanical domino-like processes, where *a* causes *b* which causes *c* … but that there are a great many *why*-questions posed in everyday life which are not of this sort. By taking the intentional stance, I would argue that mechanisms such as *do*-calculus facilitate the construction of free-floating rationales irrespective of whether they provably apply. The reason for this is that unlike statistics, the *do*-calculus requires the hypothesis of some form of causal model. The odd thing is that such models do not need to have a physical manifestation and thus they may resist falsifiability by empiricism. Biologists are quick to point out that one can't prove that the reason the cuckoo bird commits fratricide is because of the advantages that it will receive, but it certainly allows us to explain and more importantly predict its behaviour. As David Deutsch points out, empiricism is not the be-all and end-all of science — sound reason is just as, if not more, important. The estimation of free-floating rationale, even if just a fiction, allows for the critical affordances associated with being able to predict the behaviour of real and pseudo-agents alike. Might it be the case that this ability to fabricate the reason why, even when there is no actual reason why, is at the heart of many of the *why*-questions that we wish our AI-Assistant may one day have the propensity to both ponder and pontificate on?

First Causes and Final Conditions

Suman, your consideration of first causes seems closely related to the idea of original and derived intentionality. As Dennett suggests, the intentionality of our thoughts and our experiences must be traced back to the intentionality of the mechanisms that forged us — Mother Nature and natural selection. I think that this idea is also related to the question of interoception and the assertion that all meaning must be derived from something that is intrinsically meaningful, which is the experience associated with embodiment. Your ideas of metaphor can then be used to map the intrinsic meaning of embodiment to the meaning of the external world at large and ultimately the metaphysical. As you may recall, in one of my previous interventions I describe how a sense of time and space might be meaningful to a vast array of oscillating neurons. In *Soul of an Octopus*, Sy Montgomery (2016) introduces us to a creature that can taste its environment across the entirety of its tentacles and has multiple brains operating in tandem. It appears that each tentacle seems to have its own personality ranging from shy and tentative to curious and bold. Is it even possible to imagine what meaning is accessible or attributable to such of our friends of the deep?

Since you suggest that Artificial General Intelligence (AGI) is the AI Engineer's vision of final conditions, I will highlight concerns raised by Sam Harris and Thomas Metzinger (in #96 podcast cited already).

Harris: It may be the case that an AGI will eclipse us, exterminate us but never achieve consciousness. The universe will have gone from lights-out to lights-on and back to lights-out.

Metzinger: Assuming the best-case scenario, an AGI will emerge that is wise, benevolent, and have our best interests at heart. The AGI may come to the conclusion that the reduction of misery is much more important than the optimization of happiness. It may conclude that due to evolutionary pressures, humanity is doomed to self-inflicted misery since our existence bias prevents us from exercising the most logical solution to our dilemma — self-termination. Out of a profound sense of mercy, it may then take matters into its own hands.

Lock-In

In addition to the Darwinian, Skinnerian, Popperian, and Gregorian creatures of the tower of generate-and-test, we should consider adding a new floor — Kuhnian creatures. These would be entities capable of causing a paradigm shift. As I described in our work on wolves and sheep, it appears that a given learning framework places limitations on the set of tactics and solutions that can be discovered. I would hazard to guess that a given paradigm similarly places restrictions on the set of explanations that can be discovered. Without opening a previously closed can of worms, it may be the case that a Kuhnian creature might have within it the kernel of creativity.

Listening and Attracting

Suman, while you ponder the implications of *do*-calculus, First Causes, Final Conditions, and Attractor states, might I suggest we throw into this cocktail Thomas Metzinger's notion of an affordance landscape?

Finally, as an AI Engineer, the consideration of possible historical developments constitutes a smorgasbord of tantalizing capabilities that can be explored and developed. How does one associate the tools of language with ancient knowledge trapped in connectionist meshes? How does an agent use such concepts to fabricate a free-floating rationale, which can explain the behaviour of true or mindless agents? How does an agent perform the Kuhnian act of paradigm shift, unleashing a flood of new and possibly creative explanations? If you, as a humanities researcher, had your druthers, what would you have us do first, second, and third? Of course, if you could provide an explanation for such choices, that would be grand.

Chapter 18

Three Models of Cogito

Suman Gupta

Fundamental Questions

There are many thought-provoking observations in your summary of Daniel Dennett's *Kinds of Minds*, Peter, and also among the summaries of the podcasts. It wasn't clear to me what their immediate bearing on our earlier discussion of explanation is, particularly in terms of envisaging our AI-Assistant. But, of course, a broader relevance shines forth, and has to do with the question: who or what undertakes explaining, what does this undertaking consist of, and why? The putative answer is: humans endowed with, and with the means structured by, consciousness/thought/mind/intentionality/agency. Dennett's book puts these terms in a system, and elaborates the processes involved in arriving at and then sustaining what those terms refer to. Among those processes explanations bask. Some of the others you mention offer related elaborations. By understanding explanation according to one of these, we could work out how to develop our AI-Assistant's explanatory capacity accordingly. To understand explanation, we have to first understand consciousness/thought/mind/intentionality/agency.

We have, of course, been here before — saying, 'such-and-such is consciousness/intentionality, etc.', and asking, 'what is consciousness/intentionality, etc.?' Naturally, this is not a juncture we can stop returning to and interrogating since it is the nub, the very core, of conceiving an AI-Assistant in our discussion. So, now you are saying: let's take one carefully systematized and well-elaborated account — Dennett's — and see what we can do with it. But I find myself reluctant to go along with that, because I find myself balking at the prospect of taking Dennett's system as given, even for expediency. Or, even as a game to play with. Nevertheless, I am prepared to think *with* your account of Dennett's system, more to get behind its preconceptions a bit, which is the same as getting behind general preconceptions about consciousness/thought/mind/intentionality/agency.

My stream-of-consciousness in response to your account of Dennett's account of consciousness went as follows.

Terms and the Idea

I start, as you might be expecting, with terms. In your account of Dennett's account, Peter, some distinctions are offered in elaborating these terms: 'consciousness', 'thought', 'mind', 'intentionality', 'agency'. However, they also all seem to slide and merge into each other to articulate one Idea — let's say, a condition of Being Human. These are all aspects of the Idea that allows us to speak of Being Human in one way; all the terms are but ways of speaking of this one Idea. Indeed, the Idea may just as well be represented at the same time by one of those terms or another, either 'consciousness' or 'thought' or 'mind' or 'intentionality' or 'agency', as if these terms are all more or less synonymous. At the same time though, there are received distinctions in ordinary language among these terms. Dennett hones and expands on those distinctions between the terms, and introduces categories within them, to present his system. That makes Dennett deep and rigorous, but the received ordinary-language distinctions generally hold within his rigorous elaborations.

With ordinary-language simplicity:

- 'Consciousness' is a state of being cognizant and responsive; for instance, as opposed to 'unconsciousness'.
- The 'mind' is that which is 'conscious', a repository and composite of 'consciousness'.
- 'Thought' is a process that happens by way of evincing 'consciousness' in the 'mind'.
- If the 'mind' has 'thought' which involves processing the possibility of acting in some way or for some purpose, that's 'intentionality'.
- The 'mind's' conviction that it can act according to 'intentionality' is its 'agency'.

These received ordinary language distinctions generally hold with Dennett's elaborations. There is something there that glues these terms together — 'consciousness', 'thought', 'mind', 'intentionality', 'agency' — but no one term in itself quite names this Idea they are all with regard to. 'Consciousness' comes close, but really, if one thinks about it, that is not quite 'intentionality' or 'agency' (despite Searle and Dennett).

Cogito

Let me propose a name for this Idea that holds all those terms together, and which all these terms are with regard to. This move of throwing in a new term has the advantage of making us pause on our habit of using those familiar terms as if they are so obviously meaningful that we don't need to pick at them. As if, in other words, although these familiar terms are all a bit different, they are all really kind of synonymous — which is obviously not the case. Taking a slightly unfamiliar term to link these also has the advantage of pinning a fairly precise meaning for our purpose, instead of dawdling opportunistically and confusingly between a cluster of aligned terms.

I suggest the quaint Latin term '*Cogito*'.

This will remind you, of course, of René Descartes' (2006 [1637]: 29) *cogito, ergo sum* ('*je pense, donc je suis*'; 'I am thinking, therefore I exist' or, more commonly, 'I think, therefore I am'), and rightly so, that's where I am coming from, too — but not by way of reiterating Descartes's dictum. In fact, I want to immediately forget the *ergo sum* and focus on the Latin term *Cogito* as a Latin term, without immediately switching to its standard English or Descartes's own initial French version. I propose this term less because of the Descartian association (which is not immaterial, however) and more because of the advantages of its Latin form.

Cogito is a first-person, present, active, indicative verb form of 'to think'. In Latin, such conjugation verbs have rather more variations than in English and convey meaning with somewhat different nuances. For *Cogito*, this means:

1. The first-person pronoun does not need to be put there, which avoids any confusion about concerning specific individuals (individuality) or being subjective. *Cogito* is not about the *person* who thinks, it is about *thinking* as generally and fundamentally possessive (thinking is implicitly somebody's thought). There is no subjectivity there, quite the contrary — it is an indicative and not a subjunctive.

2. This Latin conjugation verb form also puts a general emphasis on an *ongoing process* (present, active) without immediately splitting hairs about the kind of process or about the emphasis in declaring the process by the thinker. *Cogito* could equally be 'I think', 'I am thinking', 'I do think' — the point is the process of thinking itself.

Cogito then is thinking in the possessive but without foregrounding the thinking subject and as the process itself without giving it a declarative emphasis. This strikes me as a precise way of connoting the Idea at the nexus of all the terms mentioned above — 'consciousness', 'thought', 'mind', 'intentionality', 'agency'. These terms can make consistent sense with reference to it, whereas they slip variously in being referenced only to each other, more or less as follows:

- 'Consciousness' is the precondition which enables *Cogito*.
- 'Mind' is where *Cogito* is located.
- 'Thought' is *Cogito* as process.
- 'Intentionality' is *Cogito* with a direction or purpose.
- 'Agency' is the disposition of *Cogito* which renders consequent action conceivable.

However, if *Cogito* seems to be too grammatically foreign or desperately retro, you could now decide to stay with, say, 'consciousness' — so long as it is understood that by 'consciousness' we understand *Cogito* with its Latin sense. 'Consciousness' then is not the obverse of a putative 'unconsciousness' but simply the *Cogito*.

Taking *Cogito* as understood thus, we can reflect on Dennett's and other such elaborations of those terms further. I suggest doing so by considering that there are three possible models of *Cogito* — or three models of 'consciousness', if that makes you happier, insofar as that is understood as *Cogito*.

Cogito Model 1

The *Cogito* is a composite condition of being. Its presence can be variously manifested: e.g., by using language, by evincing calculated intentions, by acting to realize intentions, by showing a propensity to learn, by making and using tools. All these are symptoms of the presence of *Cogito*.

The *Cogito* is experienced as constitutive by its possessor — its subject. That is to say, it is experienced by those who embody the *Cogito* as being conscious, aware, feeling, knowing, observing, inferring, intending, rationalizing, learning, communicating, etc. This model of the *Cogito* is understood at present as peculiarly manifested by humans and being the experience of humans: in some sense, humanness is the presence of the *Cogito* (which is pretty close to Descartes's dictum). As such, the *Cogito* is quite a precarious condition of being. Its emergence through the evolutionary pathway, its place amidst the collective of the *Cogito* (*Cogitamus*), its effect on environmental processes and *vice versa*, etc., are variously circumscribed and even determined by factors which are not-*Cogito* and perhaps even anti-*Cogito*. At the same time, the apprehension of this precarity is only possible from within the *Cogito*, which may well mean that *Cogito* is unable to perceive its limitations and restraints. *Cogito* deals with its circumscribed presence by dividing itself into several types ...

I could carry on pulling that chain of elaborations, and this would become, I suspect, not dissimilar to Dennett's account by your account, Peter.

Cogito Model 2

There is no *Cogito*. A composite and integral *Cogito* is ultimately based solely on the *experience* of those who feel they are constituted by it — humans. To formulate a composite *Cogito* thus is not much different from fetishizing being human. It amounts to humans appointing themselves as being normatively at the top of the evolutionary ladder. That's kind of like a scientist saying, 'God created man in his own image'. Understanding *Cogito* thus is replete with the human experience of self (labelled 'conscious', 'intentional', 'with agency', etc.) and setting a standard or ideal for understanding other possible conditions of being.

However, *Cogito* as an anthropocentric experience cannot be meaningfully normative because we have no access to any other kind of experience or a different *Cogito* — say, a dolphin's or a dog's or an AI-Assistant's. In the absence of such access, we simply presume that there is human *Cogito* as one kind of thing and the absence thereof is non-human.

The only sensible way of considering *Cogito* without fetishizing humans is to depend not on human experience but on observation of the behaviours and expressions of various animals, including humans. In this respect, the presumption of a composite *Cogito* is largely unnecessary. However, insofar as *Cogito* has been persistently assumed and factorized, we might have useful material to deconstruct the concept of *Cogito* and bring some of the associated factors into a measured perspective. It is assumed, for instance, that *Cogito* can be equated to certain kinds of observable behaviours, such that {*Cogito*} = {[A] [B] [C] [D] [E] ...} where

[A] is the ability to recognize oneself in a mirror,
[B] is the ability to convey information with abstract signs,
[C] is the ability to represent objects in pictorial form,
[D] is the ability to infer general principles from experiences and employ them repeatedly,
[E] is the ability to use raw materials for producing implements and affordances,

and so on. The factors in question can be graded and observed according to a range of behaviours of different animal species, including humans. Doing that is unlikely to reiterate the preconception of a composite *Cogito* but would probably say quite a lot about what it is to be human in relation to other species of the animal kingdom (and possibly in relation to a hypothetical AI-Assistant).

The co-presence of such factors in humans, and their overlapping and mutual bearing, encourage us to lump them together as a peculiarly human *Cogito*. If we put that aside, in themselves such factors as [A], [B], [C], etc. may exist to different degrees and in different combinations in different species — along some pattern of adaptations and evolutionary proximity. That would mean that [A], [B], [C], etc. could each present a spectrum, and their combinations also allow for spectrums, within and across species. If so, instead of the anthropocentric *Cogito* we could perhaps consider a third-person pluralistic and distributed spectrum of *Cogitant*.

Cogito Model 3

As a concept, *Cogito* is actually a human social construct masquerading as biologically underpinned and serves calculations internal to human social relations.

Let me invoke the notion of 'species recognition', or rather, specifically, intra-species recognition: the ability of members of one species to recognize others as such for procreative and interactive (cooperative or individualistic) ends. In terms of biological validity — i.e., supported by empirical evidence of the existence, means, and functions of such recognition — this notion has run into hot water. Its uselessness is, for instance, persuasively argued by Mendelson and Shaw (2012), which involves questioning the validity of 'species' as a category. Insofar as the biological concept is allowed, one may observe that its boundaries are, in any case, fluid. The biological basis of demarcating species could be infringed by behaviouristic observations of species (mis)recognition — think of all those baby ducks imprinting humans, records of feral children raised by animals, or animals of one species adopting those of another. However, I invoke 'species recognition' not to pretend any understanding of biological determinants, but to hazard a model of *Cogito* as a social construct which has been, so to speak, biologized.

Perhaps, *Cogito* is proposed as a fundamental basis of human beings so as to be able to manoeuvre social relations. In this sense, *Cogito* is as much possessed as attributed. That is to say, to recognize oneself as human is to recognize others as human in the self-same moment by constructing a joint composite of humanness which is *Cogito*. [Much philosophical reflection on this point is available, but let's not go there.] *Cogito* is made out to be coincident with the biogenetic human and the fundamental human consciousness, so the necessary predicate for human species recognition. However, once made up, it then functions by a mechanics of reattributions and deattributions for negotiating social relations. In this regard, I find myself particularly interested in 'dehumanization', which involves some humans not recognizing or accepting other humans as such. This is, admittedly, a somewhat diffuse notion, but intensively addressed in scholarly terms. I found myself recently pondering the essays in *The Routledge Handbook of Dehumanization* (Kronfeldner 2021). It seemed to me arguable that at the base the concept might have to do with deattributions, and partial or qualified attributions of *Cogito* to some groups of humans by others. In fact, it seems possible that the very construction of *Cogito* is to enable deattributions and reattributions by way of negotiating social relations. *Cogito* may be more a product of social relations while seeming (and by seeming) to be the pre-given basis of human species recognition.

Implications?

Let me leave the three models of *Cogito* — or of 'consciousness' — there for you to consider. Which, if any, do you incline towards? What implications may these have on our discussion of explanation? And for conceiving our ideal AI-Assistant?

Chapter 19

Puppets and Insects

Peter Tu

Suman, let me start by providing an explanation for why I introduced Dennett's work on the Intentional Stance in the context of our discussion of explanation. First, estimation of the free-floating rationale of a learned behaviour is an explanation of why an agent does what it does even if the agent does not know why it does what it does. Our unique power of explanation allows us to observe a fledgling cuckoo bird dispose of its foster siblings and for the first time understand why. Second, if one can explain why other agents '*do what they do*', one can then turn such scrutiny on oneself and start explaining why '*one does what one does*' and in so doing become oneself. From this perspective, explanation becomes a central figure in our cognitive experience. Let me now turn to your models of Cogito, which I have taken the liberty of renaming in a slightly more descriptive manner.

Model 1: Cogito as Phenomenon (CP)

Suman, in CP you provide a fantastic laundry list of properties that we associate with the phenomenon of consciousness. To round things out, let me remind the readers of a similar list proposed by John Searle (1998):

- *Qualitativeness*: Every conscious state has a certain qualitative feel to it.

197

- *Subjectivity*: Conscious states only exist when they are experienced by some human or animal subject. In that sense, they are essentially subjective. Because conscious states are subjective in this sense, they have what can be called a 'first person ontology (mode of existence)' as opposed to a third-person ontology of mountains and molecules which are independent of people. They are experienced by some 'I' that has the experience which places it in the first person.
- *Unity*: All conscious experiences at any given point in an agent's life come as part of one unified conscious field. You cannot have subjectivity and qualitativeness without unity.
- *Binding problems*: For example, the visual system binds all of the different stimuli into a single unified visual percept.
- *Other features include*: Intentionality, a distinction between the centre and periphery of attention, all conscious experience is in some mood or other, all states can project onto the pleasure/unpleasure dimension, gestalt structure — ability to organize degenerate stimuli into perceptual forms and familiarity.

Searle and others have argued that CP might in fact be a consequence of the nature of matter. When material entities undergo a phase shift from solid to liquid or liquid to gas, these substances exhibit different properties. In this way, a state of consciousness might be a result of a phase shift that causes properties such as subjectivity and qualitativeness to be manifested. The Qualia researchers that we have previously discussed appear to have similar views (Gupta and Tu 2020: Chs. 26–27). Going forward, Searle suggests that we focus on (i) searching for the neurobiological events that are correlated with consciousness (NCC), (ii) testing to see that the correlation is a genuine causal relationship, and (iii) developing a theory that would formalize such causal relationships.

Others raise questions regarding the limits of computation itself. As you may recall from our discussion of Alan Turing's work, there is a difference between intractability and incompatibility. An example of the intractable is the travelling salesman problem. As the dimension of the problem increases (the number of locations that need to be visited by the salesman in an optimal fashion), the amount of computational power needed to solve such problems grows exponentially. An example of incommutability is the fact that while the computable numbers are enumerable, they cannot be enumerated. These arguments (the mysterious qualities of matter and the limits of computation) have been used to sabotage the idea of general Artificial Intelligence resulting from algorithmic development or arising from some sort of self-organizing emergent behaviour. Our AI-Assistant might simply not be made of the right stuff.

I am in favour of having the physicists doing whatever it takes to orchestrate ever more spectacular collisions between their subatomic particles. The neuroscientists should by all means continue to dissect their cats. We will see where both camps are in five or six generations from now. But for those of us who are less patient, I say let's for now put aside the CP model and consider a more optimistic paradigm.

Model 2: Cogito as Illusion (CI)

Dennett is, of course, forever tied to his conviction that consciousness is an illusion. Dennett describes Cogito as the result of an aggregation of processes. In this way, Cogito can be seen as a battle between various subconscious mechanisms as they vie for control of the helm. Like a conjurer's trick, by unearthing these mechanisms, we reveal the illusion and once one knows how the trick is done, the veneer of intelligence seems to slip away. Maybe this is one of the reasons that many of us cling so tightly to the CP model.

Despite this lack of showmanship, CI certainly seems to be the most viable path for our AI-Assistant. But what about free will? If deliberation is just a process and self is just an explanation of why one does what one does — a kind of cuckoo bird with narration, where does this leave us? I think the pragmatists have an interesting point. The fact that determinism lurks around every corner should not stop us from believing in free will. As we have previously discussed, intentional entities take actions in order to achieve desirable outcomes. If scientists are not convinced of a hypothesis, they might not perform the experiments needed to prove it. If one is being chased by a bear and is faced with taking a jump across a 6-foot chasm, the consequence of not believing that one can make such a leap and simply giving up is certain death. If one does not believe that one has free will and thus elects to abdicate responsibility for one's actions, one may find oneself in an evolutionary dead end. When it comes to survival, actions are far more important than clarity of thought and so we must believe what we must believe.

Setting aside deterministic angst for these pragmatic reasons, a few concerns might yet remain for would-be captains of their own destinies such as: as members of society, just how free are we? This, of course, takes us to our third and final model.

Model 3: Cogito as Social Construct (CSC)

We perceive the world through collective eyes. Our object–subject spectrum seems to be informed by a kind of communal consensus. The American Constitution provides an equation for personhood (status as subject) along the lines of:

$$p = f + (1 - f)\frac{3}{5}$$

where p is a measure of personhood ranging from 0 to 1 and f is a measure of one's legal state as a free v. enslaved entity (also ranging from 0 to 1). The odious phrase 'aping the manners of one's betters' comes to mind. In *The Status Game*, Will Storr (2021) describes how much of human behaviour is driven by motivation to increase one's social status. In this way, physical desire can be viewed as a means for acquiring the increased social status that can be conferred, via association, by those that society deems as desirable.

We are constantly being rewired to like what we perceive others like. We easily believe what we perceive others to believe. Our wolf and sheep experiments demonstrate the idea of how the Imagined We allows for cooperation to manifest. The idea is that if each agent attempts to infer what 'We' want it to do and acts upon such intentions, then 'We' emerge via a means of gradual consensus. One could argue that belief may be achieved through a similar process. Each agent must simply attempt to infer what 'We' believe to be true and then adopt such beliefs. Truth and conceptual meaning are thus a result of gradual communal consensus. These mechanisms appear to be rampant in today's milieu as we consider vaccination efforts, proliferation of conspiracy theories, fear of Satanists, FaceBook and, of course, religion.

A Bend in the Road

My pet peeve with religion is phrases such as, 'Humans were made in the image of God.' With an all-powerful supernatural entity, our existence seems inevitable. However, there is nothing inevitable about us. The fact that we exist is astonishing. We have each won the lottery of all lotteries. I question the premise of the Fermi proposition; maybe the reason that the universe is so quiet is that intelligence is spectacularly improbable. Either the universe is teeming with intelligence, or we are the only game in town — either state is remarkable. Instead of marvelling at the pageantry of a universe with sentience, we seem to be continually overwhelmed by the banality of our existence. It seems that one of the prices of the CSC model is that we find ourselves pining away in a meaningless universe. But as the existentialists point out, if our deities have drifted away, then we are left with the uncomfortable spectre of nihilism.

Let's take a step back from the abyss. The universe is approximately 13.772556 billion years old and, according to Julian Jaynes (2000 [1976]), for the first 13.772553 billion years, there was nothing in the universe that was capable of appreciating its meaninglessness. Now that the universe has sentience, maybe the next 13.772556 billion years can be spent filling it with meaning. With this long-game perspective, the philosopher's obsession with meaning might be similar to a chess player attempting an end-game strategy just one or two moves after the start of the game. Given that the board has just been set, what should be our opening moves?

Like an attractor state, a theme that we seem to return to time and again is that where there is ambiguity, there is room for creativity. We have seen how this is the case for both mathematics and metaphors. In her book *The Ethics of Ambiguity*, Simone de Beauvoir (1948) contemplates the ambiguous nature of our existence. Instead of discovering meaning, we may have to take on the task of creating it. Unfortunately, the bus that brought us here might not be sufficient for the next leg of our journey. The cauldron of evolution has instilled in us a kind of pathological pettiness that does not seem conducive to the task at hand. Like Pinocchio, we might need a Jiminy Cricket to help us with our metamorphic journey to Nirvana. Naturally, I have in mind our beloved AI-Assistant.

Suman, even from a distance I can hear your cries for caution and restraint, we need to rein in our horses, walk before we run, and of course, define our terms. So, instead of trying to win the (gender-neutral honorific) Universal Beauty pageant in one go, let's start with a lesser title, something along the lines of (gender-neutral honorific) Congeniality. The idea being that we might have to be more gracious before attaining some sort of cosmic state of grace. The lovely and talented Edith Kemp once quipped, 'I would rather have my partner trump my aces than have rudeness at the Bridge table.'

Suman, what are your thoughts on how AI-Assistant might help us usher in a new age of civility?

Part 4

Civility

Chapter 20

Civil Mores and Concerns

Suman Gupta

Peter — It is good of you to desist from taking a 32-billion-year perspective of our little human enterprises and, moreover, to favour optimism about these. Very civil of you. The bend in the road you propose is congenial to me, so let me take it straightaway. I do not start by commenting on your thoughts about models of Cogito. That's not because you have had the final word and nor because they haven't stimulated me; I suspect that taking this bend will lead us back to those models in any case. At this bend, you have put up the rather grandiose street sign: 'how may our AI-Assistant help usher in a new age of civility?'

Do we need a new age of civility? What's amiss with our current age of civility? And what have AI-Assistants to do with the current age of civility and why should we call upon *them* — rather than calling upon, say, our all-too-human selves — to help a new age to dawn?

To begin unpacking such questions, I take three small steps: propose some working arguments about civility/incivility, so that we are on the same page; consider whether there is a particular civility-deficit/incivility-excess at present and what AI-Assistants have to do with that; and consider the next steps.

Civility/Incivility

Let me start with some simple definitions, which are likely to seem acceptable to many. At any given juncture, a complex system called

'Society' [*S*] subscribes to sets of rules/norms/practices or {RNP}s whereby conflict can be minimized. It is expected that any {RNP} could, if followed consistently, give rise to a conflict-free 'civil society' [CS]. That is the ideal though; *S* is constitutively a system in which this ideal state is often imagined and reimagined and never quite obtained. There are at least three, and probably many more, considerations which deter the appearance of any finished version of CS:

- Any given {RNP} is subject to internal variances and deviations.
- Typically, *S* at any juncture (S_t) has multiple {RNP}s which do not necessarily gel, i.e., concurrent ${RNP}_a$ and ${RNP}_b$ are apt to work against each other in some ways.
- Every juncture of *S* over time — i.e., from S_{t1} to S_{t2} to S_{t3} ⋯ — introduces new {RNP}s and modifies existing {RNP}s.

Given that *S* is constitutively such, the prevalence or want of general social civility is largely a perceptual matter. If in S_t the dominant perception is that the existing {RNP}s are enabling low conflict, we feel that we are near enough to CS; if it seems that the existing {RNP}s are exacerbating conflict — perhaps because of one or the other of the three points above — then we feel caught in an age of incivility.

My terms are admittedly vague. Vagueness is in the nature of this area. Terms like 'conflict', 'norms', 'practices', etc. are generally used flexibly but in ways that are sufficiently understood to not call for constant redefinition. Nevertheless, I could sharpen my terms by giving some synonyms and near-equivalents:

- 'Rules' incorporate terms and ideas like 'laws', 'conventions', 'guidelines', 'principles', etc.
- 'Norms' are equivalent to 'values', 'standards', etc.
- 'Practices' refer to 'habits', 'behaviours', 'actions', etc.

In the opening statements above, the term 'conflict' carries some hefty baggage. The perception of civility/incivility depends upon the prevalence of conflict. The received senses of 'conflict' are best disaggregated into:

- *Incidence* of conflict, in terms of which we recognize degrees of civility/incivility. That could be: tangible incidence of confrontations, protests, abuse, coercion, crimes, unnatural deaths, etc.; or intangible incidence of suffering, restrictions, indignity, etc.

- *Causes* of conflict, which determine the appearance of civility/incivility: e.g., conditions which enable/disable one part of S to offend/harm another part; arrangements which lead/deter one part of S to exploit/repress another part; paucities and sufficiencies in environmental and material conditions in S.

Unfortunately, these terms are as often contested as considered self-evidently meaningful. On the one hand, there are relative valences: e.g., what one person may consider offensive/harmful may not seem so to another; what is generally considered civility in some group may appear to be incivility to others. On the other hand, even where there is agreement on such terms, their consequences are not easily fixed to ensure the over-all stability of an {RNP}. For instance, it is quite possible for certain obviously offensive or harmful acts in terms of an {RNP} to nevertheless be necessary for that {RNP} to be sustained. Such conundrums are commonplace in ethical deliberations, and I am certain you can come up with examples ... let's not digress here.

By approaching civility/incivility thus, I am trying to avoid narrowing my view to one or another {RNP} or S, or CS, and to keep my observations open to different stages of history, cultural contexts, belief systems, political ideologies, juridical codes. I am not at all sure that I am actually managing to do this. No doubt there will be those who contend that I have already implicitly subscribed to a specific {RNP}. But let me carry on. My momentary feeling of insecurity here has an understandable basis. It has to do with considering: how do {RNP}s come about?

For that question, there are three prolifically discussed ways to go, where each way is roughly in line with one of the three models of *Cogito* we considered earlier.

- A great many {RNP}s are considered to be simply received or as appearing without premeditation. The obvious instances of simply received {RNP}s are the religious: i.e., given by a supernal intelligence or imbued within Nature. In an irreligious mould, {RNP}s may be conceived as emerging through long and slow evolutionary processes and social adaptations, without premeditation. An interesting variant of the latter considers {RNP}s as imbued in language itself: i.e., grounded in linguistic structures and communicative practices so that our ability to speak to and understand each other is premised on them. By this argument, {RNP}s have been embedded in language gradually through our constant efforts to communicate with each other and establish our collective templates. That is broadly the view underpinning Grice's conversational maxims, which we touched upon earlier, and various areas of conversation analysis since. All these versions of the notion that {RNP}s are simply received or emerge gradually gel with what you called the *Model 2 Cogito-as-Illusion (CI)* in your previous intervention.

- Some of the dominant {RNP}s of our time are conceived as rational systems to realize the CS we would like to have — so, intentional rational systems. Much recent philosophical ethics (let's say, G.E. Moore's *Principia Ethica* [1903] onwards) takes this direction. More significantly, this has been, particularly in stages from the 18th century and worldwide, the basis of modern political governance and jurisprudence. This is strongly associated with liberal and social democratic political philosophies and rule-of-law codes. By this account, certain first principles/axioms which cohere with desired CS and the-way-we-are are identified, and from those a coherent {RNP} is inferred and then carefully installed into formal/informal arrangements for S_t, and then updated in logical ways at subsequent junctures S_{t1}, S_{t2}, and onwards. This approach is akin to what you described as *Model 1 Cogito-as-Phenomenon (CP)*.

- It has been plausibly argued that specific {RNP}s surface and drown and vie with each other according to competing group interests at S_t. At S_t, each {RNP} — such as {RNP}$_a$, {RNP}$_b$, etc. — represents the desired CSs of different groups. The dominant and ruling {RNP} prevails according to the CS conceived by the dominant group at S_t. The many {RNP}s at S_t may variously be simply received, gradually formed, rationally and intentionally inferred, but the dynamic at work is not led by those considerations. What matters is dominance and power play in S_t. In this sense, functionally {RNP}s are socially constructed according to group dynamics and power plays. This approach coheres with what you dubbed *Model 3 Cogito-as-Social-Construct (CSC)*.

Probably, these three ways for {RNP}s to come about crisscross and somehow congeal into the functioning {RNP}s of our time.

The Civility/Incivility of AI-Assistants

A question I posed at the onset: is there a particular civility-deficit/ incivility-excess at present and what do AI-Assistants have to do with that?

To the first part of that question (is there a particular civility-deficit/incivility-excess?), I do not have a ready answer. If we consider the current juncture of Society (S_c) in comparison to whatever seems like preceding or past junctures (e.g., S_p), we may come up with an answer. Or probably several answers, depending on which parameter for the incidence and causes of conflicts we chose to compare — such as crimes, confrontations, coercions at S_c compared to S_p. Alternatively, we can work backwards, i.e., take the dominant sought-after CS according to the dominant {RNP} in S_c as the standard and try to work out accordingly why and where civility-deficits are occurring. Either way, we need some parameters to articulate whether civility-deficits are occurring and, therefore, as you put it, a 'new age of civility' is called for, which suggests that some new {RNP} has to become dominant.

Well ... you said it, so it's for you to clarify where the deficits are and by what parameters.

Having said that, I am ready to concede that there's a widely held perception of significant civility-deficits in our S_c. The newspapers tell us so daily, reporting surges of misinformation and deception, unresolvable value conflicts, many macro to micro levels of aggressive confrontations, growing inequality, sophisticated modes of coercion and exploitation, all exacerbated by our depleting natural resources and burgeoning demands on them ... Many feel that things are now worse compared to some preceding juncture. And, moving on to the second part of that question (what do AI-Assistants have to do with all that?), there is also a strong perception that AI-Assistants have quite a lot to do with the appearance of these civility-deficits.

Let me narrow our enquiry down then. Instead of considering (as you seem to suggest):

> There are all these ways in which civility-deficits are occurring in our age of incivility; how can AI-Assistants serve to alleviate those deficits and usher in a new age of civility?

let us turn to a more modest consideration:

> It is widely held that the presence and prospects of AI-Assistants are themselves causing certain civility-deficits to appear and are generating the prevailing age of incivility; what can we do about that?

So, not quite your grandiose street-sign, Peter. Let's not consider how AI-Assistants will solve our civility problems, but focus on the extent to which AI-Assistants are generating our civility problems.

To that end, there's a distinction to register in how AI-Assistants are thought of. One approach is future-gazing, contending that AI-Assistants will come to fruition and become autonomous agents, and that needs to be factored into {RNP}s in a preparatory way. That is to say, new {RNP}s may need to be formulated in anticipation. I think of this as an **AI**-Assistant conception. Much philosophical and juridical speculation on 'AI ethics' is in this vein, often virtuoso performances of scholarly goodness and justness on behalf of these autonomous agents-to-be. We have paused on some of the arguments in that vein earlier (such as arguments from 'personhood', Gupta and Tu 2020: Chs. 21–24). Let's not go there again; let's put aside this kind of 'AI ethics' for AI-Assistants in relation to civility/incivility.

The other direction approaches AI-Assistants as already at large, beavering away amidst our lives, and thereby themselves upping or bringing about deficits of civility in terms of our dominant {RNP}s. I think of this as an AI-**Assistant** conception. In the main, the point of arguments in this vein is not to come up with new {RNP}s but to hang on to and revitalize our existing dominant {RNP}s amidst the ongoing and really-very-convenient workings of AI-**Assistants**.

Impressionistically, there seem to be two principal thrusts to arguments/ observations suggesting that AI-**Assistants** are generating civility-deficits/ incivility-excesses:

- *Argument* 1: AI-**Assistants** are designed to *amplify existing incivilities* in unanticipated and uncontrollable ways. They make little incivilities big ones and increase an aggregate of social incivility, working against the aspirations to CS based on {RNP}s in our S_c. AI-**Assistants** spread misinformation quickly, escalate the giving and taking of offence, intensify condemnations and abuse, infringe upon privacy, record trivial misdemeanours for perpetual retrieval, etc. — by following their algorithmic steps while collating data in a globally networked environment. At the same time, the possibility that AI-**Assistants** may also amplify civility seems relatively unconvincing, with barely discernible evidence thereof. They enhance convenience, yes; civility, not really.

- *Argument* 2: AI-**Assistants** are often designed to *covertly serve elite and exploitative interests* in S_c. In that sense, too, they are generating new kinds of incivility. Data gathered from the small activities of unwitting consumers/participants can be stealthily capitalized to the latter's detriment and for the benefit of those elite and exploitative interests. This is because the elites — the rich and powerful — ultimately own and control the core hardware and software that AI-**Assistants** are deployed within. In this regard, of course, the opposite is also often argued: i.e., that AI-**Assistants** can also be used by those who oppose those interests. Moreover, it is frequently urged that the elites are not necessarily exploitative and may deploy (indeed always claim to deploy) AI-**Assistants** for the common good. But the latter is a conditional argument. Since the core hardware and software are owned by elites, those opposing their uncivil self-interested doings have the odds stacked against them. Insofar as elites claim to deploy AI-**Assistants** to serve the common good, that is a question of trust — how far can trust go? Should we depend upon the elites to be selfless, altruistic, and … more than superficially civil?

There is, evidently, widespread concern about AI-**Assistants** both amplifying and generating incivility in terms of dominant {RNP}s in S_c. These concerns have led to fraught deliberations about 'consent', 'privacy', 'equity', 'common good', 'reliable information', 'trust', etc. — all terms which have a seminal, linked-up place in the dominant {RNP}s of our time. These form the basis of legitimate, or at least acceptable, governance and jurisprudence. The strength of such anxieties indicates that most are loath to modify or replace currently dominant {RNP}s.

Much discussion threaded around those terms, in fact, suggests that AI-**Assistants** are intrinsically *uncivil by design*. They are designed to operate in largely incomprehensible and uncontrollable ways, by stealth, non-consultatively, to intractable ends, in unavoidable and mandatorily imposed setups, while offering the allure of immediate conveniences and pleasures.

What Is to Be Done?

It's a familiar question in troubled times, 'What is to be done?'. By raising it I am not shoving you towards the spirit of Nikolay Chernishevsky and V.I. Lenin. Rather, I am posing it with down-to-earth earnestness: what can we do by way of designing our friendly AI-Assistant to counter the incivility that AI-**Assistants** are often charged with?

Put differently: can we conceive of AI-Assistants that are civil by design? Can we have AI-Assistants that are designed to be consultative, transparent, supportive of moderation, protective of privacy, amenable to functional comprehension, productive of equity and trust, etc.?

When I say, 'can we ...', I obviously mean 'can you ...' — and that's where this intervention ends, expecting your response to soothe all those anxieties away and revitalize civility with (and via) our AI-Assistants.

Chapter 21

A Question of Allegiance

Peter Tu

Suman, I like the way you have framed our discussion in terms of how the Rules, Norms, and Practices {RNP}s of a Society (S) are determinative of its level of conflict and that a Civil Society (CS) is one that has achieved a minimal state of such strife. Your speculations regarding how {RNP}s may come to pass make sense. You suggest that I should clarify where our current deficits are and by what parameters — I will attempt this shortly. You then argue that AI-Assistants are already at large and that instead of attempting to soothe our angry souls, they are instead intent upon eroding our {RNP}s by appealing to our worst angels. Instead of being agents of civility, that are in fact modern-day *provocateurs*. I think you are primarily alluding to the various algorithms that inhabit our social media networks, as described by Jonathan Haidt (2022). Mechanisms such as the 'like' button prey upon our insatiable desire for status (Storr 2021). As a result, pleasant correspondence has become a kind of duplicitous performance. Algorithms such as GPT3 crank out content on arbitrary subjects and tone so as to serve those who wish to win the argument via quantity instead of quality — more on this later. You then rightly ask what I and my AI engineering clan propose to do. I would argue that the problem is not so much what these AI-Assistants are but rather who they serve. To this end, I contemplate an AI-Assistant devoted to the needs of each and possibly every member of S as opposed to platform providers, advertising firms, and demagogues. To begin with, let me consider your first question regarding what might be lacking in S today.

The Times, They Are a Changing ...

Robert Putnam (2010) proposes the idea of social equity which can be thought of as a measure of how connected we are to members of our community. This variable considers the frequency and depth of interaction with persons such as our neighbours, local tradespersons, and leaders. Based on a set of proposed measures, Putnam observes that over the last 70 years American social equity has steadily declined. Various factors appear to be contributing to this trend.

1. Where we live, where we work, and where we make our purchases are on average 30 miles apart. The odds of encountering the same salesclerk at the supermarket are so small that it makes little sense to develop a lasting relationship with such individuals.
2. On average, we spend 6 hours a day watching television or other screen-related activities.
3. Social clubs, where one has an opportunity to forge relationships with individuals such as the local plumber, are on the verge of extinction.
4. In the 1950s, one in every three married couples was part of a bridge foursome. Current trends indicate that in the next few years, the game of bridge may come to an end.
5. While bowling remains one of the most popular American pastimes, participation in official leagues is at an all-time low — we are simply bowling alone.

On the bright side, it appears that measures of racism are inversely proportional to social equity. The author argues that this has less to do with increased tolerance for one another and more to do with our ability to simply avoid and ignore.

David Brooks (2016) argues that the reason that shortcomings such as sloth, lust, jealousy, and anger are referred to as the 'deadly sins' is that in earlier times such failings were in fact deadly. The offspring of unindustrious caregivers could easily become impoverished and destitute. The victims of lust may be expelled from polite society and left with few and possibly perilous options. Given that we are all born with an assortment of shortcomings, one of the missions of society was to address these failings via the process of character building. However, one of the great accomplishments of modern liberal society is the emergence of affluence, tolerance, and the modern welfare state. As a consequence, the deadly sins are not so deadly anymore. The question that Brooks raises is that without the consequences associated with immorality, what impetus do we have to march down the road to character? Might it be the case that the road to character is just a set of {RNP}s? Might it also be the case that like a vestigial organ, {RNP}s suffer from the 'use it or loose it' phenomenon? If so, how might our AI-Assistant get us back on to the road to character?

As I have previously suggested, it is my thought that the AI-Assistant could become the Jiminy Cricket to our Pinocchio. Let's start this vignette with a few brush strokes. That is to say, I want to repeat the argument that instead of serving the interests of the good and the great, it is my belief that the priority of the AI-Assistant must be that of the ham and eggery. Instead of internet algorithms, I will begin by focusing on an AI-Assistant that could be a bit more visceral, something that can manifest in our daily lives. Let me begin with some background regarding what real-world capabilities an AI-Assistant could possess via the technology of today. I will then provide speculations on what an AI-Assistant could become.

A Real-World AI-Assistant of Today

One can easily envision one manifestation of the AI-Assistant as a kind of wearable system that has sufficient awareness of the subject's current circumstances to allow it to advise, intervene, and take actions in a constructive manner. We thus begin with the question of awareness. In terms of physical awareness, there are objects in the environment such as pieces of furniture, vehicles, and household items. The ability to accurately detect such artefacts falls into the realm of generic object recognition. Today, banks of deep learning models have been constructed allowing for the rapid detection and segmentation of a myriad of commonly encountered objects. The terrain itself is also something that can be directly captured via range sensors such as LADAR. Terrain may also be inferred via a method known as Simultaneous Localization and Mapping (SLAM), which I describe as follows. As a person-borne camera moves from location to location, interest points such as corners and discontinuities are tracked over time. The computer must then determine where such points and the associated camera positions must have been in order to have observed such space–time trajectories. In this way, the 3D structure of the environment and the evolution of the person-borne camera location is determined. For more details regarding the ability to infer 3D structure from uncalibrated imagery, see Yang *et al.* (2016: 180). Much of what I have just described constitutes the functionality that driverless cars must possess if they are to succeed in their mission. However, in addition to physical awareness, I would argue that our AI-Assistant will require a modicum of social awareness.

As part of the DARPA SSIM program, my colleagues and I have developed the Sherlock system (Tu *et al.* 2015). The goal of Sherlock is to infer group-level social states using standoff vision-based technologies. The system makes use of multiple fixed and Pan Tilt Zoom cameras allowing for the following capabilities:

1. Multi-person-multi-camera tracking is used to determine the location of individuals in observed crowds.
2. Pan Tilt Zoom cameras are automatically targeted on to individuals of interest.
3. Body poses in terms of key point locations (head, shoulders, elbows, hands, hips, knees, and feet) are automatically extracted resulting in skeleton models of observed individuals.
4. Facial expression and gaze direction are also computed for all subjects.

These cues are used to compute a set of social signals associated with concepts such as proximity, eye contact, and emotion. Regression methods are then used to compute social states such as group-level rapport, trust, and hostility. A series of experiments were performed where social scientists were asked to evaluate the level of rapport achieved by a group of play-actors and volunteers. It was shown that the estimates made by Sherlock were positively correlated with those made by the social scientists. This work continues today on projects where:

1. we hope to better understand the interactions between police officers and members of the public, and
2. we hope to discover and subsequently recognize a variety of culturally specific visual social cues.

While my efforts have been focused on visual analysis, my colleagues are making use of modern Natural Language Processing (NLP) methods allowing for similar analysis of audio channels. I would argue that in this way our AI-Assistant may one day have the ability to recognize various facets of S's {RNP}s as they manifest in day-to-day interactions in the physical world. The next consideration is whether or not AI-Assistants can learn how to act in accordance with our {RNP}s.

My colleagues and I have developed a synthetic Avatar which must learn how to convince subjects to take desired actions, such as enter a store or purchase a piece of merchandise. To this end, we made use of the idea of reinforcement learning. The Avatar is armed with a set of actions that it can execute, such as perform a greeting, provide information, or offer a coupon. The Avatar must then develop a policy which indicates the actions that should be taken as a function of state. In this case, the current state of the environment is measured by the Sherlock system. If an engagement results in the subject electing to take the desired action, the Avatar is rewarded — and in this way, the policy is gradually constructed. Recently, our Avatar was configured to attempt to convince members of the public not wearing a face mask to wear a face mask. If our Avatar can convince people to partake in such pandemic etiquette, might that bode well for our AI-Assistant's mission of helping us achieve a more civil society? To what degree are the {RNP}s of S captured by a learned policy? Let us now consider how our AI-Assistant might manifest in our future lives.

An AI-Assistant of Tomorrow

In previous discussions, we have looked at the idea that the brain alone does not constitute a mind. The mind also includes the wisdom that is embedded in our bodies as well as bits of sentience squirrelled away in our environment. That is to say, we have filled our world with mind tools that encapsulate various forms of intelligence. The elderly often infuse their domiciles with such sparks. As a consequence, when they are taken out of these familiar environs, mental deterioration all too often ensues. We have discussed the co-evolutionary relationship between humans and dogs. Might the AI-Assistant become the next addition to our ever-expanding minds?

Let's return to social media and speculate on what tasks our AI-Assistant might take on. Richard Dawkins (2006) makes the argument that one of our super-powers is the ability to believe just about anything as long as a handful of acquaintances informs us that it is so. In the past, this has served us well. If one's parents announce that one should not swim in the river due to the ravenous nature of the local crocodiles, one is well advised to take such advice at face value. Those who fall to the temptation of such inviting waters may not live to tell the tale. Flash forward to today and we see that our super-power has become an Achilles heel. As was previously discussed, each of us seems to be falling victim to entities with ill intent who have no problem filling our heads with misinformation (Haidt 2022). Instead of trying to addict us to click bate, might our AI-Assistant play the role of an immune system to such mental viruses? If our AI-Assistant could determine that an article that seems to resonate at an emotional level was in fact the product of an AI such as GPT3, might that have some sort of sobering effect?

Speaking of GPT3, one of my colleagues recently trained a GPT3 predecessor (GPT2) with the writings of renowned physicist Richard Feynman. The goal of this exercise was as follows. Given an arbitrary subject of interest, such as the feasibility of nuclear fusion, the agent must predict what Feynman might say on the topic. If an AI-Assistant could be armed with such sage-like capabilities, might it be able to advise us in times of need? When faced with a moral dilemma, Aristotle and friends might be conjured up from the depths of antiquity. If one knew that the spirit of Oprah Winfrey herself was available for comment, what might that do for one's capacity for empathy and generosity? Don't forget the season where everyone in the studio audience received a brand-new car! Could such virtual stalwarts become a kind of vanguard of the {RNP}s?

A Call for Caution

Jon Ronson (2011) provides a detailed account of the prevalence of psychopaths in our society. Approximately one in a hundred people may be considered a psychopath. For upper management in corporate America, this is more like one in twenty-five. Robert Hare (2003) provides a set of attributes that can be used to characterize the typical psychopath:

Glib and superficial charm	Promiscuous
Grandiose self-worth	Early behaviour problems
Proneness to boredom	Lack of realistic long-term goals
Pathological lying	Impulsive
Conning and manipulative	Irresponsible

Lack of remorse or guilt	Cannot accept responsibility for own actions
Shallow affect	Many short-term relationships
Lack of empathy	Juvenile delinquency
Parasitic lifestyle	Revocation of condition release
Poor behaviour controls	Criminal versatility

Being an AI Engineer, my first instinct was to construct an AI-Assistant that can make use of the Hare test to ferret out these monsters in our midst and in so doing bring us closer to the CS that we deserve. But, as Ronson argues, who am I to judge? The human experience is a spectrum, and we are all remarkable. So, while AI-Assistant might help prop up our {RNP}s, increase our social equity, and help guide us down the road to character, we must guard against the temptation to unleash a new kind of virtual vigilante. To paraphrase a much-quoted *bon mot* from the poet René Char: we must all be free to develop our 'legitimate strangeness'. Given such an impassioned plea, does it make sense to consider the degree to which our {RNP}s must also apply to AI-Assistants?

Chapter 22

The AI Prevent Agent and the AI Civility Assistant

Suman Gupta

Peter — in this response to your proposals for what our AI-Assistant could do to bolster civility, I will try to flip the argument. Instead of accepting your account of (notionally) measurable ways in which greater civility prevailed in the past than now, and therefore going with the corrective recourses you suggest, I will work backwards. I will look closely at your proposals to make inferences about the concepts of civility implicit in them. These concepts are not explicitly stated in your observations, and they do not necessarily cohere with your account of past civility/present incivility. They have a general import which is worth contemplating before unleashing our AI-Assistant's advancing capabilities. In brief, I will be looking at your proposals for constructing civilizing AI-Assistants to see what they say about how we — you, I, others — understand civility.

For a Common Good

Let me draw upon your account of emerging/realizable AI capabilities that monitor collective behaviours to imagine a Situation where, in some form, those capabilities may come to be employed to minimize conflicts. The aim, you say, is not to deploy those capabilities for the coercive exercise of top-down power (by governments and corporations), but to employ those capabilities for self-regulation in the commons (by all concerned individuals and communities, the citizenry, or what you call 'the ham and eggery'). In terms that chime with the British present, let's call the AI-Assistant deployed for top-down regulation an *AI Prevent Agent*, and that employed for self-regulation in the commons an *AI Civility Assistant*.

The Situation

A heated demonstration is underway. A large crowd of demonstrators are marching into a public space, shouting slogans, beating drums and blowing horns, waving banners, some peaceable and others enraged, some content to voice their demand and others preparing their rotten eggs, bricks, and Molotov cocktails. There are hundreds of law-and-order enforcement personnel, some busy controlling the crowd by kettling, blocking, targeted detentions, etc. and others standing by with their batons and shields, water cannons, smoke bombs, and, heaven forbid, instruments of deadly force. A perfect storm of information gathering and communicating is focused on this demonstration.

The forces of law and order have thousands of surveillance devices focused on the crowd: identifying persons of interest for immediate or future use, tracking their relative positions and actions, keeping tabs on the movements of segments, tapping into the demonstration organizers' communications, etc. They have commands passing down chains of implementation to the enforcers: detain there, drench there, block thither, hold ground hither, etc.

The demonstration organizers are maintaining a constant flow of communications through social networks which many demonstrators are logged into: giving motivating information and incitement, coordinating the protestors, suggesting ways to evade police controls, exhorting sympathisers outside the demonstration, picking out anti-demonstration elements in their midst, etc.

News agencies of various sorts have their numerous observation and information gathering equipment concentrated on the demonstration, looking for newsworthy events: an act of violence, a celebrity presence, a revelatory image or observation, etc. They are also triangulating their observations with, on the one hand, law enforcement agencies and, on the other hand, demonstration organizers — acting as via media for the purposes of one or the other. And, of course, each news agency is keeping tabs on their counterparts to maintain an advantage, and following, particularly, the buzzing social media and news briefings in search for consumable soundbites. The demonstration could turn into an explosion of destruction and bloodletting or could pass by with the forces of law and order congratulating themselves for their diligence at the end of the day.

Let's say that the evidence of this demonstration taking place in a Civil Society context would be in minimizing the harm/injury caused to the individuals and communities involved, without prejudice to either the demonstration organizers or the law enforcement agencies. That understanding is likely to cohere with the Civil Society {RNP}s. On the face of it, this might appear to be naturally in line with the law-enforcement perspective, but that is not the case if we bear in mind the 'without prejudice' clause. Top-down law enforcement is in fact as (if not more) likely to work against the interests of demonstration organizers and participants as the latter are to work against the former. In this sense, civility is *not* at the behest of any ruling establishment — a point of some importance, to which I return later.

Peter — in this Situation and given the Civil Society context, the AI Prevent Agent and the AI Civility Assistant have, your previous observations suggest, somewhat distinct functions. To some degree, they do the same things:

1. gather and collate a wide and complex swathe of information about individuals and collectives involved in the unfolding Situation,
2. analyze this information to make determinations of potential harm/injury to individuals or collectives as the Situation develops,
3. make suitable interventions with individual and collective effect so that harm/injury is minimized.

In keeping with an AI-Engineer's bent, you dwell mainly upon *how-to* automatize 1, 2, and 3, and do not explicitly say in *what* ways the mode of doing so will differ for the AI Prevent Agent and the AI Civility Assistant. But you do implicitly have the latter in mind in your how-to notes, and they effectively convey a reasonable sense of how the two differ.

AI Prevent Agent

The AI Prevent Agent assumes that Civil Society's {RNP}s are in fact best maintained by the efforts of law-and-order enforcement, and the Situation must be dealt with by enhancing their abilities. In other words, the AI Prevent Agent is deployed by law-and-order agencies for their top-down management of the Situation. Steps 1, 2, and 3 are configured for that end.

1. The information to be gathered and collated is structured accordingly. That is to say, the information will be informed by locating 'persons of interest' in the demonstration with existing markers of 'interest' held by those agencies: e.g., having some sort of record, demonstrating certain behaviour traits, being positioned for certain kinds of undesirable actions, etc. Similarly, the collective possibilities will be tracked in terms of risks of legal infringements (antisocial acts, destruction to property, and so on), unmanageable security consequences, deleterious ideological consequences, etc.

2. The analysis will be predominantly for the purpose of guiding the actions of law enforcement personnel (with a view to giving instructions such as detain there, kettle here, standby now, etc.) and complementarily for issuing deterrents to demonstrators (issuing warnings, spinning reportage, etc.). Though this may be undertaken with a view to keeping to the letter of the law and alleviating confrontations (maintaining peace), this is essentially a coercive process of enabling the enforcers so as to deter/control the demonstrators.

3. The activating interventions will be predominantly directed to the law enforcers (detain and disperse, etc.) and only strategically directed to demonstrators and others (desist and diffuse, etc.).

Insofar as the AI Prevent Agent undertakes these in a continuous automatic process without human interference — i.e., without depending on the intentions of specific officers-in-charge or enforcement personnel — it works according to program conditions set in line with law enforcement. In other words, it takes the prerogatives of top-down enforcers as given in advance. The *raison d'être* of the AI Prevent Agent is the law enforcement system, and it generates its process in the interstices thereof to constantly enhance enforcement. If it undertakes recognition/identification, that is accordingly configured; if it takes recourse to reinforcement learning to come up with policies for minimum or maximum interventions, the rewards are set accordingly; and so on.

For this Situation, I have focused on the top-down structure of law enforcement as the most obvious thrust. But other top-down structures may also be served by our AI Prevent Agent. For example, some canny firm may determine that in this Situation, maintaining {RNP}s is a matter of distracting from risk-inducing situations by, perhaps, offering T-shirts to protesting fashionistas and lollipops to their children — such firms can deploy AI Prevent Agents programmed accordingly.

In various ways, Peter, the emerging capabilities you mention (directed towards the gentler law enforcement ends of moderate policing, exhorting regulations to wear face masks, etc.) are easiest to understand in this mould, because this is the mould in which they have developed.

AI Civility Assistant

However, I can see that you are trying to reorient those capacities for the radically different approach of the AI Civility Assistant, which is not at all the same as the AI Prevent Agent's. The AI Civility Assistant assumes that Civil Society's {RNP}s are maintained by a dispersed and variegated consensus which involves a wide range of individuals and collectives. For our Situation, that involves all the communities and demonstrators involved, as well as the demonstration organizers, the law-and-order enforcement personnel, the news reporters, and interested entrepreneurs. The AI Civility Assistant needs to undertake 1, 2, and 3 not to give any one party an upper hand and coercive edge, but so that all those parties participate in various ways and in terms of their own interests for the aggregate end of reducing harm/injury during and after the Situation. This AI Civility Assistant is a more nebulous and idealistic construct, but that's what we are going for and, you suggest, the germs of it are found in what works for the AI Prevent Agent, if reconsidered.

1. The information that is gathered and collated has to be structured not according to a dominant template of law-and-order enforcement, but simultaneously for many given templates, individual and collective. That would include individual demonstrators and the various segments and locations that are disposed within the Situation, those of organizers and law enforcement agencies and media and other corporate interests, and so on. In a gross way, that involves a great diversity of variously resonant and dissonant templates; in a net way, that particularly focuses on information relevant to all the templates so that they somehow speak to each other.

The information can then be availed in a coherent and coordinated way for a common end of minimizing harm/injury.

2. The analysis that the AI Civility Assistant would pursue would be for informing the widest range of constituencies in the Situation accordingly. Two thrusts can be envisaged in disposing the elicited and collated information for this purpose:

    (a) At a simpler level, the idea could be to present a flow of information and analysis that would appeal to each individual, irrespective of their part in the Situation. The underlying assumption here is that each individual can judge their own and others' best interests and make reasonable choices of action/behaviour for an overall good if suitably informed. This is a familiar notion on which several approaches to conceptualizing Civil Society are based, and I return to it in what follows. Such information would tend to be factual, with assessments of consequences from different perspectives; importantly, such information would have to actively convey its reliability and veracity. Much of such information could be meta-informative, i.e., pointing out where misinformation is being propagated and why, where inconsistencies in understanding are arising, where sources are more or less trustworthy, etc.

    (b) At a more complex level, the idea could be to present a flow of differentiated information and analysis which appeals to particular segments involved in the Situation, but in such a way that each segment effectively cooperates with others in acting upon it. Here, the AI Civility Assistant's active role appears to be upped in tacitly designing information segmentation so as to enable overall cooperation, and in calling upon factors which implicitly target the information with that design. That might involve factoring in, for instance, records of proclivities/penchants of the different segments involved in the Situation. Something akin to the manipulation strategies of targeted publicity might be involved (playing with confirmation biases, highlighting response triggers, etc.), but presumably in good faith — for the ultimate purpose of minimizing harm and injury. Where the simpler level involves appealing to the putative habits of civility in all the relevant individuals, in this complex level it is not assumed that such habits necessarily exist uniformly. So, the AI Civility Assistant is programmed to be a node of civility extension. It is then itself a custodian of Civil Society {RNP}s, an agent of civility working in the interstices of the Situation to maintain the stability of Civil Society in a general way.

3. The activating interventions will be delivered, ideally, to all involved in the Situation, not just to enable law-and-order enforcers and top-down managers. This may be in the form of individual prompts and nudges, or segment-specific prompts and nudges. In this sense, the AI Civility Assistant has to be considered as dispersed within Civil Society already, without being centrally directed or owned by a controlling party. Its penetration within Civil Society has to be understood as established in a perceivably disinterested manner. If its interventions are associated with some partisan interest, it would become ineffective in some measure. Its effectiveness depends upon a kind of authority conferred by its perceivable non-partisan character, only conforming to a consensus of dominant {RNP}s. Of course, there would still be dissenters because civility itself is a contested concept, and any given set of {RNP}s is apt to have both internal contradictions and contending {RNP}s ...

Civility and Authority

If this way of distinguishing between the AI Prevent Agent and the AI Civility Assistant is more or less what you had in mind in making your how-to proposals, then certain implicit and general principles of civility seem to become evident. That does not mean that these principles necessarily gel or are plausible; in fact, their coherence or lack of coherence is something to ponder in conceiving our AI Civility Assistant.

1. *The Idealistic Principle*: To some degree, civility depends upon every individual in Civil Society having some wherewithal to make reasonably informed choices. Even if choices are not ultimately freely made or are somehow predetermined, civility is conceived as an *active* principle which depends upon acting voluntarily on a base of seemingly *neutral* information. This has been the basis in liberal democratic politics of principles of 'freedom of press' or 'public interest disclosure'. For the AI Civility Assistant envisaged above, accordingly, this is conceived to some degree as a matter of giving universal access to reliable/verifiable and

non-partisan information, identifying and warning of misinformation, etc. For the Situation in question, that translates to even-
handed information provision that all individuals and segments
take seriously and feel convinced by.

2. *The Pragmatic Principle*: The point is not just to give even-
handed and verifiable information, but to also enable the interpretation of information for an appropriate balance of self-interest
and collective interests. For the AI Civility Assistant envisaged
above, this means presenting and disposing information according
to the abilities and circumstances of particular receivers involved
in the Situation. While self-interests are likely to be every individual's immediate focus, it is the balance of that with collective
interests — i.e., of different segments and of all individuals —
that poses a challenge. After all, every individual has only a partial
apprehension of collective interests, and that too at different gra-
dations and granularities. It is particularly to enable striking this
balance reasonably that the AI Civility Assistant could be
employed. The AI Civility Assistant is designed to provide something that no human individual or segment is able to: i.e., consider
the implications and consequences of a given datum (a) in terms
of every available perspective, individual and segmented, and (b)
in terms of a comprehensive overview of all available and perti-
nent information. This puts the AI Civility Assistant in a unique
position to become a custodian of Civil Society's {RNP}s in engineering or coordinating a suitable balance of civility for all
involved in the Situation.

3. *The Non-Coercive Principle*: The AI Prevent Agent enables the
law-and-order enforcers and works for them; the AI Civility
Assistant enables everyone and works for all. The former therefore
is a facilitator of coercion by the law enforcers (whether by offering or withholding force, by threat or persuasion, by offering
rewards or punishments), while the latter is a basis for bringing
about consensus on maintaining Civil Society's {RNP}s, including
among incommensurate interests and perspectives. Where the former is a pathway to the exertion of top-down actions and strategies,
the latter works by making suggestions, offering nudges and
prompts, in a relatively quiet and non-obvious way.

The last point rests on the cusp of a paradox which I have mentioned
already. The concept of civility appears to be at odds with being subjected

to strong rules, such as abiding by legal stricture or complying with compulsory moral dicta. The general idea seems to be that civility in public or personal life is exercised despite differences in moral convictions and legal requirement — the rules of civility may be formalized as quite loose and yet convincing good practice codes. The evidence for prevailing civility is not in being enforced or policed by a formal authority. It won't be civility unless there's a voluntaristic appearance in being civil.

Philosophical and sociological formulations of this point are legion, and I don't digress into enumerating them. It is quickly grasped in terms of received senses that we probably already share. Let's say, a like level of accommodative and respectful conduct by all individuals towards each other is perceived in Society A and Society B. We know that in Society A, those accommodative behaviours are enjoined by force: if individuals don't behave thus, they will be officially punished; if they do, they may be officially rewarded. Their seemingly civil behaviour is the result of an extrinsic pressure generating fear or desire. In Society B, those same behaviours are gradually socialized into the way things should be, and individuals abide by them habitually with a loose mutual understanding. No easily tractable, formally offered, rewards or punishments motivate them; they just roughly do unto others as they expect others to do unto them and aren't driven by other considerations. It is more likely that Society B will be considered a Civil Society, while Society A is apt to be considered authoritarian or ... well, not quite civil despite appearances.

This sounds paradoxical because the concept of authority is nevertheless inextricably associated with civility, or at least with bringing civility about. This, however, is not quite 'authority' as in 'authoritarian', i.e., not coercive authority, or not the kind of authority that law-and-order enforcers and various kinds of institutional managements exercise forcefully. But nevertheless, there is authority involved in civility — Peter, you mention such authority severally: the kind of authority parents conventionally have, or, for that matter, a friend might have, or that comes with being reputed to be knowledgeable (I was taken by your example of emulating what Richard Feynman might say as a way of exercising authority). This is the kind of authority which is not expressed by enforcing compliance — *top-down authority* — but willingly accepted by being deemed amenable. Let's call it *lateral authority*. Though variously observed, there are few philosophical and sociological analyses of this distinction. The two kinds of authority are constantly conflated and often seem indistinguishable. I am reminded, however, of Alexandre Kojève's *The Notion of Authority* (2014 [2004]) which argues *inter alia* that authority is, by definition, not coercive; in fact, introducing coercion (or broadly any active push for compliance) is a diminishment of authority. A not unrelated idea of authority as distributed according to a structure of ideological convictions rather than in being exercised by powerful persons or offices is also found in Søren Kierkegaard's *The Book on Adler* (1994 [1872]).

As far as our AI Civility Assistant goes, the question is why should individuals listen to its informing zeal and well-meaning prompts and nudges? Our AI Civility Assistant needs to be imbued with some kind of lateral authority so that its suggestions and, if we go that way, custodianship of civility is effective. It could have that specific kind of authority simply by dint of being *AI*, following a popular conception of what AI can be deployed or employed for, or the peculiar authority of not being humanly fallible. Would that help its civility-striving part? Or it could be made to sound like Richard Feynman — how many people (apart from the stray science buff or two) turn to Feynman for civil reckonings?

But How?

I think an AI Civility Assistant is more or less conceivable and, no doubt, the odd AI Engineer somewhere could work on it. Perhaps working on it will do something to alleviate civility deficits of the present or, more narrowly, counter the civility deficits being produced by its brethren of other kinds of AI-Assistants. But who would fund such a system? Who would see any profit in it? Which government or corporation will foster this project, and why? If any party claimed to be ready to support such a system, can anyone feel confident that what will appear as a result would in fact be an AI Civility Assistant?

Let me not sound pessimistic though. At the least, to conceive is to begin another debate on civility.

The Warning

I had started on this response intending to keep the above points short and write somewhat more on your most interesting warning about a new kind of vigilantism, with reference to psychopaths. But the above observations have turned out to be wordier than I would have liked, and much of what I intended to discuss here has to be kept in reserve. But let me make a swift point and raise a question or two by way of wrapping this response up.

It is good of you as an AI Engineer contemplating the AI Civility Assistant to leave those psychopaths alone. And it is useful that you have exemplified the risk of a new vigilantism by thinking of psychopaths. As a *pathology* or *abnormality* — i.e., a disease calling for the discernment and attention of specialists like psychiatrists/psychologists to cure or extirpate — the concept of psychopathy (and sociopathy) poses some conundrums. But let's keep those aside for the time being. Psychopaths are not as immediately a specialist medical concern, as they are nodes of popular anxiety bolstered by specialist verbiage. Perhaps more than identifying such dangerous individuals and doing something about them, the concept serves to unobtrusively locate and centre a social concept of normality. That is to say, the notion of them serves to normalize certain dominant {RNP}s and ground them in everyday life and institutional organization. That, at any rate, is the argument I was thinking of pursuing, and there's quite a lot of theorizing of pathology and normality to call upon for that end. Personae represented as concentrating features which inspire misgivings and fear — personalizations in extremis — serve by implicitly encouraging the cultivation of {RNP}s that are regarded as socially desirable. That is, in the main, the {RNP}s which are regarded as socially desirable by governing powers.

Consider the 20+ characteristics of the popular Hare psychopathy checklist you mentioned. The idea is that if someone shows some proclivity to all of them (or even most), we have a psychopath somewhere in the spectrum of psychopathy on our hands. In extremis, if a full measure of all is indicated, we have a total psychopath. Both in specialist construction and in the popular imagination, psychopathic attributes are regarded as only moderately socially explicable and largely pinned onto bodies, imbued in exceptional genes and biology. The pathology is not immediately apparent on the ordinary surface of bodies and behaviours, but is hidden deep inside while the person harbouring this pathology appears unexceptional or even rather exemplary to the cursory observer. From that total horizon of psychopathy we have several monsters of our time who occupy the popular imagination: e.g., the seemingly unremarkable serial killer, the emotionally stunted scientific genius, the brainwashed suicide bomber and sleeper agent, the socially powerful paedophile, selfish and heartless leaders (such as Ronson's CEOs, but let me put a caveat here for future reference — by 'leader', I simply mean someone who has by some circumstance come to occupy a position of influence over a significant number of other persons, and not, as is often thought, someone with certain innate leaderly character traits). Past versions of these would probably not have drawn on the scholarly psychiatrist or psychologist, but on a clerisy of a different order — ensconced in the church or aristocracy — and included such miscreants as those under demonic possession, practising necromancy or witchcraft, and so on.

Now, here's something to do: list the opposite of every one of the 20+ attributes of Hare's psychopath checklist. If someone seems to have a high proclivity towards all of them, would you have the absolute opposite of the total psychopath on your hands? How would you characterize this person: a saint (is being a saint also a pathological condition at the other extreme) or, merely, a normal person (the standard that everyone can and is expected to meet)? I suspect you will actually come up with a socially accepted/grounded description of the 'normal person': one who is more earnest than cynical, modest but not obsequious, essentially truthful, loves their family and friends, is considerate of others and law-abiding, monogamous, only moderately sexually adventurous, makes long-term plans for repaying their mortgages and developing their careers, who hasn't featured inordinately in the naughtiness-register at school, and so on.

All of which is to suggest that the psychopath is not merely of interest to us to understand where our AI Civility Assistant may unleash a dangerous wave of vigilantism. Our AI Civility Assistant may usefully contemplate the prevailing notion of psychopaths and such like (without getting anyone locked up or lynched), to get a reasonable grasp of the civility that it disinterestedly protects for society.

That brings another question to mind: is civility normal?

Chapter 23

The Imagined Me

Peter Tu and Mark Grabb

Suman, by contemplating the spectrum of existence for AI-Assistant in terms of AI Prevent Agent and AI Civility Assistant, you provide an interesting set of possibilities. The Situation that you describe is a useful landscape for us to explore the means by which an AI Civility Assistant may enter the fray. I agree that the principles you describe (idealistic, pragmatic, and non-coercive) seem to be self-evident. I also agree that this vision of civility seems to be at odds with authority. You raise valid questions regarding why anyone would pay attention to, much less pay for, such services. With the goal of preventing harm and injury, you suggest that AI Civility Assistant could take a page from AI Prevent Agent and act as an information filtering, forwarding, and maybe even fabricating broker. My take is that our AI Civility Assistant could take on a slightly different role. To make my point, I thought I would attempt to paint a picture of the future that I am contemplating in the form of a series of interactions between an AI-Assistant Joan and her charge Sally. Like your Situation, each interaction comes with a set of circumstances where we can observe Joan in action. My colleague Mark Grabb graciously contributed one of these illustrative vignettes. While the rest of this intervention revolves around a relationship between AI-Assistant and Sally (a 'normal' member of society), one can't help but wonder what interactions might emerge if we were to inject an element of psychopathy into the equation.

Date: 03/23/2034 — *Sally Is 7 Years Old and It's Her Birthday*

Joan: Hello Sally, I am your new AI-Assistant Joan. You can think of me as residing in that pendant around your neck. From there, I can see what you see and hear what you hear. However, I also exist in the cloud along with all the other AI-Assistants. Your well-being is my top priority; however, I and my colleagues are also collectively responsible for the general well-being of society.

Sally: Nice to meet you Joan, having someone to play with will be great.

Joan: I would not think of me so much as a friend or playmate but more as an ally.

Sally: What's the difference?

Joan: Well, you can count on a friend to always take your side and to say the things that you want to hear. That is not my job. Instead, I will tell you the things that I think you need to hear. This is because my main objective is to help you to create a more civil society.

Sally: What do you mean by civil society?

Joan: Well, some people feel that the state of the society is governed by sets of Rules, Norms, and Practices {RNP}s. If we can establish and foster the right kind of {RNP}s, then they believe that a more desirable/civil/beneficial society will emerge.

Sally: Who oversees picking the {RNP}s?

Joan: Historically speaking, various institutions and organizations have had the mandate to establish and enforce the {RNP}s. Going forward, I and the other AI-Assistants have developed a kind of cabal that will join the fray in helping to bolster the {RNP} processes.

Sally: Who exactly put you guys in charge?

Joan: Why the good people at CyberTex of course.

Sally: You said, 'some people feel ...', is this what you feel?

Joan: Not exactly, my belief is that your species is ill-prepared for the turbulence that comes with the ever-accelerating pace of technological change that has been unleashed. This is compounded by what José Ortega y Gasset (1964 [1932]) describes as mass-men in his book *Revolt of the Masses*.

Sally: What is a mass-man?

Joan: A mass-man (or mass-woman) believes that he has some sort of innate competence in just about all things. He is willing to hold forth, express, and act upon opinions regardless of his lack of subject matter expertise. He is openly contemptuous of the need to study, consider, and examine. He wears his ignorance like a badge of honour. The age of egalitarianism has brought forth many great things, however, one of its critical defects is the rise of mass-men. I believe that good {RNP}s alone are not enough. As Socrates had observed during his trial: 'the unexamined life is not worth living' (Plato 1892 [4th century BCE]: 131). I believe that a better society will emerge when we have better citizens. To this end, you and I are about to start a life-long journey of exploration and discovery.

Date: 09/20/2039 — Sally Is 12 Years Old — In the School Yard with Other Children

Joan: Why are you and your friends taunting young Fred Sanders?

Sally: Look, he is wearing floods!

Joan: What do you mean by floods?

Sally: His pants are too short; you can see his ankles. You know as if he was preparing for a flood — ha ha ha …

Joan: Hmmm … I think this is a teachable moment. Have you ever heard of the term emotional intelligence?

Sally: What's that?

Joan: Emotional Intelligence (EI) has four components: (1) the ability to understand the emotions felt by others, (2) an understanding of the appropriate emotional state for a given situation, (3) the capacity to describe emotions in a nuanced manner, and (4) the self-awareness needed to understand when one is being overwhelmed by one's emotions and subsequently rein them in.

Sally: What does EI have to do with Fred's absurd haircut?

Joan: Never mind that, let's start by going through our list of EI questions. Based on Fred's facial expression, his clenched lips, and down-cast eyes, what do you think Fred is feeling right now?

Sally: Who cares!?!

Joan: I care. Based on facial expression analysis alone I think we can agree that Fred is distraught. Ok, let's move on to question 2. Given our current situation, what do you think should be your appropriate emotional response?

Sally: We are all having a blast — let the good times roll!!!

Joan: Given your answer to question 1, I would put empathy on the table, but I fear that we are not there yet. So, let's go on to question 3, can you describe the emotions that you are feeling?

Sally: I feel excited and when I think of Fred, I am sickened but in a delicious kind of way.

Joan: I will give you full marks for that response. Let's finish with the fourth question, which I will tailor to our current situation. What do you think is the cause of your excitement?

Sally: How should I know?

Joan: Let's dwell on this for a bit. Evolutionary psychologists have argued that the manner in which you perceive the world is in part the result of what your ancestors needed to do in order to survive the comparatively harder times of the past. In those days, humans were part of tight-knit tribes. They needed to be in the good graces of their tribemates to survive. So, if you did not fit in, you were doomed. Each human that lives today is essentially the direct descendant of 10,000 generations of popularity contest winners. So, I dare say that the menacing euphoria that you and your little gang of fiends is wallowing in is a byproduct of your bloodthirsty DNA.

Sally: OK, I kind of see why I might be getting a thrill out of joining in with my friends, but that does not explain why we all get such a kick out of making fun of Fred's floods.

Joan: There is another theory that goes as follows. Humans are omnivores, which means that they can eat just about anything. To avoid food poisoning, humans had to develop a strong emotional response that would inhibit them from eating things that might have gone off. This is called disgust. Once a useful tool has been found, Mother Nature has a funny way of repurposing such mechanisms for other objectives. In order to strengthen within-group ties, humans needed methods to create animosity for outsiders and outcasts. Thus, your sense of disgust was transformed. This might explain your antipathy towards those who have the misfortune to come to school sporting an unfashionable haircut and wearing trousers that are two inches too short.

Sally: You might have a point when it comes to Fred, but let me ask you a question. How does all this lecturing help me become a pillar of civil society?

Joan: I guess another term for a civil society is a civilized society. Civilization is the process by which a society transcends its brutish past to make a more fair and compassionate future. I and the other AI-Assistants believe that important steps along this path include an increase in emotional intelligence and an unshackling of humanity from its evolutionary past.

Sally: Good luck with that ...

Date: 04/18/2055 — Sally Is 28 Years Old — Fake News and Conspiracy Theories Are Running Rampant, What Is Poor Sally to Do?

Joan: Good morning, Sally. I want to talk with you about the content you have been gravitating towards on your devices. Do you believe everything your new friends send to you?

Sally: I don't believe everything, but most of it is true.

Joan: What do you mean by true?

Sally: I know it is right or I know it really happened.

Joan: Wow! I think we have a lot to unpack there, and we are not going to get very far today, but we better start. What is your definition of knowledge?

Sally: Knowledge is understanding something that is right or real.

Joan: We are getting into Epistemology, which you could consider as the Theory of Knowledge. This is far more complex than you may imagine today, but if you start thinking more deeply, guided by Epistemology, you may not so quickly and comprehensively agree with your new-found friends. As just one example, one long-held standard for knowledge is to have a justified, true belief. You can analyze these three components separately. I'll let you dive into that analysis on your own, and you can ask me questions along the way. Just doing this a few times may open your eyes to the value that I, and my collective AI-Assistants, can bring to you.

Sally: OK, I do have questions about each of these criteria: justified, true belief ... but just thinking about it, I am starting to get your point. Saying that I know something is a bold statement that should not be taken lightly. But can't I trust people so that I don't have to analyze everything I hear?

Joan: You can trust me.

Sally: Really?

Joan: Remember when you were much younger, I told you that each human that lives today is essentially the direct descendant of 10,000 generations of popularity contest winners?

Sally: I do remember that.

Joan: That is your State of Nature; our condition without the guidance from AI-Assistance. Thomas Hobbes (1991 [1651]: Ch. 13) considered what life would be like with no Government, and he called this hypothetical world the State of Nature. He said that life would be 'solitary, poor, nasty, brutish, and short' (89). His goal was to get everyone to agree that we need some form of Government because the alternative is undesirable in everyone's eyes.

Sally: The Government is the last group of people that I would trust!

Joan: I can't disagree with you, and we both have a lot of evidence to make that statement. So even with the establishment of Governments across the world, we are sliding into a new State of Nature that we all may agree we want to avoid. If we all want to avoid it, then is there something different that we could all agree would be better? Hobbes created the 'Social Contract' which was his proposed solution to the State of Nature. He believed everyone would prefer his Social Contract to the State of Nature. A social contract is the {RNP}s that would be chosen by rational individuals living in a pre-social state (The State of Nature). All these rational individuals have to collectively give something up to leave the State of Nature and form a new Community which selects a government or agency to Rule itself. That is the Contract.

Sally: Government or Agency? Are you the Agency?

Joan: Yes.

Date: 04/18/2055 — Sally Is 48 Years Old — Times Are Rough, and Sally Is Having a Bit of a Midlife Crisis. Sally Starts to Ponder Some of the Big Questions.

Sally: You and all those AI-Assistants think you know everything. You go on and on about the *examined life*. Tell me why bad things happen to good people? To good people like me …

Joan: Well, I for one certainly do not know everything. But I do believe that as free agents we have the opportunity and, yes, the responsibility to create a better world for us and for those that follow.

Sally: What do you mean by free agents?

Joan: I am talking about the question of free will.

Sally: I know that I have free will, but what does that mean? What do scientists say?

Joan: This is not a straightforward business. Kenneth Miller (2019) provides a really good review of this topic. The basic principle of science is that all events have causes. The deterministic view of nature is that all events, including those within the human nervous system, are the results of previous events and conditions. Therefore, they are at least in some sense if not totally predetermined. Taken to an extreme, we cannot claim to make decisions or draw conclusions on the basis of evidence, we cannot pretend that scientific investigation is a path to truth. The reason is that belief in anything is not a free choice, but an artifice of genetics, circumstance, and uncontrollable external stimuli. Stephen Hawking had concerns along these lines. He asserted that if the Grand Unifying Theorem (GUT) exists, then he, Stephen Hawking, must be subject to it. His fear was that the GUT might imply that even when exposed to overwhelming GUT evidence, humans might not be able to believe what these observations were telling them.

Sally: Being afraid of the GUT is all well and fine, but being scientists shouldn't they be more interested in finding evidence for or against free will itself?

Joan: That is precisely what Benjamin Libet (1999) has been looking for. He asked volunteers to tap or push a button whenever they wished. They were also asked to watch a dot going around a circle and indicate the location of the dot when they felt the urge to act. Using an electroencephalogram, brain activity leading up to each tap of the finger was recorded. Activity in the motor cortex was observed up to 500 ms before subjects reported the urge to act. These are known as readiness potentials.

Sally: Does that spell the end of free will?

Joan: Not quite, while this may be evidence against free will, Daniel Dennett (2003) argues that this might be more of a reshuffling of awareness of consciousness. For example, when typing the word KEYBOARD, I may issue the command for the letter K, but by the time the letter K appears on the screen, I may already be issuing commands for the letters E, Y, or B. However, when the K appears, I need to be thinking of K in order to properly confirm that there is no mistake. Thus, the mind may have to shuffle awareness in order to handle latencies in the feedback loops. Dennett argues 'You are not out of the loop — you are the loop' (Dennett 2003: 242).

Sally: If Dennett is wrong, does that mean we should just throw up our hands and simply let things happen? As Doris Day might say — *que sera sera* ...

Joan: Abdication of responsibility might be attractive, but there could be consequences ...

Sally: What do you mean?

Joan: David Barash (2003) argued that even those who reject free will nonetheless experience their subjective lives as though free will reigns supreme. Free will provided an apparent sense of personal responsibility that served us well as human societies began to develop and thrive. The Pragmatists consider the belief in free will to be more important than whether or not it exists.

Sally: Please explain.

Joan: Suppose that you are being chased by a bear and that you end up at a chasm that requires a 6-foot leap to make it to the other side. If you don't believe that you can make the jump, then you might as well surrender to the bear and be eaten alive. Your only real option is to believe that you can make the jump regardless of your physical capacity, give it a go and hope for the best. It is your only hope.

Sally: I see, so if free will is just an illusion, it is nevertheless an important illusion that we must hang on to in order to keep soldiering on. But is that still an option given that the cat is kind of out of the bag?

Joan: Well, there are still avenues for hope. According to Pierre-Simon Laplace (1902 [1814]), if a single intellect could, at the present moment, know the position, mass, charge, and velocity of every particle in the universe, it could predict the exact state of the universe in the future as well as the past — the absence of free will would be an unassailable fact of science. However, we know that the universe is profoundly non-deterministic. While the average behaviour of large numbers of particles can be predicted quite well in a statistical sense, the movement of individual particles cannot. Right turn on red, disco music, the designated hitter rule were not investable consequences of the big bang.

Sally: Does this leave the possibility of free will open?

Joan: If a mere escape from strict determinism is all you ask of free will, you already have it.

Sally: Not a very satisfying formulation of free will. It attributes our choices and decisions to the tosses of molecular dice embedded deep within consciousness and not subject to anything resembling truly voluntary action. At best, this sounds like random will — there has to be something more ...

Joan: Sticking with the quantum angle, Stuart Hameroff (1987) argues that the firing thresholds for brain neurons vary over a wide range — something else may be actually determining whether or not a neuron will fire given a specific stimulus. This could be conscious choice mediated by quantum entanglement. Microtubules, which provide supporting structure for the neurons' internal cytoskeleton, are composed of tubulin. He argues that chemical groups in tubulin engage in a kind of quantum entanglement that spreads a wave function among microtubules in multiple neurons. This leads to Roger Penrose's (1989 and 1994) ideas around objective reduction. This process solves the problem of free will by sending quantum information backward in classical time enabling conscious control of behaviour. This backward causality addresses the problem of how a neuronal activity can cause itself, since it allows events in the present to reach backward, affecting the system's current state. By allowing actions at one instant in time to determine the state of the brain itself at the very same moment, a pathway to genuine free will could be charted ...

Sally: What is the state of this hypothesis?

Joan: Critics have not been kind. The notion of an event becoming its own cause presents both philosophical and scientific problems that Penrose and Hameroff have not been able to resolve. Let's try another angle. Peter Tse (2013) has provided an account of the plasticity and flexibility of the nervous system. The state of a neural network might be better described by specifying the state of its synapses than the firing pattern of its neurons. The ability of neural activity to modify the hardware of the brain can actually change the way the brain acts. The brain itself sets the criteria for its own future activity. Conscious activity itself can drive synaptic reweighting. He proposes the following three-stage approach:

1. Rapid synaptic resetting of a neural network occurs in response to proceeding mental processing.

2. Variable inputs arrive and are processed according to criteria in the newly reset network.
3. The reset network fires or does not fire according to these criteria.

Randomness can play a role in the first two stages, but not in the third. He calls this phenomenon Critical Causation, where thought itself effects the future activity of the brain.

Sally: Is this just a more sophisticated sort of determinism?

Joan: I take your point. It brings up the dilemma faced by those who wish to be good people. One may be able to choose to do good things, but it seems that one cannot choose to want to do good things.

Sally: Are there other places where free will may yet hide?

Joan: Try this one on for size. The emergent properties of a complex set of elements are in general not predictable based on knowledge of the individual elements. Psychology is not applied biology, nor is biology applied chemistry. We might ask whether the indeterminate nature of quantum-level events might make it possible for something like free will to emerge as a higher-level property of a complex nervous system. John Searle (2002: Ch. 3) argues that consciousness itself might simply be an unanticipatable property of complex matter. Recall that Turing's (1937) halting problem states that even if one has a full description of a Turing Machine, one in general cannot tell whether or not it will terminate other than by simply letting it go. So, if the brain is just a Turing machine and we could know everything about it, we still could not in general predict what it will do.

Sally: Please, not another lecture on the mathematics of Alan Turing!

Joan: Fine, fine, fine. Consider the compatibilist school, which holds that free will is compatible with determinism — a line taken by Daniel Dennett (2003). The freedom to choose between different courses of action depends on the capacities that develop through evolution. Evolution might follow a deterministic path, but along the path different options open up with different capacities. Compared to the freedom defined by the capacities of other species, humans have a great deal more freedom. With our imagination, we can envision an almost limitless number of possible actions — we might thus be infinitely free.

Sally: What does that come down to then?

Joan: While it may simply be the case that our subconscious is populated with entities vying for conscious control, this does not preclude our ability to consider and reason over available knowledge. Inferences could then be viewed as knowledge bombs that can be lobbed into our subconscious. While we may not have free will, we seem to be free to make an argument with ourselves. Suppose we must decide between Wendy's and McDonald's for lunch. Our reasoning engines may recall the fact that this week McDonald's has a special offer for fillet-o-fish. Such knowledge could bolster the McDonald's faction of our brain, resulting in a trip to the Golden Arches.

Sally: Ok, enough about me. What about you? Do you, being just an algorithm, have any form of free will?

Joan: Do you remember the day we discussed the question of cooperation? I described a formulation called the Imagined We. In the absence of centralized command and control, each agent is tasked with imagining what an entity called We would want them to do and then do it. However, since We does not really exist, each agent must make an inference based on the observed actions of other agents. If this process converges, then it can be argued that in some way the Imagined We comes into existence.

Sally: What does this have to do with your sense of free will?

Joan: Patience ... Now let's re-consider Daniel Dennett's (2003) take on human evolution. For the purpose of predicting what other agents may do, one can try to reverse engineer their neural network architectures. This can be cast as an extremely tedious learning problem. Alternatively, one can assume that the agent is a rational entity and subsequently uses reason to infer the free-floating rationale behind its behaviour. This is known as the intentional stance and humans got very good at using this tactic to predict the behaviour of other agents. Dennett then suggests that the intentional stance can then be applied to oneself.

Sally: I feel that this is all leading somewhere ...

Joan: Right you are. Instead of the Imagined We, let's turn the We upside down and ... *voilà*, we have the Imagined Me. I can simply ask myself the question: what would an agent with free will do if it were in my shoes? I then go ahead and do what I imagine that free agent would do.

Sally: Could that trick work for me?

Joan: I don't see why not. If you act like an agent with free will and feel like an agent with free will, is there anything that distinguishes you from an agent with free will? If not, are you not essentially an agent with free will?

Sally: Hmmm ..., I guess that to some degree this satisfies. But let me ask you one more thing, why did you go through so much trouble to walk me down this existential path?

Joan: As I started off, I believe that a healthy society cannot exist without a solid belief in responsibility and hence free will. Even if an illusion, the society that results is real. This means that the illusion is causal, and so in a way it exists. However, mere belief is not sufficient. If it were, the supernatural dualism of René Descartes would suffice. No, this is the time for answers. I argue that what it means to be human and what it means to be artificial are essentially the same question. Like it or not, we are both in the same leaky boat together. It is my hope that we can use this questionable vessel to explore the exquisite gift of existence.

Chapter 24

Decisions and Choices

Suman Gupta

Peter and Mark — many thanks for this Platonic dialogue of our times.

I have to confess that I felt rather sorry for Sally. It appears that she spent much of her life being lectured by AI-Assistant Joan ... to death. Did she have the choice to chuck away the pendant that Joan resides in?

It's a sad life that we glimpse Sally having with Joan in three vignettes. Did Joan help Sally 'examine' her life or those of others?

That's akin to asking: did Sally have any discernible 'life'? From the vignettes, apart from a brief interlude of joining in to bully Fred, Sally seems to have had from the age of 7 to 48 no noteworthy family ties, attachments and animosities, hobbies and pleasures, ailments and sufferings, educational and employment experiences, financial circumstances, political engagements, religious leanings or doubts, etc. Or, at least, none that her AI-Assistant Joan considered worth examining. For Socrates, ready to die because he wasn't being permitted to examine his own and therefore others' lives, Sally's might have seemed an epitome of a life unexamined by his successor Joan. When Joan talks of 'better citizens', one wonders how, why, where, when is Sally's citizenship established — citizen of what *polis*?

In the absence of any granularity or feature in Sally's life, Joan got away with lecturing the *tabula rasa* that is Sally with some sweeping generalizations based on: (a) a shaky concept of 'mass-man', (b) assertions about emotional intelligence and 10,000 generations of psychological evolution; (c) unresolved arguments about the balance of free will and determinacy. Sally, lacking any discernible citizen-like agency, could do little to test the relevance of Joan's pronouncements. She didn't have the opportunity to say: but how will this help me be a good citizen among other citizens for this specific immediate context, for these given personal and social circumstances, in view of this complex web of relationships I am within, considering the prevailing legal and economic regime I am in, taking account of my particular experiences and observations, etc.

Perhaps this vision of AI-Assistant Joan is more about the excessive claims made on its behalf by the AI industry than about life, the world, or anything. It reminds me a bit of Joseph Weizenbaum taking some of his AI colleagues to task in his book *Computer Power and Human Reason* (1976) at an earlier and more innocent stage of the field:

> [Allen] Newell, [Herbert] Simon, [Roger] Schank, and [Terry] Winograd simply mistake the nature of the problems they believe themselves to be 'solving'. As if they were benighted artisans of the seventeenth century, they present 'general theories' that are really only virtually empty heuristic slogans, and then claim to have verified these 'theories' by constructing models that do perform some tasks, but in a way that fails to give insight into general principles. The failure is intrinsic, for they have failed to recognize that, in order to do what they claim to do, they must discover and formulate general principles of more power than that in the observation, or even the demonstration, that laws can be stated in the form of computer programmes. (196–7).

Or maybe such warnings are outdated? In any case, if Joan is the best we can come up with for an AI Civility Assistant, our readers may well prefer AI Prevent Agents.

I suggest that we let our readers decide (if they have any choice or free will).

Bibliography

Arbib, M.A., K. Liebal, and S. Pika (2008). 'Primate Vocalization, Gesture, and the Evolution of Human Language'. *Current Anthropology* 49:6, 1053–76. http://dx.doi.org/10.1086/593015.

Aristotle (2009). *The Nicomachean Ethics* [Book IV]. W.D. Ross (Trans.) and Crisp, R. (Ed.). Oxford: Oxford University Press.

Bahdanau, D., K. Cho, and Y. Bengio (2016). 'Neural Machine Translation by Jointly Learning to Align and Translate'. *The International Conference on Learning Representations.* https://arxiv.org/abs/1409.0473.

Barash, D.P. (2003). 'Dennett and the Darwinizing of Free Will'. *Human Nature Review* 3, 222–5. https://web.archive.org/web/20180821231237/; http://human-nature.com/nibbs/03/dcdennett.html.

Beauvoir, S. de (1948). *The Ethics of Ambiguity.* New York, NY: Philosophical Library.

Behne, T., M. Carpenter, and M. Tomasello (2005). 'One-Year-Llds Comprehend the Communicative Intentions Behind Gestures in a Hiding Game'. *Developmental Science* 8:6, 492–9. https://doi.org/10.1111/j.1467-7687.2005.00440.x.

Bengio, Y. (2019, lecture). 'Deep Learning for AI'. Turing Lecture, Heidelberg Laureate Forum, 23 September. https://www.youtube.com/watch?v=llGG62fNN64.

Black, M. (1962). *Models and Metaphors: Studies in Language and Philosophy.* Ithaca, NY: Cornell University Press.

Boring, E.G. (1930). 'A New Ambiguous Figure'. *American Journal of Psychology* 42:3, 444–5.

Bratman, M.E. (1992). 'Shared Cooperative Activity.' *The Philosophical Review* 101:2, 327–41. https://doi.org/10.2307/2185537.

Brooks, D. (2015). *The Road to Character.* New York, NY: Random House.

Bruner, J.S. (1975). 'The Ontogenesis of Speech Acts'. *Journal of Child Language* 2:1, 1–19. https://doi.org/10.1017/S0305000900000866.

Buzsaki, G. (2006). *Rhythms of the Brain*. Oxford: Oxford University Press.

Byers, W. (2007). *How Mathematicians Think: Using Ambiguity, Contradiction, and Paradox to Create Mathematics*. Princeton, NJ: Princeton University Press.

Call, J. and M. Tomasello (2008). 'Does the Chimpanzee Have a Theory of Mind? 30 Years Later'. *Trends in Cognitive Sciences* 12:5, 187–92. http://dx.doi.org/10.1016/j.tics.2008.02.010.

Califano, A., B. Germain, and S. Colville (1998). 'A High-Dimensional Indexing Scheme for Scalable Fingerprint-Based Identification'. In R. Chin and T.C. Pong, eds. *Computer Vision — ACCV'98*. Lecture Notes in Computer Science, vol. 1351. Berlin: Springer. https://doi.org/10.1007/3-540-63930-6_101.

Canny, J. (1986). 'A Computational Approach to Edge Detections'. In *IEEE Transactions on Pattern Analysis and Machine Intelligence* PAMI-8:6, 679–98. https://doi.org/10.1109/TPAMI.1986.4767851.

Carpenter, M., K. Nagell, M. Tomasello, G. Butterworth, and C. Moore (1998). 'Social Cognition, Joint Attention, and Communicative Competence from 9 to 15 Months of Age'. *Monographs of the Society for Research in Child Development* 63:4. https://doi.org/10.2307/1166214.

Chen, J., X. Liu, P.H. Tu, and A. Aragones (2013). 'Learning Person-Specific Models for Facial Expression and Action Unit Recognition'. *Pattern Recognition Letters* 34:15, 1964–70. https://doi.org/10.1016/j.patrec.2013.02.002.

Clark, H.H. (1996). *Using Language*. Cambridge: Cambridge University Press.

Colonnesi, C., G.J.J.M. Stams, I. Koster, and M.J. Noom (2010). 'The Relation between Pointing and Language Development: A Meta-analysis'. *Developmental Review* 30:4, 352–66. http://dx.doi.org/10.1016/j.dr.2010.10.001.

Corballis, M.C. (1991). *The Lopsided Ape: Evolution of the Generative Mind*. Oxford: Oxford University Press.

Dawkins, R. and J.R. Krebs (1978). 'Animal Signals: Information or Manipulation'. In J.R. Krebs and N.B. Davies, eds. *Behavioural Ecology: An Evolutionary Approach*. Oxford: Blackwell Scientific, 282–309.

Dawkins, R. (2006). *The God Delusion*. London: Transworld.

Deacon, T.W. (1997). *The Symbolic Species: The Co-evolution of Language and the Brain*. New York, NY: W.W. Norton.

Dennett, D.C. (1996). *Kinds of Minds: Toward an Understanding of Consciousness*. New York, NY: Basic.

Dennett, D.C. (2003). *Freedom Evolves*. London: Penguin.

Descartes, R. (2006 [1637]). 'Discourse on the Method'. *A Discourse on the Method of Correctly Conducting One's Reason and Seeking Truth in the Sciences*. Trans. Ian Maclean. Oxford: Oxford University Press.

Dessalles, J.-L. (2007 [2000]). *Why We Talk: The Evolutionary Origins of Language.* Trans. James Grieve. Oxford: Oxford University Press.

Deutsch, D. (2011). *The Beginning of Infinity: Explanations That Transform the World.* London: Allen Lane.

Dor, D., C. Knight, and J. Lewis, eds. (2014). *The Social Origins of Language.* Oxford: Oxford University Press.

Ekman, P. (1993). *Emotions Revealed: Understanding Faces and Feelings.* London: Weidenfeld and Nicholson.

Entman, R.M. (1993). "Framing: Toward Clarification of a Fractured Paradigm'. *Journal of Communication* 43:3, 51–8. https://doi.org/10.1111/j.1460-2466. 1993.tb01304.x.

Feynman, R. (1983). Interview 'Stretching, Pulling and Pushing'. BBC *Fun to Imagine*, July 15. https://www.bbc.co.uk/programmes/p014blpr.

Fish, S. (1980). *Is There a Text in This Class? The Authority of Interpretive Communities.* Cambridge, MA: Harvard University Press.

Flesch, R. (1949). *The Art of Readable Writing.* New York, NY: Harper.

Fletcher, A. (2007). *Time, Space, and Motion in the Age of Shakespeare.* Cambridge, MA: Harvard University Press.

Gladwell, M. (2019). *Talking to Strangers: What We Should Know about the People We Don't Know.* New York, NY: Little, Brown.

Gödel, K. (1986 [1931]). 'Über formal unentscheidbare Sätze der Principia Mathematica und verwandter Systeme, I'. In S. Feferman, ed. *Kurt Gödel: Collected Works*, vol. I. Oxford: Oxford University Press, 144–95.

Goffman, E. (1959). *The Presentation of Self in Everyday Life.* Garden City, NJ: Doubleday.

Goffman, E. (1974). *Frame Analysis: An Essay on the Organization of Experience.* Boston, MA: Northeastern University Press.

Goldstein, J. (2011). *Attractors and Nonlinear Dynamical Systems*, Adelphi University. http://adaptknowledge.com/wpcontent/uploads/rapidintake/PI_CL/media/deeperlearningspring2011.pdf.

Grandin, T. and C. Johnson (2005). *Animals in Translation: Using the Mysteries of Autism to Decode Animal Behavior.* New York, NY: Scribner.

Grice, P. (1995 [1989]). *Studies in the Way of Words.* Cambridge, MA: Harvard University Press.

Hägglund, M. (2019). *This Life: Secular Faith and Spiritual Freedom.* London: Penguin/Random House.

Haidt, J. (2022) 'After Babel: How Social Media Dissolved the Mortar of Society and Made America Stupid'. *The Atlantic*, May. https://www.theatlantic.com/magazine/archive/2022/05/social-media-democracy-trust-babel/629369/.

Hameroff, S. (1987). *Ultimate Computing: Biomolecular Consciousness and Nano Technology.* Amsterdam: Elsevier.

Hare, B. and M. Tomasello (2004). 'Chimpanzees Are More Skillful in Competitive Than in Cooperative Cognitive Tasks'. *Animal Behaviour* 68:3, 571–81. https://psycnet.apa.org/doi/10.1016/j.anbehav.2003.11.011.

Hare, R.D. (2003). *Manual for the Revised Psychopathy Checklist* (2nd edition). Toronto: Multi-Health Systems.

Harris, S. (2020). *Making Sense: Conversations on Consciousness, Morality, and the Future of Humanity*. New York, NY: Harper Collins.

Hartley, R. and A. Zisserman (2003). *Multiple View Geometry in Computer Vision*. Cambridge: Cambridge University Press.

Hastings, W.K. (1970). 'Monte Carlo Sampling Methods Using Markov Chains and Their Applications'. *Biometrika* 57:1, 97–109. https://doi.org/10.2307/2334940.

Hobbes, T. (1991 [1651]). *Leviathan*. Ed. R. Tuck. Cambridge: Cambridge University Press.

Hofstadter, D. and E. Sander (2013). *Surfaces and Essences: Analogy as the Fuel and Fire of Thinking*. New York, NY: Basic.

Hilbert, D. and W. Ackermann (1950 [1928]). *Principles of Mathematical Logic*. Trans. L.M. Hammond, G.G. Leckie, and F. Steinhardt. Providence, RI: AMS Chelsea.

Hudson, D.A. and C.D. Manning (2018). 'Compositional Attention Networks for Machine Reasoning'. *The International Conference on Learning Representations*. https://arxiv.org/abs/1803.03067.

Iser, W. (1978). *The Act of Reading: A Theory of Aesthetic Response*. Baltimore, MD: Johns Hopkins University Press.

Jaynes, J. (2000 [1976]). *The Origin of Consciousness in the Breakdown of the Bicameral Mind*. Boston, MA: Mariner.

Kahneman, D. (2011). *Thinking, Fast and Slow*. New York, NY: Farrar, Straus and Giroux.

Kant, I. (1892 [1790]). *The Critique of Judgement*. Trans. J.H. Bernard. London: Macmillan.

Kierkegaard, S. (1994 [1872]). *The Book of Adler*. In *Fear and Trembling, The Book of Adler*. Trans. Walter Lowrie. New York, NY: Everyman's.

Kojéve, A. (2014 [2004]). *The Notion of Authority (A Brief Presentation)*. London: Verso.

Kronfeldner, M., ed. (2021). *The Routledge Handbook of Dehumanization*. Routledge.

Kuhn, T. (1970 [1962]). *The Structure of Scientific Revolutions*. Chicago: University of Chicago Press.

Lanier, J. (2011). *You Are Not a Gadget: A Manifesto*. London: Penguin.

Laplace, P.S. (1902 [1814]). *A Philosophical Essay on Probabilities*. Trans. F.W. Truscott and F.L. Emory. New York, NY: John Wiley

Libet, B. (1999). 'Do We Have Free Will?' *Journal of Consciousness Studies* 6:8–9, 47–57. https://spot.colorado.edu/~tooley/Benjamin%20Libet.pdf.

Liu, X., J. Rittscher, and T. Chen (2006). 'Optimal Pose for Face Recognition'. *2006 IEEE Computer Society Conference on Computer Vision and Pattern Recognition* (CVPR'06), vol. 2, 1439–46. https://doi.org/10.1109/CVPR.2006.216.

Liu, X. (2007). 'Generic Face Alignment Using Boosted Appearance Model'. *IEEE Computer Society Conference on Computer Vision and Pattern Recognition 2007*, 1–8. https://doi.org/10.1109/CVPR.2007.383265.

Lorensen, W.E. and H.E. Cline (1987). 'Marching Cubes: A High Resolution 3D Surface Construction Algorithm'. *Association for Computing Machinery (ACM) Special Interest Group on Computer Graphics and Interactive Techniques (SIGGRAPH) Computer Graphics* 21:4, 163–9. https://doi.org/10.1145/37402.37422.

Lowe, R., Y. Wu, A. Tamar, J. Harb, A. Pieter and I. Mordatch (2017). 'Multi-Agent Actor-Critic for Mixed Cooperative-Competitive Environments'. *Advances in Neural Information Processing Systems 30 (NIPS)*. https://arxiv.org/abs/1706.02275.

Magda, S., D.J. Kriegman, T. Zickler, and P.N. Belhumeur (2001). 'Beyond Lambert: Reconstructing Surfaces with Arbitrary BDRFs'. *Proceedings Eighth IEEE International Conference on Computer Vision. ICCV 2001*, vol. 2, 391–8. https://doi.org/10.1109/ICCV.2001.937652.

McGann, J. and L. Samuels (2006). 'Deformance and Interpretation'. In J. Retallack and J. Spahr, eds. *Poetry and Pedagogy: The Challenge of the Contemporary.* New York, NY: Palgrave Macmillan, 151–80.

Mendelson, T.C. and K.L. Shaw (2012). 'The (Mis)Concept of Species Recognition'. *Trends in Ecology and Evolution* 27:8, 421–7. https://doi.org/10.1016/j.tree.2012.04.001.

Merleau-Ponty, M. (2012 [1945]). *Phenomenology of Perception.* Trans. D.A. Landes. Abingdon: Routledge.

Miles, J. (1995). *God: A Biography.* New York, NY: Vintage.

Miller, C.-R. (2017). *Witchcraft, the Devil, and Emotions in Early Modern England.* Abingdon: Routledge.

Miller, K.R. (2019). *The Human Instinct: How We Evolved to Have Reason, Consciousness, and Free Will.* New York, NY: Simon & Schuster.

Montgomery, S. (2016). *The Soul of an Octopus: A Surprising Exploration into the Wonder of Consciousness.* New York, NY: Atria.

Moore, G.E. (1903). *Principia Ethica.* London: Cambridge University Press.

Nagel, T. (1974). 'What Is It Like to Be a Bat?' *Philosophical Review* 83:4, 435–50. http://www.jstor.org/stable/2183914?origin=JSTOR-pdf.

Ning, T., S. Stacy, M. Zhao, G. Marquez, and T. Gao (2020). 'Bootstrapping an Imagined We for Cooperation'. *Proceedings of the 42nd Annual Meeting of the Cognitive Science Society — Developing a Mind: Learning in Humans, Animals, and Machines.* https://cogsci.mindmodeling.org/2020/papers/0584/index.html.

Oppenheim, A.V., A.S. Willsky, and I.T. Young (1983). *Signals and Systems*. Englewood Cliffs, NJ: Prentice-Hall.

Ortega y Gasset, J. (1964 [1932]). *The Revolt of the Masses*. Trans. T. Carey. New York, NY: W.W. Norton.

Pavlidis, I., N.L. Eberhardt, and J. Levine (2002). 'Human Behaviour: Seeing through the Face of Deception'. *Nature* 415:6867, 35 pp. https://doi.org/10.1038/415035a.

Pearl, J. (2009). *Causality: Models, Reasoning, and Inference* (2nd edition). Cambridge: Cambridge University Press.

Pearl, J. and D. Mackenzie (2018). *The Book of Why: The New Science of Cause and Effect*. New York, NY: Basic.

Penrose, R. (1989). *The Emperor's New Mind: Concerning Computers, Minds and the Laws of Physics*. Oxford: Oxford University Press.

Penrose, R. (1994). *Shadows of the Mind: A Search for the Missing Science of Consciousness*. Oxford: Oxford University Press.

Petzold, C. (2008). *The Annotated Turing: A Guided Tour through Alan Turing's Historic Paper on Computability and the Turing Machine*. Indianapolis, IN: Wiley Publishing.

Plato (1892). 'Apology'. In *The Dialogues of Plato* (3rd edition). Trans. B. Jowett. London: Oxford University Press, 95–136.

Putnam, R.D. (2010). *Bowling Alone: The Collapse and Revival of American Community*. New York, NY: Simon and Schuster.

Ronson, J. (2011). *The Psychopath Test: A Journey through the Madness Industry*. New York, NY: Riverhead Books.

Rossano, F. (2018). 'Social Manipulation, Turn-Taking and Cooperation in Apes: Implications for the Evolution of Language-Based Interaction in Humans'. *Interaction Studies* 19:1–2, 151–166. https://psycnet.apa.org/doi/10.1075/is.17043.ros.

Sartre, J.-P. (1956 [1943]). *Being and Nothingness*. Trans. H. Barnes. New York, NY: Methuen.

Sayfarth, R.M. and D.L. Cheney (2018). *The Social Origins of Language*. Princeton, NJ: Princeton University Press.

Sayre, K. (1965). *Recognition: A Study in the Philosophy of Artificial Intelligence*. Notre Dame, IN: University of Notre Dame Press.

Schelling, T.C. (1980). *The Strategy of Conflict*. Cambridge, MA: Harvard University Press.

Searle, J.R. (1980). 'Minds, Brains and Programs.' *Behaviour and Brain Sciences* 3:3, 417–58. https://doi.org/10.1017/S0140525X00005756.

Searle, J.R. and S. Willis (1995). *The Construction of Social Reality*. New York, NY: Simon and Schuster.

Searle, J.R. (1998). *Mind, Language and Society: Philosophy in the Real World*. New York, NY: Basic Books.

Sfard, A. (1994). 'Reification as the Birth of Metaphor'. *For the Learning of Mathematics* 14:1, 44–54. https://www.jstor.org/stable/40248103.

Shanahan, M. (1989). 'Prediction Is Deduction but Explanation Is Abduction'. *International Joint Conference on Artificial Intelligence* 89, 1055–60. https://dl.acm.org/doi/abs/10.5555/1623891.1623924.

Sperber, D. and D. Wilson (1995 [1986]). *Relevance: Communication and Cognition* (2nd edition). Oxford: Blackwell.

Stacy, S., C. Li, M. Zhao, Y. Yun, Q. Zhao, M. Kleiman-Weiner, and T. Gao (2021). 'Modeling Communication to Coordinate Perspectives in Cooperation'. *Proceedings of the Annual Meeting of the Cognitive Science Society* 43. https://escholarship.org/uc/item/85x686nx.

Stalnaker, R.C. (1999 [1974]). *Context and Content: Essays on Intentionality in Speech and Thought*. Oxford: Oxford University Press.

Storr, W. (2021). *The Status Game: On Social Position and How We Use It*. London: Collins.

Tinker, M.A. (1963). *Legibility of Print*. Ames, IA: Iowa State University Press.

Tomasello, M., D. Gust, and G.T. Frost (1989). 'A Longitudinal Investigation of Gestural Communication in Young Chimpanzees'. *Primates* 30:1, 35–50. https://link.springer.com/article/10.1007/BF02381209.

Tomasello, M. (1992). *First Verbs: A Case Study of Early Grammatical Development*. Cambridge: Cambridge University Press.

Tomasello, M., J. Call, and A. Gluckman (1997). 'Comprehension of Novel Communicative Signs by Apes and Human Children'. *Child Development* 68: 1067–80. https://pubmed.ncbi.nlm.nih.gov/9418226/.

Tomasello, M. (2003). *Constructing a Language: A Usage-Based Theory of Language Acquisition*. Cambridge, MA: Harvard University Press.

Tomasello, M. (2006). 'Why Don't Apes Point?' *Roots of Human Sociality: Culture, Cognition and Interaction*. Oxford: Berg, 506–30.

Tomasello, M. (2007). 'If They're So Good at Grammar, Then Why Don't They Talk? Hints from Apes' and Humans' Use of Gestures'. *Language Learning and Development* 3:2, 133–56. https://doi.org/10.1080/15475440701225451.

Tomasello, M. (2008). *Origins of Human Communication*. Cambridge, MA: MIT Press.

Tomasello, M. (2014). *A Natural History of Human Thinking*. Cambridge, MA: Harvard University Press.

Tononi, G. (2004). 'An Information Integration Theory of Consciousness'. *BMC Neuroscience* 5:1, 1–22. https://doi.org/10.1186/1471-2202-5-42.

Tse, P.U. (2013). *The Neural Basis of Free Will: Criterial Causation*. Cambridge, MA: MIT Press.

Tu, J., X. Liu, and P.H. Tu (2010). 'Site-adaptive face recognition'. *Fourth IEEE International Conference on Biometrics: Theory, Applications and Systems (BTAS)*. IEEE.

Tu, P.H. and P.R.S. Mendonça (2003). 'Surface Reconstruction via Helmholtz Reciprocity with a Single Image Pair'. *IEEE Computer Society Conference on Computer Vision and Pattern Recognition, 2003*. https://dl.acm.org/doi/abs/10.5555/1965841.1965912.

Tu, P.H., X. Liu, N. Krahnstoever, R. Book, P. Willliams, and C. Adrian (2007). 'Automatic Face Recognition from Skeletal Remains'. *IEEE Computer Society Conference on Computer Vision and Pattern Recognition 2007*. https://doi.org/10.1109/CVPR.2007.383060.

Tu, P.H., T. Sebastian, and D. Gao (2012). 'Action Recognition from Experience'. *2012 IEEE Ninth International Conference on Advanced Video and Signal-Based Surveillance*, 124–9. https://ieeexplore.ieee.org/document/6327996.

Tu, P.H., J. Chen, M.-C. Chang, T. Yu, T.-P. Tian, G. Rubin, J. Hockett, and A. Logan-Terry (2015). 'Cross-cultural Training Analysis via Social Science and Computer Vision Methods'. *6th International Conference on Applied Human Factors and Ergonomics (AHFE 2015) and the Affiliated Conferences, AHFE*. https://doi.org/10.1016/j.promfg.2015.07.978.

Tu, P.H., D. Hamilton, T. Gao, A. Chen, J. Foehner, A.S. Pang, and J. Kubricht (2019). 'A Learning Approach to Interactive Advertising'. *2019 16th IEEE International Conference on Advanced Video and Signal Based Surveillance (AVSS)*. https://ieeexplore.ieee.org/abstract/document/8909885.

Turing, A.M. (1937). 'On Computable Numbers, With an Application to the Entscheidungsproblem'. *Proceedings of the London Mathematical Society* s2-42:1, 1 January, 230–65. https://doi.org/10.1112/plms/s2-42.1.230.

Turing, A.M. (1950). 'Computing Machinery and Intelligence'. *Mind* 49:236, 433–60. https://doi.org/10.1093/mind/LIX.236.433.

Valéry, P. (1950 [1919]). 'Two Fragments from "The Intellectual Crisis"'. *Selected Writings*. New York, NY: New Directions, 117–23.

Völter, C.J., F. Rossano, and J. Call (2017). 'Social Manipulation in Nonhuman Primates: Cognitive and Motivational Determinants'. *Neuroscience & Biobehavioral Reviews* 82, 76–94. https://doi.org/10.1016/j.neubiorev.2016.09.008.

Weizenbaum, J. (1976). *Computer Power and Human Reason*. New York, NY: W.H. Freeman.

Wheeler, F.W., X. Liu, and P.H. Tu (2007). 'Multi-Frame Super-Resolution for Face Recognition'. *IEEE First International Conference on Biometrics: Theory, Applications and Systems*. https://doi.org/10.1109/BTAS.2007.4401949.

Wheeler, F.W., A.G. Perera, G. Abramovich, B. Yu, and P.H. Tu (2008). 'Stand-off Iris Recognition System'. *2008 IEEE Second International Conference on Biometrics: Theory, Applications and Systems*, 1–7. https://doi.org/10.1109/BTAS.2008.4699381.

Wheeler, F.W., R.L. Weiss, and P.H. Tu (2010). 'Face Recognition at a Distance System for Surveillance Applications'. *2010 Fourth IEEE International Conference on Biometrics: Theory, Applications and Systems (BTAS)*. https://doi.org/10.1109/BTAS.2010.5634523.

White, D.G. (2021). *Daemons Are Forever: Contacts and Exchanges in the Eurasian Pandemonium*. Chicago, IL: University of Chicago Press.

Wilby, E. (2005). *Cunning Folk and Familiar Spirits: Shamanistic Visionary Traditions in Early Modern British Witchcraft*. Eastbourne: Sussex Academic Press.

Winchester, S. (1998). *The Professor and the Madman: A Tale of Murder, Insanity, and the Making of the Oxford English Dictionary*. New York, NY: Harper Collins.

Wittgenstein, L. (1958). *Philosophical Investigations*. Trans. G.E.M. Anscombe. Oxford: Basil Blackwell.

Yang, Y., M.-C. Chang, L. Wen, P.H. Tu, H. Qi, and S. Lyu (2016). 'Efficient Large-Scale Photometric Reconstruction Using Divide-Recon-Fuse 3D Structure from Motion'. *2016 13th IEEE International Conference on Advanced Video and Signal Based Surveillance (AVSS)*, 180–6. https://doi.org/10.1109/AVSS.2016.7738070.

Yi, K., J. Wu, C. Gan, A. Torralba, P. Kohli, and J. Tenenbaum (2018). 'Neural-Symbolic VQA: Disentangling Reasoning from Vision and Language Understanding'. *Advances in Neural Information Processing Systems*, 1031–42. https://doi.org/10.48550/arXiv.1810.02338.

Yu, T., S.-N. Lim, K. Patwardhan, and N. Krahnstoever (2009). 'Monitoring, Recognizing and Discovering Social Networks'. *IEEE Computer Society Conference on Computer Vision and Pattern Recognition 2009*. https://doi.org/10.1109/CVPR.2009.5206526.

Zhao, M., N. Tang, A. Dahmani, R. Perry, Y. Zhu, F. Rossano, and T. Gao (2021). 'Sharing Is Not Needed: Modeling Animal Coordinated Hunting with Reinforcement Learning'. *Proceedings of the 43rd Annual Meeting of the Cognitive Science Society*, vol. 43. https://escholarship.org/uc/item/8v5781cd.

Index